Lone Stars Rising

Lone Stars Rising

The Fifty People
Who Turned Texas into the
Fastest-Growing, Most Exciting,
and, Sometimes, Most Exasperating
State in the Country

HARPER WAVE

An Imprint of HarperCollins*Publishers*

HarperCollins books may be purchased for educational, business, or sales promotional use. For information, please email the Special Markets Department at SPsales@harpercollins.com.

Cover illustrations by Israel G. Vargas
Chapter illustrations by Israel G. Vargas
Previous page: photograph by James H. Evans
Credits and permissions are continued on page 238–239

FIRST EDITION

Designed by Leah Carlson-Stanisic

Library of Congress Cataloging-in-Publication Data has been applied for.

ISBN 978-0-06-306861-2

23 24 25 26 27 TC 10 9 8 7 6 5 4 3 2 1

contents

The 1980s

The 1990s

The 2000s

The 2010s

The 2020s and Beyond

Foreword

by Dan Goodgame

Texas Monthly was founded fifty years ago with a simple mission: to publish the best storytelling about the Lone Star State—about its events, its places, and, especially its people. That remains our mission today, even as we've expanded onto the web and into videos, podcasts, live events, newsletters, Hollywood productions, and books like the one you're holding.

Our focus on interesting Texans reflects the nature of the state that we cover. It has always been defined by big personalities, from Sam Houston and Quanah Parker to Lyndon Johnson and Ann Richards; from Mary Kay Ash and Herb Kelleher to Selena and Beyoncé. We're home to many of America's boldest entrepreneurs and inventors, chefs and architects, film directors and musicians. So when my colleagues and I decided to publish a book to celebrate our golden anniversary, we thought it made sense to highlight fifty or so of the fascinating personalities we've been blessed to write about over the past half century.

During that period, Texas has experienced

a profound transformation. Its population has risen from twelve million to thirty million, including millions of newcomers from all over the globe. Contrary to popular stereotype, most live not in rural areas but in vibrant cities and increasingly diverse suburbs. The state's economy ranks ninth in the world, just behind that of Brazil and ahead of South Korea. Its political and cultural influence has expanded apace, in every sphere from hardball politics to hip-hop. And at every turn, *Texas Monthly* writers have chronicled the state's growth and its growing pains.

TM published its first issue in February 1973, shortly after former president Lyndon Johnson died, Houston's Barbara Jordan took her seat as the first Black woman elected to Congress from a southern state, and the Supreme Court overthrew state bans on abortion in a Texas case called *Roe v. Wade.* That first issue included reviews of books, films, restaurants, theater, and weekend getaways. But most of its pages—like those of the six-hundred-plus issues that would follow—were devoted to engaging stories about Texans: the effervescent president of Dr Pepper, the colorful sportscaster and former Dallas Cowboys quarterback Don Meredith, and the feuding families who ran the high-end department store chains Neiman Marcus and Sakowitz.

That first issue is where we began our research for this book. We started by making lists of who we might feature, which was fun and easy. We included famous figures such as Matthew McConaughey and Solange Knowles. Amusing ones such as Woody Harrelson and Dennis Rodman. Ones nurtured here who found fame elsewhere, such as Walter Cronkite and Melinda Gates. Ones who made their names elsewhere and then got here as soon as they could, such as Elon Musk and Joe Rogan. Our potential profile subjects soon numbered in the hundreds. That's where the going got tough. We had to find a way to cull the herd.

We decided to focus on the men and women who had *shaped* the state in some lasting manner over the past half century, rather than those who were simply well known or whose significant accomplishments occurred elsewhere. (Jeff Bezos may have grown up in Houston and spent his summers on his grandfather's ranch in Cotulla, but his impact is global, not Texas-specific.) To winnow our list, we consulted with historians and experts in fields ranging from business and politics to the arts, food, medicine, and sports. We debated at length and went back to read more about scores of Texans, both little known and famous. Then we argued some more.

In the end, we tended to choose directors over actors, entrepreneurs over corporate CEOs, and musicians and sports figures who expanded our sense of what was possible in those fields rather than those who were merely popular.

Though this book covers individuals who shaped the state between 1973 and 2023, the complex process of influence doesn't necessarily respect the rigid borders of decades. In our first chapter, on the 1970s, you'll see a few figures who made major contributions years earlier but whose influence continued to be felt many years later. Likewise, in our afterword, on the 2020s—a decade that was still unfolding as we put this book together—we decided to loosen our criteria a bit and include Texans who, based on their early contributions, look likely to have lasting impact.

One beneficial effect of that decision is that we were able to include a more diverse range of folks in our list of fifty influential Texans than we otherwise might have. Of course, there are limits to how far we can bend in that direction without distorting history; the realities of who has wielded power in Texas are, unfortunately, what they are. Every one of the state's forty-eight governors, for instance, has been white, all but two of them white men. The founders of most of our iconic brands have been white men, too. But that was then. Texas is now a majority-minority state, and the afterword's diverse roster provides a glimpse of our future. Twenty-five years from now, our seventy-fifth anniversary book will almost certainly look very different from this one.

For our brief profiles of each of the Texans featured here, we drew on nearly fifty years of *Texas Monthly*'s reporting. Roughly half of these articles have been freshly written, in several cases by authors who have covered the subjects for decades. The other half are stories from our archives that have, in many cases, been substantially updated and otherwise revised. In cases where the authors of our original profiles are alive and well, we have either enlisted them in the editing and updating or consulted closely with them. Sadly, four of the finest writers in *TM*'s history—Gary Cartwright, Jan Reid, Paul Burka, and Al Reinert—have passed on in recent years and a couple of others are ailing. In adapting their work, we've done our best to preserve each writer's voice and style.

Dozens of *TM* staffers, as well as freelancers and alumni, have enthusiastically contributed to this book, and I'm grateful to each of them. Spe-cial thanks are due to Stephen Harrigan, a distinguished *TM* alum who wrote *Big Wonderful Thing*, the definitive history of Texas. His introduction to this book provides colorful and insightful perspective on our past half century. Special thanks are also due to *Texas Monthly*'s deputy editor Jeff Salamon, who expertly directed this project on a tight deadline. Both rank high on my personal list of top fifty Texans.

I think you'll find, as I have, that our writers and editors have created a remarkably entertaining and enlightening work. Though it is, narrowly defined, a collection of fifty unrelated profiles, this book also functions as an intimate, personality-focused history of America's most fascinating state during an era of sweeping change. Reading through these pieces, you get the sense of time unfolding, of institutions rising and falling, of political and cultural forces emerging and pushing against one another—and of the magazine that chronicled all of it.

Lone Stars Rising

TM

Introduction

by Stephen Harrigan

Lyndon Johnson placed his last phone call, and spoke his last words, on the late afternoon of January 22, 1973. He was alone, in the bedroom of his ranch house, when he dialed the Secret Service and, in a stricken tone, asked for help. Two agents rushed to his room, but when they arrived they found the former president, the man who had held sway over Texas history as no one had since Sam Houston, already dead of a heart attack.

He was buried in the family graveyard on the Pedernales River three days later. Only a few days after that, the first issue of *Texas Monthly*—the February 1973 issue, with the former Dallas Cowboys quarterback Don Mer-edith on the cover—appeared on newsstands. That May, *Texas Monthly*'s fourth issue included an account of LBJ's funeral by Bill Porterfield, written in a lush elegiac key ("Never in memory," it began, "had the hill winter been so hard and insistent and the sun so shy") that signaled that the magazine was savvy to the literary dimensions of what was then called the New Journalism.

Texas Monthly was created in time to memorialize Johnson, but too late to cover him. It had missed that era. But with the state's most commanding personality now laid to rest, another Texas era was beginning, and *Texas Monthly* was on hand to document it. LBJ's passing represented, in a way, a clean break with history. There was no reason to doubt that Texas would always be teeming with characters to write about, but a gigantic, overshadowing Texan like Lyndon Johnson already seemed like an emblem of the past.

In some ways, however, the past was still tenaciously with us. Even though it had produced a president (two, if you count Dwight Eisenhower, who was born in Denison but brought to Kansas before the age of two), Texas in 1973 felt far removed from the national stage. By the 1970s, nearly 80 percent of Texans were city dwellers—twice as many as there had been four decades earlier—but the state was still grounded in, and hobbled by, its own insistent clichés. Recent movies like *The Last Picture Show* had moved the needle a bit when it came to realistic depictions of Texans, but we were still conditioned to recognize ourselves in the panels of Ace Reid cartoons about lanky, bowlegged cowboys.

Living in Texas back then, you felt cut off from a wider and presumably more cosmopolitan world. Blue laws, for instance, were still very much in effect. It wasn't just that you couldn't buy liquor on Sunday. If you needed a new mop, the housewares section of your local grocery store was literally roped off, for fear you might profane the Lord's Day by buying something that would lead you to commit labor. It had only been two years since the Texas Legislature overturned the law forbidding you from ordering a drink in a restaurant, and if you happened to be in the lounge car of a train, service was still suspended when you passed through one of Texas's one-hundred-or-so dry counties. You learned about what was happening beyond the borders of Texas from thirty-minute news segments on the three broadcast networks or from your local newspaper. There wasn't yet a national edition of the *New York Times*, or a self-appointed national

newspaper like *USA Today*. Flights outside of the state were expensive. Travel outside of the country remained, for a penurious freelance writer like myself, a maybe-one-day, once-in-a-lifetime dream.

Even so, you had the sense that things were starting to loosen up, that Texas's borders wouldn't always be such a hard barrier and that the state had something important to say to the rest of the country. Nineteen seventy-three was also the year that a sprawling soon-to-be-international airport the size of Manhattan debuted between Dallas and Fort Worth, opening up Texas to the world in much the same way that the cattle trails had a hundred years earlier. During the construction of DFW, workers unearthed the fossilized bones of a seventy-million-year-old marine reptile called a plesiosaur. In a vivid demonstration of how Texas was emerging into the ether of the modern age, the plesiosaur was put on display in the Braniff terminal.

Braniff itself would soon become a fossil, going out of business in 1982. But at about the same time that a young lawyer named Mike Levy began traveling around Texas pitching potential investors on the idea of a statewide magazine, a new venture called Southwest Airlines, with a tiny fleet of three Boeing 737s, began flying passengers to and from Houston, Dallas, and San Antonio. A low-cost airline connecting Texas's biggest cities was the vision of an investment banker and recreational pilot named Rollin King, but it was co-founder Herb Kelleher's raucous, try-anything personality that gave

Lady Bird and Lyndon Johnson at the Lyndon B. Johnson Library on the University of Texas campus in Austin.

3

the airline its renegade identity and helped cement its customer loyalty. Southwest also served as a binding force for Texans, reflecting to us an image of our long-cultivated identity as a world unto ourselves.

That prideful parochialism still exists, but Texas—like Southwest, now one of the biggest airlines in the world—is no longer as containable as it once seemed. In the last half century, the number of people living here has more than doubled and Texas has climbed the charts from the country's fourth most populous state to its second. Austin, an over-

grown college town of slightly more than two hundred thousand people when I arrived in 1966, is now the eleventh largest city in the United States. Houston is now the fourth largest, and someday soon will probably be the third.

The change has been so overwhelming, so inundating, that it's puzzling to remember that when *Texas Monthly* published its first issue my rent in central Austin was a hundred dollars a month, that I had not yet tasted Chinese food, that the downtown bus station was a thriving portal for state and national travel, that barbecue was not the object of hipster obsession or the subject of foodways scholarship but just something that people ate because it was a good, cheap lunch. The Astrodome and the Shamrock Hotel were still major landmarks in Houston, Dallas was still the radioactive site of the Kennedy assassination, and a twelve-year-old amusement park in Arlington was still called Six Flags Over Texas for a reason, since it was mostly divided into six themed sections focused on the six nations Texas had been a part of during its history.

Visitors to Six Flags could embark on La Salle's River Adventure, named for the doomed explorer who had tried to establish a French colony in the 1680s near Matagorda Bay. "Indians!" the guide called out as the boat passed a village of conical thatched huts where human skulls were displayed on poles. "Every one of these Indian braves has sworn a blood oath to kill any white man he sees." He alerted the passengers to the presence of a hideous-looking medicine man but lasciviously called their attention to a beautiful "Indian chick" and instructed them: "Hands off!"

Someone at Six Flags must have noticed the squeamishness potential of some of the attractions as Texas was beginning its evolution into a majority-minority state. The demeaning robotic representations of dancing tamales and grinning campesinos wearing giant sombreros and riding undersize donkeys that you passed on the Fiesta Train in the Mexico section had recently been relocated to another part of the park, and there was no longer a "recruitment station" in the Confederacy section, or mock executions of Union spies. But the Old South plan-

tation vibe was undisguised and Six Flags continued to fly the Confederate battle flag without asterisk or apology.

There was, though, no hiding the fact that Texas was shedding the old cultural tropes that no longer fit. As this book vibrantly demonstrates, it was people, not just time itself, that transformed Texas over the last fifty years. Fifty of those people are featured here. They are not necessarily the people who, in 1973, you might have predicted would change our state the most or who would test the parameters of Texas identity. Some of the people who once seemed like sure bets for the final draft of Texas history aren't even included in the pages of this book.

The first public figure, other than Don Meredith, to appear on the cover of *Texas Monthly* was John Connally. This was in September 1973, fewer than ten years since Connally was almost fatally shot while riding through Dealey Plaza with President Kennedy. He had by then joined Richard Nixon's cabinet, switched to the Republican Party, and begun to set his own course for the White House. His national popularity, according to a Gallup poll cited by Ann Fears Crawford and Jack Keever, the authors of the piece, was "second only to Teddy Kennedy's. It is not out of the question that this Texan with a strong personality and an almost nineteenth-century view of formality and style could be the next president."

Not out of the question, but not in the

4

cards. The same was true for Lloyd Bentsen, depicted on a cover the next year languidly reaching out to touch the finger of God (Lyndon Johnson) in a parody of Michelangelo's *Creation of Adam*. The closest he got was the vice presidential slot in Michael Dukakis's failed 1988 presidential bid.

In 1987, I wrote a profile of Henry Cisneros in which I overspeculated on the possibility of the San Antonio mayor being the first Hispanic occupant of the Oval Office.

"Do you think you could do it?" I asked while I sat next to him on an airplane.

"Do what?"

"Be president?"

"Yeah," he said. "I could do it."

But he never got the chance to prove it. Neither did Ross Perot, Phil Gramm, or (so far) Rick Perry, Ted Cruz, or Beto O'Rourke. But of course George H. W. Bush and George W. Bush both did, and both cycled through the pages of the magazine for decades.

But *Texas Monthly* was never all about politics; it was all about Texas. The same is true of this book, which, in its carefully chosen but inevitably debatable list of the most influential Texans of the last half century, aims to cast the Texas identity net as wide as possible.

I don't have any interest in trying to nail down what a real Texan is or is not. Wouldn't be prudent, as the one of our two former Midland residents who occupied the Oval Office might have phrased it (if he had actually said it in the first place). But when you look back upon a half century of successful or sometimes pernicious Texas humans, you're helplessly alert for commonalities. If I had to make a guess, I'd say that many of the fifty people who ended up being singled out in this volume—out of the thousands who appeared in the magazine during the last five decades—share a talent for self-creation. "Wildcatter," the off-the-shelf Texas descriptor for nonconformists with a tolerance for long odds, is as good a word as any to apply to Willie Nelson or Herb Kelleher or Mary Kay Ash—people who defy the rules, reinvent the rules, or who may not have been aware that there were rules in the first place.

Like LBJ, whose political power originated from humble and neglected sources like college activity societies and congressional secretaries' organizations, the people who changed the course of Texas during the last half century seized opportunity in unlikely places: from the UT dorm room where Michael Dell began assembling computers, to the flailing Mexican restaurant in Lake Jackson where nine-year-old Selena Quintanilla first sang for the public, to the vegetarian housing co-op in Austin where a philosophy and religion student named John Mackey met a young woman—Renee Lawson Hardy—who would become his girlfriend and partner in creating Whole Foods.

I suppose the same is true of entrepreneurs, politicians, and artists no matter where they come from. But the bet that *Texas Monthly* made long ago is that it had found an inexhaustible incubator of colorful people to write about. Texas would loom larger and larger in the world's sight, not just because it was a giant state that became an economic powerhouse, but because it held on so jealously to its historical imperative of seeming special. And because its people—not all of them, but enough to count—were either quietly or noisily self-reliant.

Whether Texas—its manners, its landscape, its history—created those people, or whether it was they who keep re-creating Texas is the sort of slippery thought experiment some of us have engaged in over the decades in the pages of *Texas Monthly* without reaching any conclusion that would bear scrutiny. But it's impossible to read Larry McMurtry without feeling the isolating West Texas world that shaped him. In the soft, hesitant tones that underlie Brené Brown's Texas accent there's a hint of the vulnerability that became her calling card as a motivational speaker, just as the career of Mary Kay Ash—who started her own cosmetic company after she grew tired of watching men she had trained advance faster and make more money—broadcasts a particular kind of Texas confidence and bravado.

In the early decades of *Texas Monthly,* staff members would receive every year a thick volume, bound in red, of the past year's issues of the magazine. When I look up from the desk on which I'm writing this, I can see twenty or so of these volumes marching across the room at the top of my bookshelf, spanning eventful Texas years from the mid-1970s to the early 1990s.

I'm not someone who can bear too much re-reading of my own ancient work, so over the years I haven't had that much occasion to climb up to the top of the bookshelf and haul down one of those heavy tomes. But that was before I began the chore of writing a heavy tome of my own, a sprawling history of Texas from prehistoric times to the dawn of the twenty-first century that was eventually published by UT Press in 2019. After grinding away for about

five or six years and amassing six or seven hundred pages, I began writing about the 1970s and beyond. As I read through those old issues that had been gathering dust in my office, I realized that *Texas Monthly* had been in business for so long that its history and the history of the state were now entwined. There were times when I even found myself crossing my own trail—when I stumbled across an article I had written many years ago that, to my surprise, was now historical source material.

And suddenly those bound volumes became, for me, not just treasured souvenirs but an active research library. Paging through them, following the columns of editorial print past the perfume ads whose long-lost smells readers had once complained about, past images of miniskirted airline stewardesses and leisure-suited department store models, I encountered story after story about the Texans who had built banks or medical centers, or caused political scandals or created art, or fought for expanding rights for minorities or women. When I came to the end of my bound volumes, I went to the magazine's internet archives to read more recent stories about the horrors of the Branch Davidian siege, the dragging murder of James Byrd Jr., the fall of Enron, the rise of lifestyle and tech entrepreneurs, the ongoing shift in the state's political center of gravity from conservative Democrats to Republican culture warriors.

If only, I wished sometimes, *Texas Monthly* had started in 1873, rather than in 1973. That would have given me a hundred more years of world-class journalism to inspire and inform the epic story I was trying to write. As it was, I was grateful enough for what I could read in those bound volumes. The pages themselves might be moldering a bit, but the writing on those pages was still bright. The context in which events unfolded was still vivid.

I never expected *Texas Monthly* to last fifty years when I saw that first issue in 1973, or when my first story—about an alien spacecraft that had supposedly crashed into a field near the town of Aurora in 1897—appeared six months later. But the magazine caught

on, just like Southwest Airlines caught on. It too was a binding force, something that helped sustain the centripetal power of the Texas identity even as it relentlessly set about questioning it: how it had come about in the first place; what it meant, for good or ill, to claim it.

Texas is a staggeringly different place than it was in 1973, when it was not just in thrall to its frontier past but in some ways a hostage to it. Now it's a state from which the future seems to radiate outward in waves: the future of politics; of new modes of transportation; of scientific and technological breakthroughs; of private space flight; of energy, music, literature; of cultural conflict and medical healing. But *Texas Monthly* is still covering Texas and still challenging itself to be relevant and adaptable, worthy of its gigantic subject.

When I thumbed through that very first issue of *Texas Monthly* back in 1973, at a newsstand in an Austin bookstore, I was still young enough to be incapable of imagining the forward passage of fifty years. All I could understand in the moment is what I still understand today: that the state I lived in had found a lasting voice.

Ground controllers at the Manned Spacecraft Center in Houston watch the space walk by Apollo 15 command module pilot Alfred M. Worden on August 5, 1971.

the 1970s

In Texas, there's no such thing as an uneventful decade. But the '70s feel particularly historic; the transition from a rural to an urban state seemed to take on warp-speed velocity. In addition to the opening of Dallas Fort Worth International Airport, which radically changed Texas's relationship to the global economy, the Port of Houston underwent a major expansion, eventually becoming the second-biggest port in the country. At the same time, Houston's exploding medical sector and vibrant art scene began to draw visitors from across the world. But traces of the old Texas remained; in that same burgeoning city, a young Hispanic man named Jose Campos Torres was brutally murdered in 1977 by members of the local police force, sparking the sort of demands for racial justice that continue to this day. Perhaps most significantly, as the decade closed, Bill Clements was elected governor, making him the first Republican to hold that office in more than a century. He would not be the last. Texas, once regarded as a distant corner of the United States, had begun to edge its way to the center of the nation's identity—a process helped along by a pair of bestselling posters featuring the Dallas Cowboys Cheerleaders and Corpus Christi native Farrah Fawcett-Majors.

Willie Nelson

by Al Reinert Photograph by Michael O'Brien

Born in 1933 in the Central Texas town of Abbott, Willie Hugh Nelson is almost certainly the most beloved musician Texas has ever produced. But it would have been tough to imagine that honor back when he was plying his trade in Nashville in the 1960s. Plenty of other artists had hits with Willie's songs, but he spent those years bitter about his inability to break through as a performer. Fed up with Music City, in 1972 Willie moved back home—well, to Austin, which was close enough—and at the soon-to-be-legendary Armadillo World Headquarters created an alternative country scene that against all the odds brought together the rednecks and the hippies. In many ways, Austin's reputation as the Live Music Capital of the World began there, and the Texas country scene suddenly had the music industry's attention. The success that followed made the Nashville executives who didn't get Willie look downright foolish: the breakthrough album *Red Headed Stranger*; the annual Fourth of July picnics; the outlaw country movement; collaborations with everyone from Julio Iglesias to Snoop Dogg; and countless hours spent fighting for farmers and stoners and the environment. By the time he hit his late eighties, Willie wasn't going quite as strong as ever: the shows got shorter, the voice frailer, the guitar picking more hesitant. But old age certainly hadn't stopped him. It was tough to imagine that anything but the inevitable destiny hiding in the shadows of so many of his lyrics ever would.

I **first met Willie** Nelson on a Saturday afternoon in March 1970 when I wandered into Roy Evans's living room in Austin and found this quiet little man perched on the back of an armchair, his feet on the cushion, strumming an apparently prehistoric guitar. He was wearing gabardine slacks and a tacky yellow Robert Hall shirt and seemed terribly shy. I'd been told he was a "famous country songwriter," which didn't impress me—I was a graduate student then, very young and superior—but I liked him from the moment we shook hands and he smiled at me: it's what everybody first responds to in Willie, that tremendously embracing smile. His hair was still pretty short in those days, no beard yet, either, and his face was plain bad luck and lumps.

His home in Nashville had burned down a few months earlier, the only things rescued with a mad dash into the flames being his guitar and his dope stash. Willie was passing the winter on a deserted Bandera dude ranch with his family and the Family, his odd coalition of flunkies and friends. He did a lot of writing that winter, some of the best he'd ever done. Drawn irresistibly and practically nightly to Hill Country dance halls and honky-tonks, he was slowly rediscovering Texas, taking some readings, finding himself.

He found himself in Roy Evans's living room because Evans, then the state AFL-CIO president, had recruited his old buddy Willie to play a benefit concert for Ralph Yarborough, the labor-backed U.S. senator who was campaigning for reelection. And I was there to help promote the benefit. I'd never heard of Willie Nelson, but Evans assured me his fans were legion within the ranks of organized labor.

This was a somewhat exaggerated claim, I suspected, but it proved sufficiently accurate to surprise me: Willie drew a pretty good crowd. None of the union members had to pay, however, and since not much of anyone else came, the benefit was sort of a loser. There definitely weren't any "hippies" in attendance, not with all those hard hats around. The hottest single on the country charts that winter was "Okie from Muskogee," Merle Haggard's cheap broadside against dope-taking, free-loving, flag-burning hippies. Virtually a redneck anthem, the song was everything a Willie Nelson song was not: petty, self-righteous, and strident.

The official Nashville brand of country music was quickly fading into a pale, languid stupor at the time, suitable for funerals or *The Tonight Show Starring Johnny Carson*. When Willie went back to Nashville that summer, he attempted to stir up some excitement, or at least some trouble, but the city kept its stars on short leashes and his kept getting jerked. *Johnny Carson* just wasn't Willie's idea of night life, so after a fruitless, frustrating year he decided to quit Nashville entirely—about the most radical decision you can make in the country music business, then and now—and moved to Austin, where his sister Bobbie lived.

Playing around Texas, he began to notice occasional, presumably audacious longhairs infiltrating his familiar honky-tonk crowds and became intrigued. He looked around some more, played for and with some of them, and sent word back to his fellow Nashville troublemakers that these kids might have the makings of a fair country audience. An unlikely alliance was about to be joined.

The basic cultural distinction between rednecks and hippies, Willie once observed, is that "whiskey makes you feel like fightin', and marijuana makes you feel like listenin' to music." And so long as that's all there was to it, Willie figured he could handle things: he was a recognized authority, after all, on the whiskey-and-fightin' scene, and he'd been fairly well acquainted with the marijuana scene ever since helping his folks plant it in the cornfields south of Waco. It was merely one more approach to all-night dancing, and that was okay by Willie. He even started letting his hair grow.

And when he showed up in New York to record an album for his new label, he brought his road band along with him. It was the customary practice for a rock 'n' roll band but a brash departure for a country singer, whose backup support was virtually always provided by studio musicians. It was the first album Willie ever enjoyed any degree of personal control over, and it came out sounding more raucous and rowdy, more like his live performance, than any recording he'd done before. The album was *Shotgun Willie* and it was a runaway hit.

He celebrated the album's release, and his fortieth birthday, with a full-dress performance at Armadillo World Headquarters, Austin's answer to Caesars Palace, in April 1973. Three months later came Willie Nelson's first Fourth of July Picnic, and within the year there were landmark albums from Jerry Jeff Walker, Waylon Jennings, Michael Murphey, Doug Sahm, Kinky Friedman, and a veritable studio-full of Austin sidemen. It was the beginning of something.

And it all happened so quickly: "redneck rock," "progressive country," "Austin music," "Texas music"—whatever it is, it sure got here in a hurry. Austin hadn't had a unifying obsession like it since 1969, when the Longhorns were national champs. Of course, there was a lot of posturing and pretense involved, silly mooning over "outlaws" and such,

the embarrassments of parody. But there was also a lot of vitality in Austin, and the ripples of that moment could be felt in the city and across the state a half century later. Texas had always provided the cutting edge of country music; there was nothing new about that. But it took Willie to transcend Nashville and bring it back to where he started.

13

Lady Bird Johnson

by Jan Jarboe Russell Photograph by Michael O'Brien

When Lyndon Johnson lost the 1960 presidential nomination to John F. Kennedy, his wife, Lady Bird Johnson, expressed relief (though she immediately retracted the comment); shy by nature, she had never been one to relish the spotlight. Yet, just three years later, when she was thrust into the public eye by Kennedy's assassination, the woman born Claudia Alta Taylor took to the role of First Lady ably. During her husband's years in office, she loyally supported his policies and provided a gentle foil to his bombast, as she had done throughout his career. But she was a force in her own right as well. An unusually well-educated woman for her time and place—she received two bachelor's degrees from UT-Austin, from which she graduated cum laude—she is widely credited with creating the modern notion of the First Lady as a highly visible figure with her own, usually narrow policy agenda. Lady Bird was a lifelong lover of the natural world, and her most visible legacy is the Highway Beautification Act of 1965, which put limits on highway advertising and promoted the planting of wildflowers and native plants. In Austin, where she lived after her husband's death in 1973, the Lady Bird Johnson Wildflower Center and Lady Bird Lake are both named in her honor.

On a rainy day in November 1994 I visited Lady Bird Johnson at her home in northwest Austin to interview her on the occasion of her upcoming eighty-second birthday. We met in the kitchen, where she made coffee, leaning on a steel cane. Her hair was completely gray, her face creased with lines, and even though it was overcast and we were indoors, she wore a pair of sunglasses with large white frames. To be in her presence that day was both moving and unnerving. She was clearly arthritic and going blind from macular degeneration, and these ailments made her seem vulnerable; yet as she stood at the stove, dressed in a pleated navy skirt, cotton blouse, and black lace-up shoes with crepe soles, it was impossible not to feel intimidated.

Sam Rayburn called her "the darn greatest woman who ever lived," and Lady Bird Johnson's was indeed a remarkable life. Born in the small East Texas town of Karnack, she moved to Washington, D.C., in 1934 as the twenty-one-year-old bride of Lyndon Baines Johnson, who was then a congressional aide; twenty-nine years later she became the First Lady when John F. Kennedy was assassinated. When she died in 2007 at age ninety-four, tributes and speeches touted her graciousness and fortitude and her dedication to racial equality.

Many twenty-first-century Texans have no memory of Lady Bird at the height of her power, and those who do may be inclined to think of her as belonging to the past, a woman who brought her husband coffee and newspapers in bed, ironed his shirts, and quietly tolerated his excesses. But one of the secrets to Lady Bird's success was that she always dealt from strength, never weakness. Publicly she pretended to be a traditional stay-at-home wife and mother, but nothing could have been further from the truth. Hers was a life of cultural transition.

During the thirty-eight years she spent as Mrs. Lyndon Johnson, married life in America underwent several upheavals, and Lady Bird's public image can be seen as a bridge from the less visible roles inhabited by wives of the forties and early fifties to the era of women's liberation. Though her demeanor and style may now seem faintly anachronistic, she was remarkably effective as a First Lady, more so than some of her "modern" successors.

Ever the warm and generous host, she quickly set me at ease that day in her kitchen. "Do you take your coffee black or with sugah?" she asked, and the way she rolled that velvety *r*—not disguising her Texas accent but proudly flaunting it— completely won me over. Like her, I was born and raised in East Texas. Her traditional appearance and slow, Southern speech reminded me of all the women I'd grown up with. The fact that she felt no need to feign sophistication made her immediately real to me.

This may be impossible to fathom in today's Texas, where every place you go has Walmart, McDonald's, and all the other chains, but there was a time when character was utterly formed by the physical place in which one was born. Lady Bird was a child of deep East Texas, and I believe that the chief features of her personality— her determined graciousness, her remoteness, her ability to burn anger behind a calm veneer, her down-to-earth nature, her ambition—were all derived from that early landscape.

Like many young girls in East Texas, Lady Bird grew up isolated from the rest of the world by the insular nature of her physical surroundings. Yet the same woods that hemmed her in were a cherished retreat, especially after her mother died, when Lady Bird was only five years old. She often took to the woods for comfort and solace. "I was a child of nature," she told me in our first interview. Every year she would look for the first daffodil of spring to bloom and name it Queen.

The virtues instilled in her as a girl—practicality, thriftiness, good manners, an open mind—served her well in what may have been the most significant episode of her time in the White House: the 1,628-mile train trip she took through eight southern states following the passage of the Civil Rights Act in 1964. Her message to the gathered crowds was that unless the South accepted the Civil Rights Act, its economy would be ruined and its fate consigned to the past. In stop after stop, she faced angry white picketers with signs such as "Black Bird Go Home." But she carried on.

Where Lady Bird represented the best of Texas womanhood, Lyndon often represented some of the worst traits of Texas men. Though brilliant and astute, he could be a terrible bully, and his many alleged infidelities have been carefully chronicled by biographers. This presented me with a particular difficulty. In order to write about Lady Bird's life, I felt it was necessary to address some of her husband's darker dimensions. Yet, on that first day in her kitchen, when I brought up the subject, Lady Bird yanked off her sunglasses and snapped, "When people ask me these sort of things, I just say, 'Look to your own lives. Look to yourself, everybody. Fix yourselves, and keep your problems to yourself.'" It was the kind of stoic answer that was deeply ingrained in women of her time and place—the idea that personal problems must be borne alone.

But Lady Bird also resisted being seen merely as an individual. She saw herself as an extension of her husband and recoiled from any attempt to view her life apart from his. Her marriage was what defined her. "He was the catalyst; I was the amalgam," she said, over and over. In other words, she poured herself into the mold of his life.

Their interaction was seamless, mutual. Lyndon brought her out of her shyness, and Lady Bird gave him what he most needed: loyalty. Neither could have succeeded without the other. She took care of his personal needs, having his size 17 shirts extended so they would stay tucked in his trousers, soothing his temper. But she did more than that. She helped draft his speeches and was one of the few people close to him who could offer criticism without fear of reprisal. Love was a part of what bound them together, but loyalty, ambition, and self-interest played a part as well, from both sides. Despite her image as Our Lady of the Wildflowers, Lady Bird was tough.

Looking back, what was most impressive about Lady Bird was how engaged she was. She never shrank from the tumultuousness of her times. Like her husband, she believed in the power of government to change things for the better. The small sign on her White House desk said it all: CAN DO.

17

Michael DeBakey and Denton Cooley

by Mimi Swartz

The long-running professional feud between world-class heart surgeons Michael DeBakey and Denton Cooley had everything you could want from a real-life medical melodrama: a revolution-ary and controversial invention (the artificial heart), desperate patients hoping for a miracle, two protagonists with world-class talents and the egos to match, a blistering series of accusations and counteraccusations, and lots of petty tit-for-tat. But anyone who focused on the animus between this pair of prodigiously gifted physicians missed the big picture: by the time that they buried the hatchet, late in life, they had helped turn Houston into the world-class city it had so long sought to be.

ome people, unfamiliar with Houston's sprawling layout, think they're downtown when they're actually somewhere else entirely, and with good reason. The Texas Medical Center, which sits south of Hermann Park, is the world's largest of its kind. A city within a city of squat stone buildings and soaring glass towers, it boasts an employee population of 106,000—equal to the general population of Burbank, California, or Boulder, Colorado. Ten million patients a year are seen at its forty-five institutions. Here, ambulance sirens provide a perpetual soundtrack and doctors in scrubs crisscross its streets, their white coats flapping like the wings of gulls on the gulf breezes trapped between the buildings. There are patients in faded overalls, Chanel suits, saris, burkas, and Birkenstocks; many in wheelchairs, most wearing expressions that reveal some combination of fear and hope. The Texas Medical Center can be as dizzying and disorienting as it is inspiring, because it's the home of some of the best medical care on the planet. If that fact is well known, it is less well known, particularly outside of Houston, that the place exists today largely as the result of a bitter feud between two of its most famous surgeons, Michael DeBakey and Denton Cooley.

When Houstonians talk about the enmity between these two men, they tend to focus on their differences. DeBakey was short in stature, a dervish of unceasing energy, and possessed of a hawkish, sometimes dour mien that could be said to resemble that of a French police officer presented with a moldy croissant. DeBakey, who was born in 1908, grew up in Lake Charles, Louisiana, the child of Lebanese immigrants. Brilliant as the young, slight DeBakey was, it is impossible to imagine that such a bookish and bespectacled child avoided the taunts and worse of bigger Cajun boys. Instead of punching

back, he devoured library books, learned how to sew from his mother, and dissected the baby birds that fell from the trees near his home, all in preparation for a better life in a bigger place.

That "bigger place" would soon become the whole wide world. After acing medical training at Tulane, where he invented a device called a roller pump, a precursor part to what would become the heart-lung machine, he attended some of the finest European medical institutions and then returned to Tulane to teach. When World War II broke out, DeBakey served in the Army, where he rose through the ranks and became an expert at logistics, responsible among other things for developing what would come to be known as mobile army surgical hospitals, aka MASH units, that saved countless lives on the front lines. After the war he hired on as chair of the surgical department of the fledgling Baylor College of Medicine in 1948. Over the next few decades, he built a worldwide reputation as a surgeon while converting what he had initially called "a second-rate medical school" into one of the country's best.

During that time, he became not just a master of vascular surgery and an inventor of medical devices but a master of politics and a crucial advocate for health care as a right, not a privilege. Once awkward and stiff, DeBakey now hobnobbed effortlessly with senators and presidents, allowed his lifesaving surgeries to be televised—the

19

first time in history that had been done—and operated on heads of state. His face graced the cover of *Time* magazine in 1965. This redounded to his benefit, but not his alone; as DeBakey's reputation grew, so did Baylor's and the Houston medical sector's. The Texas Medical Center may have been founded in 1945, but it was only after DeBakey's arrival that the money started rolling in. As more hospitals and other medical institutions were built, nothing at the TMC happened without DeBakey's input. Or his blessing.

It so happened that one of the high-powered doctors DeBakey recruited to Baylor and the affiliated Methodist Hospital as a protégé was the man who would soon become his archnemesis, Denton Cooley. For Cooley, Baylor was a homecoming: he was born in Houston in 1920. Cooley grew up to be a tall, gifted athlete with an almost preternatural calm and, even into middle age, so movie star handsome, with dimples and chiseled cheekbones, that women—nurses, patients, wives of patients, virtually any female—would quiver when he graced them with his velvety voice and toothy smile. Cooley came from a prominent local family but was a child of divorce when it was still considered shameful, and he had a father and a brother who destroyed themselves with drink. Still, he described his childhood as halcyon: swimming in Houston's bayous, sneaking fruit from neighbor's orchards, repairing jalopies and driving them in his early teens, and feeling in general that rules applied to other people. From his beloved University of Texas, Cooley went on to study at Johns Hopkins and racked up a host of prestigious fellowships, so that by the time he came to Baylor in 1951, he was already developing a reputation as not just the best heart surgeon in the world but the best surgeon who ever lived. It was not an opinion he ever disputed.

Maybe, in some other universe, DeBakey and Cooley could have become partners and transformed the world of medicine together. But the problems were there from the beginning: Cooley had long suspected that DeBakey had thwarted his attempt to get a job years earlier, and harbored a grudge. So maybe it was unavoidable that their relationship started deteriorating on Cooley's first day of rounds at Baylor, when, for reasons presumably buried back in Lake Charles, DeBakey ridiculed Cooley for claiming that a patient with an aneurysm could be better served by removing the life-threatening bulge in the aorta instead of patching it, as DeBakey had been doing with a Dacron graft he'd invented. When Cooley proceeded to prove himself right by performing the newer procedure, DeBakey felt compelled to burst into the operating room for a theatrical but unnecessary rescue.

But even with an apology that never came, the two would never have found equanimity. DeBakey was a man who believed in control and authority; Cooley listened almost exclusively to his own inner directives. DeBakey was a good surgeon and a good inventor, but his greatest gifts were administrative and political. Cooley's abilities in the operating room were singular: before there were heart-lung machines to keep patients alive during surgery, Cooley repaired the tiny hearts of children so quickly and effortlessly that his assistants couldn't believe their eyes. He was a brilliant inventor, with numerous patents to his name. And while DeBakey was famous for terrorizing interns and residents, Cooley, having been a team player in high school and college sports, inspired an almost religious fervor among those who worked for and with him.

For a while, the differences between the two men didn't matter. Baylor's dedication to excellence spread to other hospitals in the medical center, including MD Anderson Cancer Center and the charity hospital Ben Taub. But, as they say in the old westerns, by the 1960s DeBakey's Methodist Hospital wasn't big enough for the two of them. Patient loads were exploding as people from all over the world arrived in Houston to see one world famous surgeon or the other. Cooley was not a man to fight over beds or wait his turn in the operating room. In 1967 he broke ground for his own place, the Texas Heart Institute, with money raised from rich Houston pals. DeBakey saw his departure as an unforgivable betrayal, on the scale of Brutus's duplicity toward Caesar.

But Cooley wasn't done. By 1969, he had grown weary of DeBakey's cautious approach to the artificial heart DeBakey had been developing in the Baylor lab. With a dying patient at the ready, Cooley commandeered—or borrowed, or stole, depending on who you ask—the device with help from one of DeBakey's researchers and put it in his patient. DeBakey heard the news of the historic surgery the next day while he was out of town, at a conference in Washington. It's safe to say that Cooley became as dead to DeBakey then as Cooley's patient was three days later.

From then on, anyone who wanted to work with DeBakey could not be seen with Cooley's associates, much less the doctor himself. Not only did they have competing staffs, they had competing hospitals. No hostess in Houston or elsewhere would even consider inviting both men to the same event. The feud became so bitter that it was the subject of a *Life* magazine cover story in 1970.

But as Cooley would later attest, their competition made everyone around them work harder and better, whether improving the quality of patient care, developing surgical innovations, or perfecting the elegance of their individual facilities. If Houston had always thrived on entrepreneurship and innovation, the feud supercharged it.

Ultimately, the similarities between Cooley and DeBakey mattered more than their differences, which perhaps they finally recognized when they publicly reconciled in 2007, less than a year before DeBakey's death and nearly a decade before Cooley's. They were vain and prideful, but the shining towers and state-of-the-art operating rooms, the research laboratories and donors' names carved in stone, reflect their outsized dreams and ambitions, the ones that showed the world what Houston medicine could do.

21

Américo Paredes

by John Phillip Santos Photograph by Jesse Herrera

Américo Paredes, one of the foremost Mexican American scholars of the twentieth century, was born in 1915 in Brownsville, where, as a child, he wrote poetry, sang, and played guitar. After earning his associate degree at a local junior college, Paredes published his first book—*Cantos de adolescencia*, a volume of poetry from his teenage years—at the age of twenty-two. Following a stint in the Army during World War II, he returned to the United States and enrolled at the University of Texas at Austin, where he completed his bachelor's degree and earned his master's degree and doctorate. It was at UT that Paredes became interested in folklore and wrote his famous dissertation, *With His Pistol in His Hand*, which was published as a book in 1958 and is avidly read today. Before his death in 1999, Paredes spent decades teaching at UT; writing books about Texas, Mexico, and the borderlands; and inspiring generations of Chicano scholars. At least three public schools in Texas are named after him.

For centuries, the lands that became Texas were a place where diverse peoples encountered strangers, interacted with them, and became someone new, sometimes for the better and sometimes for the worse. Too often those meetings flared up into violence and injustice, a deep-time backstory that belies the triumphalist myth of the Lone Star State, but offers the opportunity for future reckonings and reconciliations.

Those who see Texas through such a lens likely learned something about that past from the life and works of the folklorist Américo Paredes, who yoked literary virtuosity to a compassionate understanding of his people's complex history. His many talents brought forth song, reportage, poems, works of fiction, and a doctoral dissertation that became a movie. Taken all together, his body of work is a prophecy of what Texas might yet become.

When you're born in Brownsville in 1915 with a name like Américo Paredes—"American Walls" would be the rough English translation—it might seem that destiny was prefiguring an interesting life, especially if you were birthed into the borderlands of South Texas, which was seen by many

Texans as the farthest edge of the barely civilized world. And so it would be for Paredes, who blithely pushed his way through all manner of walls: he was an accomplished norteño guitarist and singer; a military veteran who wrote firsthand accounts for *Stars and Stripes* about the complicated aftermath of the Pacific War; the first Mexican American to receive a PhD in English from UT Austin; and a legendary professor committed to mentoring a generation of Chicano intellectuals.

Paredes's life and works remind us that the origin story of Texas began from the south, with the conquest of Mexico one hundred years before Plymouth Rock, and the settlement of northern New Spain and Mexico, including the lands that would eventually become Texas. Paredes's ancestors were Sephardic Jews who made their way to these unsettled northernmost reaches of New Spain in the late sixteenth century as they sought to keep their distance from the Inquisition in Mexico City. Other ancestors were part of the mid-eighteenth-century expeditions of José de Escandón, who settled the region of New Spain known as Nuevo Santander, founding many of the towns of today's state of Tamaulipas, as well as Laredo.

Don Américo's father, Justo Paredes Cisneros, was born in Matamoros, across the Rio Grande from Brownsville, where as a young man he joined an ill-fated uprising against the dictator Porfirio Díaz. After the rebellion collapsed, Justo gave up his

23

birthright to the family's lands to move to Brownsville, where Américo was born.

The young Américo grew up spending his summers working on that same family ranch, where he proved to be a keen observer of Mexican folkways as well as a gifted musician, learning hundreds of traditional border ballads, or corridos, that memorialized the "heroes of the people" who were ignored in history books.

One such hero, Gregorio Cortez, became the target of the largest manhunt in Texas history in 1901 after a sheriff in Gonzales County shot Cortez's brother and Cortez shot the sheriff. After a ten-day manhunt, Cortez was caught by the Texas Rangers and, over the next few years, convicted of the murders of the sheriff and two other law enforcement officers whom he likely didn't kill. Two of those convictions (and a conviction for horse theft) were eventually reversed, and Cortez was pardoned for the third in 1913 after spending a decade or so in prison. Following his release, he emigrated to Mexico, where he died in 1916 in Nuevo Laredo. This was in the midst of the period known as La Hora de Sangre, "the Time of Blood," when as many as five thousand Mexican Americans were killed in extrajudicial slayings and lynchings in south Texas, some with the involvement of Texas Rangers.

Paredes wrote his celebrated doctoral dissertation (not a commonly used phrase) about Cortez, and *With His Pistol in His Hand: A Border Ballad and Its Hero* was published in 1958 by the University of Texas Press. Paredes's book examines the story retold in many versions of the corrido, all of which celebrate Cortez's cunning in eluding the "Rinches,"as the Rangers were derogatorily known. Even more daringly, the book indicted the dean of Texas history of the time, UT's Walter Prescott Webb, the great extoller and apologist of the Texas

Ranger legacy. Reading Paredes's civilly worded assault on Webb, I'm reminded of the unforgettable line uttered by Omar Little in *The Wire*: "When you come at the king, you best not miss." Paredes did not miss.

He began by quoting Webb himself on the character of Texas Mexicans from his 1935 book *The Texas Rangers: A Century of Frontier Defense*: "Without disparagement it may be said there is a cruel streak in the Mexican nature, or so the history of Texas would lead one to believe. This cruelty may be a heritage from the Spanish of the Inquisition; it may, and doubtless should, be attributed to the Indian blood." To which Paredes wryly replied, "Professor Webb does not mean to be disparaging. One wonders what his opinion might have been when he was in a less scholarly mood and not looking at the Mexican from the objective point of view of the historian." By exposing the blatantly racist underpinning of Webb's scholarship, Paredes changed Texas historiography, opening a way for scholars in the decades since to engage with the popular histories of Mexican American communities across the state.

With His Pistol in His Hand was even made into a movie, 1982's *The Ballad of Gregorio Cortez*, starring a young Edward James Olmos as Cortez. How many dissertations become movies? Still, though Walter Prescott Webb's historical oeuvre is irreversibly tainted by Paredes's 1958 intervention, he is the one who has an endowed chair at UT named in his honor.

Why is Don Américo Paredes's legacy so important today? Though his book came out in the late 1950s, it wasn't until the 1970s that Chicano scholars, some of them his onetime students, began teaching it—ironically, not at first in Texas but at the University of California, Los Angeles. Paredes would become the unsuspecting *padrino* of Texas Chicano cultural studies, influencing diverse key figures such as the longtime UT professor José E. Limón and the Chicana scholar Gloria Anzaldúa. He was a cultivated Tejano gentleman who helped to ignite a cultural and intellectual uprising reflected in such pivotal works of revisionist scholarship as David Montejano's *Anglos and Mexicans in the Making of Texas, 1836–1986*, and the MacArthur "genius" grant winner Monica Muñoz Martinez's *The Injustice Never Leaves You: Anti-Mexican Violence in Texas*.

Though Paredes wasn't a literal activist, his work and life served to awaken many Mexican American Texans to the history that was being erased as Texas became vested as a state of the American Union. At the time Paredes was born, that project wasn't altogether completed, and blood was still being spilled to determine that outcome. So his influential scholarly *testimonio* grew out of a fundamentally cleft world, out of the experience of being between worlds, between Mexico and Texas, between the past and the future. Evoking this sentiment in one of his poems, Paredes wrote, "I am homesick for a home I've never lived in . . ."

As the Chicano literature professor Ramón Saldívar—a fellow Brownsville native—has observed, one of the major impacts on Paredes was his experience as a wartime journalist in East Asia, covering the war trials of Japanese military officials and writing searing dispatches capturing everyday life in the aftermath of conquest. It was a pivotal time in his life—he met and married his second wife, Amelia Nagamine, a Japanese-Uruguayan mestiza, while he was there—and Saldívar argues that Paredes recognized something kindred with the world of the "Mexico-Texans," as he sometimes called them.

How, Paredes wondered, would the Japanese remember their history, full of defeats and dispossession? How would they find the resilience to move forward into an uncertain future? These were queries he brought back to Texas and applied to his own people when he began his undergraduate and doctoral studies at UT at the age of thirty-five.

In a poem from that era, Paredes wrote about standing at a corner between "absolute elsewhere" and "absolute future"— and the light is always red. He ends by telling us that the "people in between" are destined to "stand on the corner/Waiting for the green."

Paredes's work helped to advance a reckoning with injustices Mexican Texans endured early in the twentieth century, if only by hinting at what a reconciliation based on mutual understanding might look like. In 1999, close to the end of the century during which Paredes lived his entire life, a group of family and friends went to the beach at Boca Chica, where the waters of Rio Grande and the Gulf of Mexico mingle, and poured in the ashes of the scholar Don Américo and his wife, Doña Amelia.

25

Barbara Jordan

by William Broyles

History is full of what-ifs, few more intriguing than the question of how far Barbara Jordan would have risen if illness had not caused her to prematurely retreat from public life. Born in Houston in 1936, Jordan decided early on that she was meant for greatness and made good on that ambition quickly. In 1966, at the age of thirty, she was elected to the Texas Senate, making her Texas's first Black state senator since 1883—and the first Black woman ever to sit in that institution. Over the course of her six years there, she earned a reputation as a dogged legislator and savvy parliamentarian, and won over many of her colleagues. In 1972, when she was elected to the United States Congress, she and Georgia's Andrew Young became the first Black candidates from the Deep South to serve in the House of Representatives in the twentieth century. There, she gained fame during President Richard Nixon's impeachment hearings, when she gave a speech in defense of the Constitution that made headlines and can be quoted from memory by many people today. How much further could she have gone? Governor of Texas? Vice president of the United States? President? We'll never know, as her struggle with multiple sclerosis prompted her in 1978 to retire from Congress. By the time she died in 1996, it was widely recognized that she had blazed a path for the numerous Texas politicians of color who have since rendered our Legislature much less lily-white than it was when she first walked through its doors.

When **Barbara Jordan** was elected to the Texas Senate in 1967, she studied the institution's procedures so closely that within weeks she was recognized as one of its leading parliamentarians, not above using, as she put it, "the trickers' tricks." Politicians highly respect political skills, and Jordan, who was the first Black person elected to the Senate since the nineteenth century, quickly demonstrated that she had them. She knew the rules backward and forward, she only spoke when she knew what she wanted, she didn't preach or harangue, she concentrated on a few subjects and became the Senate expert on them, and she never embarrassed a fellow senator: she always gave the impression she understood the pressures he was under and left him room for self-respect.

Often, her exacting and aloof sense of dignity was shrewdly leavened with warm humor. Since it softens the abrasiveness of conflict, humor is one of a legislator's most valuable skills. Few politicians appreciate a somber ideologue, even if he's on their side. Jordan's status as a Black woman could have been a damper on the club's easy sexual and racial jokes. But it didn't work out that way. "She never let on," recalled her fellow senator Don Kennard. "She put up with it, participated in it, and she used it." She was, in short, one of the boys. She would laugh with them, drink with them, stay up late, go quail hunting, play the guitar, and sing songs with them.

Her political techniques were the same ones she would later perfect in Congress: deference to leadership, loyalty to the institution, hard work, humor, and an unwillingness to be typecast, all wrapped up in the power and mystery of her personality and topped off with that old standby, her voice—which could either create an easy intimacy or intimidate, seemingly at will. On hearing it for the first time, one awed young woman said, "I turned on my television set and thought I was listening to God." It sounds, as the former Georgia congressman Andrew Young said, "like the heavens have opened up." The religious parallels are apt, because her voice was an evangelical voice, a voice designed to bring to the fold the presence of the Lord. It was a voice that millions of people came to know in 1974, during Richard Nixon's impeachment hearings, when she declared, before millions of television viewers, in her unplaceable accent and cadences, "My faith in the Constitution is whole, it is complete, it is total, and I am not going to sit here and be an idle spectator to the diminution, the subversion, the destruction of the Constitution."

By deploying so many different skills, Jordan shattered grotesque stereotypes about Blacks that many of her less enlightened colleagues in the Senate held. Just as importantly, at a time when Black militancy was on the rise, she alerted her more liberal colleagues that not all Blacks were antiestablishment. She was a hard-nosed, practical politician with no patience for the politics of confrontation.

Jordan's insistence on working within the system, by the system's rules, was a hallmark of her entire career. She wasn't raised to rebel or to make a scene. Instead, she was the master of the art of the possible: the practical craft of knowing how things work and what buttons to push. And if at times her notion of what was possible was too narrow, if she occasionally gave more ground than she should have, she also had a lot to show for her efforts. In her three regular sessions in the Senate she introduced more than 150 bills and resolutions. About half of them were the apolitical meat and potatoes of legislation, from creating a new court and establishing a new medical school to closing off the street that ran through Texas Southern University and setting safety standards for people who climb into manholes. But the rest were solidly liberal: extending the minimum wage to cover nonunionized farmworkers and domestics, a fair labor practices act, pollution control, a whole range of workmen's compensation acts, equal rights, and antidiscrimination. She fought for liquor by the drink and against extending the sales tax.

She did, though, insist on not being taken for granted by her Democratic colleagues, and she had the charisma to make that insistence stick. "Even though Barbara was with us on almost every crucial issue," said one liberal senator, "somehow you never could *assume* she would be. If you had a real good bill, you know, that did everything right, that had in it all the sort of things she had been supporting, you still couldn't just check off her vote on your scorecard. You had to go see her, reason with her, make her understand what you wanted to do." She always ended up in the corral, but damned if she didn't have to be rounded up every time.

In many ways, she reminded some observers who could look beyond differences of race and gender of the similarly protean Lyndon Johnson. By the time she was elected to the Texas Senate, LBJ was struggling. The prodigious outpouring of Great Society and civil rights programs was behind him, and the Vietnam War, no matter how much he wheeled and dealed and plotted and planned, steadily kept pulling him beneath the political waves. His protégé in Texas, John Connally, didn't care about the Great Society and in fact had done some impressive footdragging on anti-poverty programs and civil rights. This pained Johnson deeply. To LBJ, these programs were more than just legislative accomplishments; they were his legacy, they were what would go beside his name in the history books. All the political operating in the world wasn't worth a damn if you didn't do something with it. So far as Johnson could tell, Connally had inherited his skills but none of his heart.

Barbara Jordan was different. She had many of the qualities Johnson admired: she had a deep respect for legislative bodies and the legislative process, she was uncomfortable with ideologues, and she had great humor and political skills. She admired and recognized what an accomplishment the Great Society programs were, how much arm-twisting and cajoling and convincing and political chips they had used up.

She understood that getting bills passed, not lofty rhetoric, was the essential work of a legislator, no matter how much lofty rhetoric she spun out. She would brush aside high-flown descriptions of her symbolic significance and insist she was just "a practical politician."

There is, though, a deep symbolic dimension to Barbara Jordan's achievement. She is a link between the dark past and a hopeful future, a bridge from a segregated society to an unsegregated one. Yet during her life she was smeared with racist stereotypes rooted in that past. She was condescended to as if she were every Black maid, every Black cook, every Black woman who lived closest with whites, the women who sustained what Martin Luther King called the "web of mutuality" between the races. She knew the forces against her and she knew she could not bring about that hopeful future single-handedly. But she never wavered in using her unique gifts to do the most possible in the here and now. Her enduring legacy is that she subverted and then destroyed those stereotypes—as if every Black woman maligned across the centuries had risen up to change the world.

29

Tom Landry

by Gary Cartwright Photograph by Ron Scott

"In Texas there is only one sport and only one team," *Texas Monthly*'s erstwhile executive editor Paul Burka used to say when the staff was discussing assigning a sports story. Burka didn't have to explain what he meant because everyone knew: in Texas, football was the only sport and the Dallas Cowboys were the only team. This was, by any measure, a hyperbolic statement, but there was an essential truth to it. If the Cowboys were known nationally as "America's Team," they were, more or less, Texas's Team, too. The Cowboys, longtime *Texas Monthly* writer Joe Nick Patoski once wrote, "were the pinnacle of Texas's infatuation with football, the one true thing that brought together fat cats and yardmen, painters and politicians." They were also ambassadors to the wider world, advertising an indelible Texas persona marked by a swaggering self-confidence. Over the years there have been many iconic Cowboys, but none was more important than the team's founding head coach, Tom Landry. The South Texas native led the team for an astonishing twenty-nine years—from 1960 to 1988—tying the record of longest-tenured coach in NFL history. Born in Mission in 1924, Landry played for the University of Texas Longhorns and then the New York Giants, where he got his first taste of coaching and developed his revolutionary "4-3 defense." During his time in Dallas, the team had twenty consecutive winning seasons, earned thirteen division titles, and won two Super Bowls. All of that came to an end in 1989 when, in the wake of three consecutive losing seasons, Jerry Jones bought the team and fired Landry on his first full day as owner. Landry passed away in 2000.

In the delirious hours of January 16, 1972, after Super Bowl VI, when the Dallas Cowboys were drunk with victory and talk of the new dynasty rained down, Tom Landry permitted himself a Virginia reel around the dressing room, then he struck a note of caution. The question, he said, was whether the Cowboys would perform at the same level the next year.

"At the championship level," he said, "there is a very narrow edge between winning and losing. You don't have to take much away from a team to keep them out of the Super Bowl. The hunger that makes a player work hard enough to win is inherent in some, but in others it has to be built in. The edge comes from trying to achieve a goal. Once you've achieved it, it is very difficult to look back at the price you've paid and then make yourself do it again."

At the bottom of the sweet cup of Super Bowl VI, Landry read the future. Though they were essentially the same team that won the Super Bowl, the next year's Cowboys were found lacking, never making it past the NFC Championship game. There is only one Super Bowl, and it's no disgrace not to get there: at that point, only Vince Lombardi's Green Bay Packers had been able to repeat as champions.

That is what hurt Landry, the fact that Lombardi had done it. Lombardi was a football legend, a vain, volatile, uncompromising dictator. Could Tom Landry afford to be something less?

Landry and Vince Lombardi had a long history. They were guiding forces behind the great New York Giants' teams of the 1950s. Jim Lee Howell was the head coach of the Giants, but it was Lombardi's work as offensive coordinator and Landry's as defense coordinator that gave the Giants character.

They were very different men. "Lombardi was a much warmer person than Landry," said Wellington

Mara, the Giants' owner. "He went from warm to red hot. You could hear him laughing or shouting for five blocks. You couldn't hear Landry from the next chair." Landry would react to a great play or a poor play in the same dispassionate manner, as though it were ancient history. When a player was down and writhing in agony, the contrast was most apparent: Lombardi would be racing like an Italian fishwife, cursing and imploring the gods to get the lad back on his feet for at least one more play; Landry would be giving instructions to the unfortunate player's substitute.

Landry once explained: "The reason I take on the appearance of being unemotional is I don't believe you can be emotional and concentrate the way you must to be effective. When I see a great play from the sidelines, I can't cheer it. I'm a couple of plays ahead, thinking. . . . The players don't want to see me rushing around and screaming. They want to believe I know what I'm doing."

"Landry was a born student of the game," says Em Tunnell, the great defensive back who played with and for Landry on the Giants. "But he was kind of weird. After a game the rest of us would go out for a beer, Tom would disappear. He was always with his family. You never knew what was going through his mind. He never said nothing, but he always knew what was going on."

By training, Landry was an industrial engineer. "I couldn't be satisfied trusting my instincts the way Tunnell did," Landry

explained of his days as a player. "I didn't have the speed or the quickness. I had to train myself and everyone around me to key various opponents and recognize tendencies."

"Most of us just played the game," recalled Landry's fellow Giant Frank Gifford. "Landry studied it. He was cool and calculating. Emotion had no place in his makeup."

In 1973 the former Cowboy Peter Gent wrote a bitterly critical pro football novel, *North Dallas* *Forty*, that is widely regarded as a roman à clef about his years with the team. "Landry is a plastic man," he once said, echoing his former teammate Duane Thomas's description. "And yet, there is this paradox—in Landry's presence you do not feel the cool platitudes of plastic and computers, you feel something more visceral. You feel fear."

Mary Kay Ash

by Skip Hollandsworth Photograph by Danny Turner

When Mary Kay Ash founded her namesake cosmetics company in Dallas in 1963 with just $5,000, few thought she would succeed. Back then, there weren't many examples of wildly successful female entrepreneurs. But Ash, who was born in Houston in 1918, knew she was onto something, and she was right. She was also well aware that her company's success was incredibly unlikely: one of the company's main symbols was the bumblebee—an insect that, urban legend has it, scientists believe shouldn't be able to fly. By the time she died in 2001, Mary Kay Cosmetics was a global and highly profitable company. Even today, without her charisma boosting the brand, it's the fifteenth largest beauty products company in the country, with annual U.S. sales of $3.5 billion, ahead of such big names as Colgate-Palmolive, Chanel, and Revlon.

Until I met her, I regarded Mary Kay Ash as the epitome of Texas feminine flamboyance. The famous cosmetics mogul wore baseball-size jewelry and piled-high blond wigs that looked like soft-serve vanilla ice cream. She drove a pink Cadillac and lived in a Dallas mansion that was also painted pink.

In 1995, I attended the annual convention she hosted at the Dallas Convention Center for her saleswomen. As cymbals crashed and timpani drums rolled, Mary Kay, wearing a long sparkly gown, strode onstage to deafening cheers. "Are you ready for the most exciting moment of your life?" she asked, holding out

her hands exactly the way the pope does when he blesses his flock. There were more cheers as Mary Kay Cosmetics' top saleswomen were escorted down a curving staircase and led to thrones, where tiaras were placed on their perfectly sprayed hair, new fur coats wrapped around their shoulders, and diamond bracelets clasped over their wrists. "You too can do it," Mary Kay proclaimed to the crowd in her sugary sweet voice. "I know you can."

When I went backstage to meet Mary Kay, I told her I was a little bewildered by the spectacle. It seemed so frivolous, I said. Mary Kay gave me a pleasant smile. "All I'm doing is giving women a chance to change their lives," she said. "My goodness, how can you complain about that?"

As I quickly learned, I really shouldn't have. Mary Kay was genuinely driven to give women— from unappreciated housewives to underpaid office workers—a chance to change their lives. Although she would never describe herself as such, she was a fierce feminist who created her company to empower women who felt frustrated and angry about their place in life and desperately longed to prove themselves.

"I want the women who sell my cosmetics to be able to make as much money as they want to make, not as much money as their male bosses want them to make," she told me. "I want them to become wealthy entrepreneurs in their own right, without worrying about men trying to hold them back."

Mary Kay knew exactly what she was talking about because it had all happened to her. Born in Houston in 1918, she was taking care of herself before she entered elementary school. Her father, an invalid afflicted with tuberculosis, spent most of Mary Kay's early childhood in a sanatorium. To pay the family's bills, her mother managed a restaurant. She woke before daylight to make breakfast

for Mary Kay and her two other children, left the house by 5:00 a.m., and sometimes didn't get home until 9:00 at night.

The grueling, thankless nature of her mother's labors never left Mary Kay's memory. She married at age seventeen, had three children, and then divorced in the 1940s after her husband abandoned her. To support her children, she had to go to work, but as she told me, "There just weren't any career options for a woman unless it was doing what my mother did. In that era, you had to walk two paces behind a man and there was no way you were allowed into an executive office unless it was to serve coffee."

In order to work from home, she got a job selling brooms, irons, and other housewife's tools, lugging a suitcase full of samples from one home to another. An amazing saleswoman, she was hired away by another direct sales company, but she soon discovered that the all-male board of directors had promoted her male assistant whom she had trained to an executive position at twice her salary. "Those men didn't believe a woman had brain matter at all," Mary Kay said, giving me a long look, trying to maintain her composure. I was astonished. All these years later, she was still brimming with anger at the way she had been betrayed.

It was that anger that drove her in 1963, at the age of forty-five, to start her own company in Dallas. Her business plan was simple. She didn't require a résumé for any woman who wanted to join the company as a "consultant" (Mary Kay's preferred term for a saleswoman). All the woman had to do was pay for a Mary Kay beauty kit, purchase some makeup from the company, and then sell the makeup for twice what she paid for it. If she recruited another woman to become a consultant, she would earn even more money, receiving a percentage of her new recruit's sales forever.

Bankers and accountants—all of whom were men, of course—told Mary Kay the company would never succeed. But Mary Kay tapped into the deep emotions of downtrodden working-class Dallas women who wanted to do more with their lives than answer the phone in an office and clean their houses on weekends.

Soon, Mary Kay Cosmetics spread across the country, where it found an entire generation of eager women. Besides getting fat commission checks, consultants who built successful sales teams were given pink Cadillacs to drive. They got to walk across the stage at the annual convention to thunderous applause. "The last time a lot of my consultants had received any applause was when they walked across the stage at their high school graduations," Mary Kay noted. "I said, 'That's not going to happen in my company.'"

As the years passed and more careers opened up for women, Mary Kay still insisted her company was the best place for a woman to work. She called corporate America the "other world" that enslaved its female employees in exhausting nine-to-five jobs and paid $0.76 for every dollar that a man made. Only at Mary Kay Cosmetics, she said, could a woman be a milk-and-cookies mom and make the kind of money that would allow her to buy her dream house and put her kids through college.

When Mary Kay died in 2001 at the age of eighty-three, there were more than eight hundred thousand women selling her cosmetics in thirty-seven countries. Sales had reached $1.2 billion

a year. I went to her funeral at a Baptist church, where the sanctuary was overflowing with pink floral arrangements. Most of the female mourners were wearing their finest pink power suits. The Mary Kay employee choir, dressed in bright pink choir robes, sang "On Silver Wings" and "I Did It My Way." And as the service came to an end, the organist struck up the company's theme song, "Mary Kay Enthusiasm," which begins, "I've got that Mary Kay enthusiasm down in my heart . . ."

Mary Kay's followers put down their purses and began clapping in time to the music. As I headed out the door, I could not help but remember a story Mary Kay had told me on the day I interviewed her. "You know," she said, "when God made the world, He proclaimed, 'That's good.' And then he made a man and said, 'That's good.' And then He said, 'But I think I can do better.' So He made a woman."

37

Dominique de Menil

by Laura Furman

When Dominique de Menil died in Houston in 1997, she left behind a city dramatically different from the one she had arrived at a half century earlier—and played a significant role in making many of those changes come about. De Menil, who was born in Paris, France, in 1908, was an heir to Schlumberger Ltd., the global concern founded by her father that brought scientific rigor to oil exploration and extraction, which until then was something more like a dowser's art. Fleeing the Nazi occupation of France, she and her husband, John, who had joined the family firm, had settled in Houston in the early 1940s. It wasn't long before the stylish couple set about elevating Houston's image from that of an oil patch jumping-off point to a metropolis with a global cultural scene and a soaring modernist skyline. She spent decades developing and refining an eye for modern art, amassing a collection of immense size, breadth, and depth. At the same time, she learned to use her wealth, power, and generosity—sometimes combined with sharp elbows—to impose her artistic sensibility on the Bayou City. The most visible and well-known artifacts of her influence are the famed Menil Collection museum and the neighboring Rothko Chapel.

Dominique de Menil always seemed to be chilly, especially in the frigid Houston air-conditioning, and she carried a large shawl to wrap around herself at meetings. In photographs before her husband John's death, she often wears flower-patterned dresses that

belt at her waist and hang obediently in a full skirt. After he died, when I knew her, she wore mono-chromatic garments that enveloped her. In my ignorance I thought that the loose-fitting dresses and suits just happened to look perfect. But it was not by chance that the garments she chose draped becomingly over her thin body: her wardrobe was created by designers such as Charles James. From Mme. de Menil I learned that it's more difficult to make something look effortless than it is to show off the design.

Mme. de Menil's expression gave away very little of what she was thinking or feel-ing. She observed the world with distant, calm attention. In the years I worked for her I must have spent hours looking at her to discern what she was thinking and what she wanted me to do.

Before Dominique de Menil hired me in the early 1970s as editor for one job af-ter another—two catalogues and the first volume of a series of heavily illustrated books, almost seven years of work—she interviewed me in her town house on Manhattan's Upper East Side, across Central Park from the neighborhood where I'd grown up and still lived. The façade of her New York home was unadorned, the interior elegant and comfortable, with just enough furniture so there was always a place to sit and to lay out a manuscript or proofs. There was nothing ostentatious about the decor. It was the opposite of the formality I'd expected. It didn't feel like a home or an office; it resembled an artist's studio, where things could be rearranged by necessity or whim.

For one project, I read proofs in the basement. When lunchtime came, I was invited upstairs to eat at the long dining-room table. A famous artist might be there, or one of Mme. de Menil's grown children with her coterie. Though I was more or less a contemporary of the Menil children, I never felt like an equal, even at the same table, the distance a product of my unease and their disinterest. It was a relief to return to my work in the basement.

Once, Mme. de Menil took me to an art gallery on Madison Avenue, a small, quiet space on the second floor of a three-story building. She had an appointment with the dealer there; to be polite, I wandered away. When I looked around, he was showing her a small painting recognizably a Monet. It shouldn't have shocked me that she could buy a Monet if she chose to, but it did. Another time, I told her about the research I was doing on her behalf in the Egyptological library of the Brooklyn Museum. The woman assigned to help me kept a variety of over-the-counter medications in her top drawer because so many researchers got headaches from the library's inadequate light. Without a word to me, Mme. De Menil saw to the installation of new lighting.

In the course of our acquaintance, she surprised me more than once.

Early in our time together Mme. de Menil asked me to work on the catalogue of a Max Ernst show that originated at the Musée de l'Orangerie in Paris, traveled around Europe, and was to open at the Institute for the Arts at Rice University, where the de Menils exhibited their collection long before the Menil Museum was built. She invited me to Houston for the opening. Max Ernst was there, along with his third wife, the artist Dorothea Tanning. Max's son, the painter Jimmy Ernst, was a friend of my parents, and as a child I was allowed to wander in his studio, but I was too shy to approach Ernst to say so.

It was the autumn of 1973, and John de Menil had died that June. Their forty-two-year alliance had demanded significant changes from Mme. de Menil. Dominique Schlumberger had been raised Protestant; she converted to Catholicism on her marriage and, characteristically, both observed and tried to improve her adopted religion for the rest of her life. The daughter of a family of industrial scientists, she was educated in mathematics and physics at the Paris Institute of Political Studies, but after her marriage she took up the study of art, one of her husband's devotions. She became knowledgeable enough to co-create a world-famous collection and to complete after her husband's death the many projects they had planned together.

One night during my visit to Houston,

Mme. de Menil and I ate dinner in a room just outside the kitchen. A painting hung above her head by Tomás Hiepes, a Spanish Baroque painter, of four pots of staked flowers, perhaps carnations. The pots were glazed white with a pattern of leaves and birds. A certain secrecy was implied by the placement of the innocent pots just inside an arch and against the dark background.

Manny Subramanian, Mme. de Menil's servant, placed a large bowl of chocolate mousse and a serving spoon between us, setting smaller bowls and spoons before each of us. Mme. de Menil murmured her refusal to Manny. He filled my bowl, then reached for hers. She refused to let him fill it and spoke more distinctly. *"No, no, Manny, none for me."* He told her she should have some, that she'd barely eaten dinner. When Manny retreated to the kitchen, she reached for her spoon and ate one slow spoonful after another from the serving bowl, pausing in between as if each would be the last.

After dinner, we went to the living room and sat side by side on a couch shaped like an overgrown squash. At one end of the living room there was an open doorway and through it Mme. de Menil's bedroom was visible. Inside was a double bed covered with a cloth that trailed to the ground. Above the bed was a wooden cross.

Manny came in with a coffee tray, and Mme. de Menil selected a book from a stack on the low table before us. She held it closed in her lap for a few moments as if she were making up her mind about something, then opened the book to a place marked by a white slip of paper. The book was about a French artist, Jean Fautrier, born in Paris in 1898, illegitimate, and raised by his grandmother. During the Nazi occupation of France, Fautrier was arrested by the Gestapo, and after he was released from prison he moved to a village about six miles from Paris. In 1943 and 1944, Fautrier painted a series he called "Hostages." One of the series, *Oradour-sur-Glane*, was named after a village in the Haute-Vienne, where, on June 10, 1944, the Waffen-SS killed 642 civilians—men, women, and children. Some were shot in the massacre; others were locked in a building and burned to death. Only a few individuals escaped.

Oradour-sur-Glane was reproduced in the book Mme. de Menil held in her lap, and at first glance the painting seemed to feature an irregular light shape against a varicolored ground. As we considered the image in silence I realized that the central shape was filled with the faint profiles of unnamed individuals. The dead of Oradour-sur-Glane were both buried and resurrected. Mme. de Menil didn't mention that Fautrier's painting was in her collection. When I learned this, I took her reticence as an example of her humility and also her desire to protect her privacy.

So much about Dominique de Menil was hidden, though perhaps others might disagree. I saw her as a hard worker who understood exactly what she wanted to achieve. She was willing to wait patiently until those who were there to carry out her vision—the architects, assistants, editors, designers, curators, even the artists whose work she honored—understood her wishes at last. Her final lesson to me is that loneliness may endure even in the presence of great beauty and plenty of company.

41

Herb Kelleher

by Loren Steffy Photograph by Pam Francis

Herb Kelleher used to remark that moving to Texas was the greatest business decision he ever made. The thirty-year-old New Jersey native came to Texas in 1961 intending to start a business or a law firm. Eight years later, Kelleher was working as a San Antonio lawyer when he and one of his clients created the business plan for what would soon become Southwest Airlines. On June 19, 1971, the first Southwest flight took off from Dallas's Love Field bound for San Antonio. Under Kelleher's leadership, the airline changed the industry with its low fares and exceptional customer service, which sometimes included Kelleher himself serving patrons on flights. Regarded as one of the best CEOs in America, Kelleher created a fun-loving culture that attracted customers and employees: Southwest has consistently been named one of the most admired companies in the United States, though it has hit some rough spots in recent years. Kelleher passed away in 2019, eleven years after retiring as chairman of the world-famous company he had built from scratch.

The boarding area at Love Field was packed, as it often was in the early morning in the late 1990s. I was waiting for a Southwest Airlines flight to Houston when a strange hush came over the terminal. Then, the murmurs began. "That's Herb Kelleher!" a lady near me said. "He's the owner of Southwest Airlines." No, Herb wasn't the owner; Southwest was a publicly traded company. But few publicly traded companies were more closely associated with their chief executive than Southwest was with Herb, as everyone called him.

At the time, Herb was making regular trips to MD Anderson in Houston for prostate cancer treatments, but you wouldn't have known it that day. He worked the room—shaking hands, slapping backs, and unleashing his raucous laughter among his loyal customers. He was on my flight that day, and he flew, as he always did, in the cockpit jump seat (smoking—a Herb trademark—was still allowed in the cockpit but not the cabin). After the flight hit cruising altitude, he emerged to help hand out the airline's famous peanut packets to passengers.

Few people have done more than Herb to change a major American industry. Congress deregulated the airlines in 1978, but Southwest democratized it. Southwest's bargain-rate fares made it possible for millions of people to fly who previously couldn't have afforded it. The U.S. Department of Transportation dubbed it the "Southwest effect": when the company entered a new market, passenger traffic soared.

The stories of Herb's pranks and carousing are legendary. There was the classic arm-wrestling match (the "Malice in Dallas") with another airline executive over the rights to a marketing slogan. And the times he reportedly flew on Southwest dressed as the Easter Bunny and a leprechaun (for Easter and St. Patrick's Day, respectively). And the time he appeared in a television ad with a brown paper bag over his head. (It's complicated.)

Herb's image as a chain-smoking, bourbon-swilling party animal masked a profound intellect, though. Born and raised in New Jersey, he was a graduate of Wesleyan University, where he majored in English and minored in philosophy and then received his law degree from New York University before moving to San Antonio, where he joined a prominent firm—hardly a typical CV for a CEO.

Yet he was also a shrewd businessman. Airlines were notorious money losers, but not Southwest.

During Herb's tenure, it was the most consistently profitable major carrier. It was relentless in its cost-cutting efforts; the company once saved hundreds of thousands of dollars a year by removing three peanuts from each packet.

What set Southwest apart from its rivals, though, was its disruption of industry norms. By the time the carrier hit its stride in the early eighties until well after Herb's retirement in 2001, it had the highest level of union representation of any airline but the least labor strife, in part because Herb was so well respected by the rank and file. It had the lowest-paid executives in the industry and the highest-paid employees. It had the best on-time performance and the cheapest fares. It was the only growth stock among the major airlines, and it issued shares to its employees. Many of the pilots, flight attendants, and baggage handlers who joined the company in its early days retired as millionaires.

Southwest spent the first few years of its life fending off lawsuits from competitors such as Braniff and Texas International. (Herb provided his legal services for free.) When Southwest started flying in 1971, its rivals tried to stunt the company's growth, convincing U.S. House Speaker Jim Wright, who represented a portion of North Texas, to restrict air travel from Love Field. The other carriers had all moved to the larger DFW International Airport by then, and the "Wright Amendment" limited commercial flights from Love Field to other cities in Texas and five surrounding states. Kelleher managed to transform the amendment into a competitive weapon, making Love Field Southwest's fortress and building the carrier into a powerhouse that for years flew more passengers than any other.

But it's Texas where Southwest made the biggest impact. As the writer Jan Jarboe Russell once put it, by making it possible to travel from any major Texas city to another within an hour, Southwest radically altered the state's psychic landscape. Texas, Russell wrote, "has never been the same."

As an executive, Herb believed in listening to passengers, even as other carriers treated them as an annoyance. He encouraged Southwest employees to help resolve customer complaints; gate agents could authorize hotel stays or rental cars for stranded passengers. In other words, he brought an old-school retail mindset to the staid world of air travel. His competitors struggled to keep up.

Reporters loved Herb because he always seemed willing to answer our questions. Once, after a luncheon in Dallas, he slipped out a side door for a cigarette, ditching his public relations staff. Several of us caught up to him in the hallway, and he regaled us with stories for probably two hours before his handlers tracked him down. He seemed to be having a good time, as if he had nothing better to do in the middle of the day than shoot the breeze with the press.

I don't remember what he told us that day, but that too is classic Herb. For all his gregariousness, he never forgot his responsibilities as CEO. Rarely did a market-moving comment escape his lips unplanned. Dan Reed, then a reporter for the *Fort Worth Star-Telegram*, once dubbed it the "Six Flags effect." Reed said he would drive to Dallas to interview Herb. He would leave thinking he had gotten a lot of great information, but at about the time he passed Six Flags in Arlington on his way back to Fort Worth, he'd realize Herb hadn't said anything newsworthy.

Thanks to Herb's leadership, Southwest was so successful that eventually every one of its major competitors filed for bankruptcy. While Southwest's competition wasn't the only cause, its frequent deep discounts made it difficult for its rivals, with their bloated cost structures, to compete. Bankruptcy allowed them to slash expenses, cutting fares in the process. They went broke and then emerged looking more like Southwest.

Herb retired as CEO in 2001, just months before 9/11 threw Southwest's model of short, frequent flights into jeopardy as new security measures made flying less attractive. He remained a guiding force, though, first as executive chairman and later as chairman emeritus. Herb was a part of Southwest and it was a part of him.

The airline has faced new competitive threats in the twenty-first century. It isn't always the lowest fare carrier anymore; its labor relations, while still good, are less amiable than they once were; and the company has had to go beyond U.S. borders to find growth markets. During the COVID-19 pandemic, it offered buyouts to thousands of employees, and executives slashed their pay, but Southwest managed to avoid furloughs, leaving unblemished its record of fifty years without a layoff. Through it all, the carrier retained its fun-loving image. YouTube videos of flight attendants singing safety briefings became internet sensations. The culture still felt like an expression of Herb's outsized personality.

45

O'Neil Ford

by Mark Lamster

Even if you've never heard O'Neil Ford's name, if you live in the Lone Star State you likely know his work. The North Texas–born architect designed numerous buildings with a high public profile, most of them in the San Antonio and Dallas areas: the campuses of Trinity University and the University of Dallas, the Tower of the Americas, the Texas Instruments Semiconductor Building, and the River Walk's Venue Villita among them. Though he did most of his work prior to the 1970s, his wedding of modernism and the Texas vernacular in both residential and commercial design has proven extraordinarily influential. He was regarded as a mentor by Dallas's late Frank Welch (aka the "Dean of Texas Architects"), and his impact can be seen in the homes and buildings of his disciples David Lake and Ted Flato, proprietors of Lake Flato, arguably the most important architectural firm of twenty-first-century Texas.

Texas has its own barbecue, its own country music, its own politics (not that it's anything to brag about), and, albeit with considerably less notoriety, its own brand of modern architecture. The man chiefly respon-

sible for its development was himself a Texas original, a fun-loving, cigar-smoking civil rights activist who got his architectural degree in the mail. His name was O'Neil Ford, and his achievement was such that he was desig-

nated a national landmark by the National Council on the Arts, perhaps the only individual ever to be so honored.

Ford was born into modest circumstances in the town of Pink Hill, near the Oklahoma border, in 1905, and those circumstances became even more modest after the death of his father, in 1917. The family moved to Denton, where Ford took courses in drafting at North Texas State Teachers College (now the University of North Texas)

and met the Dallas-based architect David Reichard Williams, joining his practice in 1926.

If Ford is the father of Texas modernism, Williams is its grandfather. He was fifteen years older than Ford, but like him an autodidact who received his architectural degree from correspondence school. He became Ford's mentor, and they traveled the state, examining its urban history and the vernacular architecture of the Hill Country and the settlements along the Rio Grande. Those journeys became the basis for a three-part essay series, "The Architecture of Early Texas," that they coauthored for the journal *Southwestern Architect*.

Those trips profoundly shaped their design thinking. The two men were still working together during the creation of Williams's landmark Elbert Williams House in University Park, which took elements of Texas architectural tradition (metal shed roofs, shaded balconies, thick beige brick walls, deep-set verandas) and translated them into a residence of elegant distinction. At a time when fashionable homes came in revival styles (Italianate, Georgian, Gothic, Tudor), it stood out as something wholly original.

"The Texas man was not a slave to academic process or to architectural conceits," Ford wrote in a later essay on the state's settler builders. "He was an original person using old precepts and old notions." He might just as well have been describing himself.

Williams dissolved his practice in the early 1930s, leaving Ford to forge his own distinctive path, which drew not just from Texas building but from the work of European modernists and Frank Lloyd Wright, whose idea of an "organic" architecture attuned to the American landscape Ford found persuasive (though he considered the man an "egomaniac").

That direction was apparent in one of his earliest commissions, the Little Chapel in the Woods, completed in 1939 on the Denton campus of the Texas State College for Women (now Texas Woman's University). From the outside, it is almost elementally simple: a crisp box articulated by horizontally set fieldstone and punched by a circular window on its front façade. That geometric clarity was carried over into the interior, an almost magical space with a series of tapered, parabolic brick arches—inspired

by the work of the Mexican engineer Félix Candela—supporting its gabled roof.

The building was completed with the labor of the National Youth Administration, one of the New Deal agencies that put Americans to work during the Great Depression. Its stained glass windows were made by the school's female students, whose contributions were indicative of an emphasis on craftsmanship that would characterize Ford's work throughout his career. Among his regular collaborators on this front was his younger brother Lynn, a carpenter of extraordinary skill.

Ford merged his interest in historical preservation and his craft-centered sensibility with a commitment to the application of advanced technology. Working under the auspices of the federal Works Progress Administration, he led the restoration of La Villita, a village of nineteenth-century adobe buildings along the San Antonio River Walk. His novel contribution to the project was a marvel of engineering wizardry, a drum-shaped assembly hall with an inverted dome for a roof. He modeled its spoke-hub structure on the wheel of a bicycle, an object he considered almost "magic" in its perfection.

Ford based his practice in San Antonio, and his presence in the city is unmistakable. His 750-foot tall, saucer-capped Tower of the Americas, built for the 1968 HemisFair, lords over downtown and remains its tallest building. But his most significant contribution to the city, beginning in the late 1940s, was his design for Trinity

University, which he set into an abandoned rock quarry on the outskirts of town. He eventually designed thirty-three buildings for the school, using a warm red brick and a pioneering "lift-slab" process, in which concrete floors and roofs were poured on site and then lifted into place by hydraulic jacks. Ford claimed it saved 9 percent of the overall construction cost.

It's somewhat ironic that Ford, who did not have a college degree, made a specialty of designing institutes of higher education. In addition to Trinity University, he designed the University of Dallas and Skidmore College, in upstate New York. He also designed buildings for several private schools in the Dallas area: a science complex for St. Mark's, academic buildings for Lamplighter, and a library for Greenhill, the last of those being a work of great delicacy, with a living room–style reading area facing a large fireplace, like something from a historic lodge.

The design of inviting and intimate private spaces might have been Ford's greatest gift, as his many residential commissions demonstrate; he's a favorite of mid-century modern architecture fans. One of his earliest, built in 1938, was for the Texas oilman Sid Richardson on the private Gulf Coast island of San José. It has the long and low proportions of a ranch house, but with a broad wall of windows fronting its living space and a curling, exposed-concrete staircase clipped to its side. Its pure white form looks like something out of Germany's austere Bauhaus movement.

By the mid-century, that aesthetic was refined into something more completely his own, a trajectory illustrated by a pair of neighboring homes built in University Park for the writer and critic Lon Tinkle and his friend, the artist and museum director Jerry Bywaters. The two houses, both modest in scale, faced each other over a small pond at the top of Turtle Creek. The great Texas writer J. Frank

Dobie dubbed the small community they created, with two other modern homes built for members of the Dallas intelligentsia, the "Culture Gulch." Both homes featured brick inside and out- and embraced the landscape on which they were perched. Tinkle's library floated on pillars above the water; the Bywaters house had a wide screened porch accessible by sliding pocket doors.

Ford's place in history books as a master of mid-century residential design and a pioneer of Texas modernism is secure, but on the ground that legacy is disappearing. The restrained modesty of his homes, in both scale and aesthetics, leaves them vulnerable to a new generation of wealthy clients who prefer larger, showier architecture. Several of his most important works have already been demolished, including the Lon Tinkle home in 2013. For Ford, who died in 1982, that would have been a bitter pill. That disappointment, however, is leavened by the fact that a new generation has embraced his ideas, and his vision of an architecture rooted in Texas history lives on.

49

Willie Velasquez

by Julian Cástro

Willie Velasquez was the son of a San Antonio union organizer, and it was clear from early on that he would follow in his father's footsteps. After graduating from St. Mary's University with a degree in economics, Velasquez immediately dived into activism, working as a boycott coordinator for the United Farm Workers in the Rio Grande Valley. He was deeply involved in the famous Starr County Strike of 1966 and 1967, a series of actions conducted by underpaid workers in the valley's melon farms. The strike, which was marked by law enforcement abuses, failed in its efforts, despite drawing national attention to the workers' plight. Velasquez, though, soon pivoted to a more successful strategy: empowering Latinos by registering them to vote in large numbers. By the time of his death in 1988 at the too-young age of forty-four, he was widely regarded as one of the nation's most transformative civil rights activists.

Growing up as the child of a Chicana activist in San Antonio's West Side in the 1980s, whenever I heard someone refer to "Willie," I didn't picture a long-haired, pot-smoking country singer strumming on his guitar. "Willie" instead called up a stout, raven-haired, and jabby-voiced political activist walking door-to-door with pen and pad in hand, a man on a mission to empower Mexican Americans by registering them to vote. "Willie" meant Willie

Velasquez, the visionary founder of the Southwest Voter Registration Education Project, who was also a product of the West Side.

The post–World War II San Antonio that Willie grew up in offered little upward mobility for Mexican Americans. High dropout rates, stifling poverty, and prejudice suffocated the community. In 1968, the CBS documentary *Hunger in America* spotlighted San Antonio's West Side, capturing one of the most heart-wrenching moments of film ever broadcast on television. In a San Antonio emergency room, a neo-natal physician cradled a tiny, emaciated brown-skinned baby as the child gasped his final breath. "He was an American," the show's host, a young Charles Kuralt, intoned as the baby's body went limp on the screen. "Now he is dead." One-quarter of San Antonio's four hundred thousand Mexican Americans "are hungry all the time," Kuralt reported.

Even though Mexican Americans made up nearly half the city's population, political power rested almost entirely in the hands of a white, business-friendly elite. By the early 1970s, however, things had begun to change. The Voting Rights Act of 1965 had boosted voter protections for people of color. The Supreme Court had struck down the poll tax as discriminatory a year later, effectively ending a tool of disenfranchisement that Texas had wielded against minorities and the poor since the turn of the century. By 1970, the Chicano Movement was blossoming in Texas. La Raza Unida, an offshoot of the Mexican-American Youth Organization, which Willie had co-founded in 1967 in San Antonio, was fielding candidates for local and statewide office. Although Willie left La Raza Unida because he didn't believe a third party was the best route to Latino political empowerment, he understood its potential to galvanize the Mexican American vote.

When Ramsey Muñiz, La Raza's candidate for governor, unexpectedly pulled 6 percent of the general election vote in 1972, he siphoned enough votes from Democrat Dolph Briscoe to scare the bejeezus out of the state's Democratic establishment.

Willie understood the enormous power Latinos could wield to improve their lives if they turned out to vote. His genius was that he knew exactly how to make that happen. He formed Southwest Voter in 1974 with the purpose of registering Latino voters and educating them about the democratic process. His vision was groundbreaking. It just wasn't being done—not in Texas and certainly not in the Latino community—with the skill, scale, or fervor that Southwest Voter brought to it. Person by person, family by family, neighborhood by neighborhood, the group helped nearly double Latino registration nationwide over the course of two decades. More Latino voters also meant more Latino candidates elected to office. In the five Southwestern states where it focused its efforts, the number of Latino elected officials jumped from 1,566 in 1974 to 2,861 in 1984.

"*¡Su voto es su voz!*"—"Your vote is your voice!"—was Willie's exhortation to Latino voters. Every time I hear it, I get a lump in my throat thinking of the generations of Latinos and Latinas who never had the opportunity to fully use their voice, either at the ballot box or in life. They labored in fields and factories, in homes as maids and gardeners, in faraway lands fighting for our country. They worked hard and often stayed quiet about the injustices around them at the risk of losing their job if they rocked the boat. Willie changed the game.

I remember overhearing my mom talk about Willie with her activist friends at Panchito's, a basement restaurant in the Plaza de Armas Building, where she worked in the city's personnel office in the mid-1980s. It wasn't uncommon for her to breathe fire, as activists are sometimes wont to do, at people she thought were hyped-up but ineffective. But she saw Willie as the complete opposite: "He gets it," she told them, her declarative words delivered in a tone of respect that she reserved for people she believed were making a difference, "and he's getting things done."

"What you are seeing is a transition from powerlessness to power," Willie declared to an audience at Harvard's Institute of Politics in March 1988, only three months before his sudden passing from cancer at age forty-four. He was right. The movement he started helped transform American politics. Today, Latinos are one of America's most sought-after voting blocs, with Democrats and Republicans routinely competing for their vote. Perhaps most importantly, the sons and daughters of those who stayed quiet are using their voices not only at the ballot box but in courtrooms as attorneys, in clinics as physicians, in classrooms as teachers, and in city halls, in state legislatures, and on Capitol Hill in numbers thought impossible when Willie launched Southwest Voter almost a half century ago. In 1981, San Antonio elected its first Latino mayor in a century, Henry Cisneros, and between 1970 and 2010 the poverty rate for Hispanics in Texas dropped from 40 percent to 27 percent.

The transition that Willie spoke of is far from complete. Too many Latinos are still cut off from the ability to reach their dreams. The Latino community still votes at lower rates than most others and Latinos hold just a quarter of the seats in the state legislature, despite accounting for almost 40 percent of the population.

In an age of election denialism, rampant disinformation, revived voter suppression, and extreme polarization, Willie's zealous faith in the democratic process should serve as a North Star. Coming from such a marginalized community, he had every reason to doubt that working within our flawed democratic system was the answer. But instead of throwing stones or storming the Capitol or trying to overturn an election, he put his faith in our Constitution's highest ideals.

"'Willie' was and is now a name synonymous with democracy in America," President Bill Clinton proclaimed as he posthumously bestowed on Willie the Medal of Freedom in a 1995 White House ceremony. Willie is one of the few Latinos ever recognized with the nation's highest civilian honor. He made a difference, and the powerless and the powerful have long known it, whether they reside in the West Side or the West Wing.

The Best of the 1970s

Books

Films and TV Shows

1. *Brewster McCloud*
   (1970)

2. *The Last Picture Show*
   (1971)

3. *The Life and Times of Judge Roy Bean*
   (1972)

4. *The Texas Chainsaw Massacre*
   (1974)

5. *Austin City Limits*
   (1974–present)

6. *The Sugarland Express*
   (1974)

7. *The Whole Shootin' Match*
   (1978)

8. *Days of Heaven*
   (1978)

9. *Dallas*
   (1978–1991)

10. *North Dallas Forty*
    (1979)

Sports

1. UT Austin Longhorns win the Cotton Bowl in 1970.

2. Garland-born golfer Lee Trevino wins the U.S. Open, the Canadian Open, and the Open Championship over the course of twenty days in 1971.

3. The Dallas Cowboys win their first Super Bowl in 1971.

4. Marshall native George Foreman beats Joe Frazier to win the 1973 heavyweight title.

5. Monahans-born golfer Kathy Whitworth wins the 1974 Orange Blossom Classic.

6. Texas Longhorns baseball wins its third College World Series in 1975, and wins again in 1983, 2002, and 2005.

7. The University of Houston Cougars win four Southwest Conference football championships in 1976, 1978, 1979, and 1984 and the 1977 Cotton Bowl.

8. After a successful career as a kickboxer, Bridge City native Randall "Tex" Cobb becomes a heavyweight boxer in 1977 and wins his first fourteen bouts by KOs or TKOs.

9. In 1977, Houston's A. J. Foyt wins the Indianapolis 500 for the fourth time.

10. UT Austin running back Earl Campbell becomes, in 1977, the first Longhorn to win the Heisman Trophy.

Music

1. **Janis Joplin,**
   Pearl
   (1971)

2. **Little Joe y La Familia,**
   Para La Gente
   (1972)

3. **Jerry Jeff Walker,**
   ¡Viva Terlingua!
   (1973)

4. **ZZ Top,**
   Tres Hombres
   (1973)

5. **Freddy Fender,**
   Before the Next Teardrop Falls
   (1974)

6. **Tanya Tucker,**
   Would You Lay with Me (in a Field of Stone)
   (1974)

7. **Willie Nelson,**
   Red Headed Stranger
   (1975)

8. **Clifton Chenier,**
   "I'm on the Wonder"
   (1975)

9. **Townes Van Zandt,**
   Live at the Old Quarter, Houston, Texas
   (1977)

10. **Joe Ely,**
    Honky Tonk Masquerade
    (1978)

the 1980s

Though *Dallas* debuted in the spring of 1978 with a brief, five-episode mini-season, it became an icon of 1980s pop culture for a reason. It was the season three cliffhanger, which aired in March 1980, that launched the "Who Shot J.R.?" phenomenon, cementing J.R. Ewing's place as a symbol of of Texas's newfound swagger—and of the brazen veneration of the wealthy that marked the Reagan years. Less than three months after J.R. took those infamous bullets to the stomach, the John Travolta vehicle *Urban Cowboy* debuted, and suddenly everyone wanted to act like a Texan; instead of hicks, we were heroes. And for good reason: an oil boom was still in effect; Southwestern cuisine was making waves nationally; ZZ Top were major stars on a nascent MTV; and a born-again Texan, George H. W. Bush, spent almost the entire decade in the White House, first as vice president and then as president. For a moment, everything about Texas just seemed cool. Americans couldn't get enough of western wear or mechanical bulls. But it didn't last, and neither did the roaring economy; when the oil boom went bust and the savings and loan crisis hit, the fall was hard. If he'd been a real person, J.R. Ewing might have wished those bullet wounds had been fatal.

Larry McMurtry

by Skip Hollandsworth Photograph by Michael O'Brien

Texas's most celebrated writer was born in 1936 in Archer City, a town of fewer than two thousand located just south of Wichita Falls. It wasn't the most obvious breeding ground for a great writer, but Larry McMurtry was a bookish and observant child, and he later immortalized his hometown as the fictional Thalia. McMurtry found success early; all three of his first novels were turned into films. But his greatest success came with 1985's revisionist western *Lonesome Dove*, which won a Pulitzer Prize and was turned into a television miniseries that is regarded as near sacred by many Texans. Cowboys were hardly the only subject that fascinated McMurtry, though. It's stunning just how much of Texas he portrayed and got right—the Old West, yes, but also mid-twentieth-century rural Texas (in the series of novels that began with 1966's *The Last Picture Show*) and modern Houston (1975's *Terms of Endearment* is the best-known installment). It's as if he laid down the blueprint for three different genres of Texas literature. Despite his sometimes scornful attitude to his home state, he remained a staunch Texan of a sort, showing up to the Academy Awards ceremony in 2006 wearing a tuxedo jacket, blue jeans, and cowboy boots. His devotion to Archer City didn't recede, either. Late in life McMurtry returned to his hometown and opened Booked Up, an antique bookstore empire that at its height carried more than four hundred thousand titles. When he died in 2021 at eighty-four, fans and fellow writers descended upon Archer City to pay tribute to Texas's most beloved writer.

Spend any time with Larry McMurtry, and it doesn't take long to be struck—no, run over—by his restless, roving intellect. During the days I spent interviewing him in 2016, he talked about the personal lives of European leaders during World War I, a Siberian leper colony, the 2016 presidential campaign, concussions among professional football players, an afternoon he spent playing tennis with Barbra Streisand in Hollywood, the problems with air travel, his love of Dr Pepper and Fritos, the geoglyphs that can be found in the Atacama Desert of Chile, and a rodeo performer he once knew whose boot was ripped off during a bull ride, then sent flying through the air until it clobbered a spectator sitting in the bleachers.

But ask McMurtry about his writing— why he became a writer in the first place, or what inspires him, or if there's an underlying meaning to his fiction, or any other such forced attempt at introspection—and he is steadfastly unreflective. "I like making stuff up," he told me, simply.

When I tried again—What about process? Did he ever get stuck developing a plot? Seize up sometimes before a blank page?—he sighed. "I just write," he replied. "You either do it, or you don't."

Nor does he have any particular desire to discuss the characters he has created or the books he has written. "As soon as I finish a novel and ship it to the publisher," he told me, "I almost immediately lose interest in it and never read it again."

"Even *Lonesome Dove*?" I asked.

"I've never reread it. I don't hang on to any of my books. If I did that, I wouldn't have time to think about what I'm going to do next."

I looked at him for a few seconds to see if he was joking. He looked right back at me, his face impassive.

That McMurtry's voracious curiosity, and his ability to spin yarns, were forged on the empty flatlands of rural Texas makes either no sense at all or all the sense in the world. He spent his early childhood on a small ranch fifteen miles outside Archer City, where his father had him riding a horse by the age of three and herding cattle at four. McMurtry told me there were no books in the house—not a single one—until a cousin heading off to World War II dropped off nineteen boys' adventure books with such titles as *Sergeant Silk: The Prairie Scout*. His parents did not read to him. "They preferred sitting on the porch, swapping tales with other relatives, or we listened to the radio," he said.

When McMurtry was six, his father moved the family to a white frame home in Archer City (population: 1,675) so that McMurtry could be close to school. Scrawny and bespectacled, McMurtry was

a good student. ("Keep in mind," he cautioned, "that a good student in Archer City was any student who actually attended class.") When he got to high school, he joined the 4-H club, played the clarinet (and later trombone) in the marching band, acted in school plays, wrote what he called "one-paragraph editorials" for the school newspaper, ran the mile for the track team, and was a starter on the school's dreadful basketball team, which had the distinction, he recalled, of losing one game, to Crowell High School, by a score of 106–4.

His greatest extracurricular interest, however, was books—the very thing he hadn't had access to on the ranch. After devouring his cousin's adventure series, he bought pulp novels from the paperback rack at Archer City's drugstore. When he was in Fort Worth one weekend for a track meet, he took a city bus downtown just so he could wander through Barber's Book Store. He read *Don Quixote* and *Madame Bovary*. He even leafed through the *Bhagavad Gita*. "Anything I could get my hands on, I'd read," he said. "Reading took me away, at least for a little while, from the drabness of Archer City."

As his dismissive description of his hometown indicates, McMurtry has never been what you might call a Texas booster. He sees his native state too clearly for that. Yet Texans can't get enough of him.

In 2014, when he appeared at the Dallas Museum of Art to promote his latest bestseller, a western titled *The Last Kind Words Saloon*, the 425-seat auditorium was filled to capacity, and dozens more ticket holders were ushered into overflow rooms to watch on simulcast. During a question-and-answer segment, audience members took turns commandeering the microphone to tell McMurtry what his books had meant to them. One woman spoke of her love of *The Last Picture Show*, his novel about teenagers coming of age in the fictional North Texas town of Thalia; another brought up *Terms of Endearment*, his novel about an indomitable grande dame in Houston's wealthy River Oaks neighborhood. A man confessed that he had read the 843-page *Lonesome Dove* three times. And then another man rose to recall, in almost reverential tones, how as a student at Texas Christian University in the early sixties, he had played a game of Ping-Pong against McMurtry, who was then teaching at the school. The man had lost.

"Yes, I was quite good at Ping-Pong," McMurtry replied, and the audience roared with laughter, as if it was the funniest thing anyone had ever heard.

Texans just love McMurtry, orneriness and all. And the book of his that they love the most is perhaps the one that most pitilessly eviscerates their mythology.

When I asked McMurtry about *Lonesome Dove*'s success, he did one of his shrugs. "It isn't a masterpiece by any stretch of the imagination," he said. "All I had wanted to do was write a novel that demythologized the West. Instead, it became the chief source of western mythology. Some things you cannot explain."

There is, perhaps, an explanation. Texans have a long memory of the brutality and desolation of our state's early years. Stories of violence and deprivation are passed down from generation to generation. So we're unlikely to give much weight to books that portray early Texas as the site of romance and

derring-do; we'll read those books for fun, but we don't take them seriously. Likewise, we probably don't want to read books that peer into that bleakness and see nothing beyond it; that just cuts too close to the bone. What McMurtry did, and what Texas will be forever grateful for, was to portray our history in all its pitilessness but reassure us that the men and women who peopled it were by turns brave and funny and sad and weak, as real to us as anyone we've ever met, and almost as familiar.

That such figures could spring up from such vacant plains was a never-ending source of wonderment to McMurtry and one of the things that fueled his drive to write. "You know, people have no idea how empty the world is out here," McMurtry told me once, late in his life, as he stood on the porch of his childhood home in Archer City. "They don't understand its bleakness."

"And yet you keep coming back," I said.

"I keep coming back," he replied. A light breeze came up, blowing wisps of his white hair across his forehead. "I admit, I always do."

H. Ross Perot

by Loren Steffy Photograph by Danny Turner

If you squint a little, you could see Ross Perot as the Donald Trump of his time: a pugnacious business tycoon who ran for president based on the unshakable belief that he knew best, and in the process shook up the political system with his sharp tongue and populist fervor. There, though, the similarities pretty much end. The man born Henry Ross Perot in Texarkana in 1930 was a bona fide business genius who built his wealth through his own entrepreneurial innovation and a disciplined, hard-charging managerial style. Though he ran for the nation's highest office twice, in 1992 and 1996, he never made it to the White House. But offsetting those losses was a trailblazing career as the founder of two Dallas-based technology businesses that he sold for billions, and a generous record of philanthropy. Not bad for a onetime enrollee at Texarkana Junior College.

When he was young, Ross Perot wanted to be a pearl—smooth, well rounded, and admired. But he realized as he got older that would never happen. He wasn't the oyster, either. "My lot in life is that of the grain of sand that irritates the oyster," he once said.

From professional services to presidential politics, Perot's legacy was built on irritation. He was a provocateur who redefined almost everything he touched. But the innovations followed often bitter fights. He clashed with his commanding officer in the Navy. He took

a sales job with IBM and did phenomenally well—until the company decided to cap commissions. His managers brushed off his ideas for selling computer time as a service, so he quit and, at age thirty-two, started his own company, Electronic Data Systems, in Dallas. Perot realized that many companies couldn't afford to buy mainframe computers, so EDS leased time on the big machines at night or on weekends—whenever the owners weren't using them—and then crunched data on them for clients.

Later, EDS bought its own mainframes—and PCs, network gear, and storage systems—to handle clients' information technology needs. If you hired EDS, you didn't have to worry about keeping up with the latest technology. The company would do it for you. Eventually, these computer services were given a name: *outsourcing*.

Despite his jug ears, five-foot, six-inch frame, and nasally East Texas twang that divulged his Texarkana roots, Perot was a charismatic leader, and EDS employees were fiercely loyal. Like many successful entrepreneurs, Perot was "utterly, absolutely convinced of his rightness," his biographer Todd Mason wrote. "Perot requires people to accept him on faith." And follow him they did, in business and later in politics.

Perot had become an Eagle Scout at age thirteen, and at EDS he created a culture that reflected the Boy Scout code of honor. Employees wore IBM-style suits and white shirts, and if they engaged in extramarital affairs, they faced termination. EDS's workforce "acted like the Marine Corps and dressed like the FBI," Mason wrote.

EDS made Perot a billionaire, and his success ushered in a new era of tech-based Texas wealth, paving the way for the likes of Michael Dell and Mark Cuban. He didn't get rich by raising cattle or drilling for oil, but he had his own brand of Texas swagger and tenacity. (Remember: another word for *sand* is *grit*.) When two EDS employees were imprisoned in Iran in 1978, Perot hired his own team of commandos to get them out—though the mission's success is a matter of some dispute.

Perot sold EDS to General Motors in 1984 for $2.5 billion. He got to keep running the company and took a seat on the automaker's board. It was not a good fit. Perot bristled at GM's bureaucratic lethargy and clashed openly with its CEO, Roger Smith. Smith had hoped Perot would help the company beat back the incursion of Japanese carmakers, who were rapidly gaining market share in the United States. Instead, Perot publicly blasted Smith and other GM leaders as ineffectual. He criticized the automaker's underfunded employee pensions while noting that management's retirement plan was fully funded. Smith wanted to make more acquisitions like EDS to diversify GM. Perot argued the company should make better cars. Eventually, GM bought him out to silence him.

In 1983, Texas governor Mark White named him to chair a committee on improving Texas public schools. The committee called for limiting class size, creating prekindergarten classes for disadvantaged children, and insisting on proficiency tests for high school graduation. But the hallmark was the "no pass, no play" rule requiring that students have passing grades to participate in extracurricular activities such as sports. Perot quickly drew the ire of football coaches from across the state, but he was unmoved. "If the people of Texas want Friday night entertainment instead of education, let's find out about it," he said defiantly.

But if he was often a thorn in the side of the establishment, he wasn't quite the figure of progressive dreams, either. He called for stronger punishments for drug possession, which swelled the state's prison population. And he reportedly suggested that Dallas police combat gang violence by cordoning off minority neighborhoods and conducting door-to-door searches. (Though he later denied saying this.)

In 1988, Perot started a new company, Perot Systems, that tried, with a fair amount of success, to replicate EDS's business model. But by then Perot had his eye on a bigger stage. In 1992, the national economy was emerging from a recession, and the effects of the late 1980s oil, real estate, and banking busts had left thousands of Texans out of work. Perot found both major political parties lacking, believing they were too beholden to wealthy donors and had turned their backs on working people. The North American Free Trade Agreement, which was ratified with bipartisan support in 1993, would, he warned, create a "giant sucking sound" as American factories and jobs went to Mexico.

Perot favored charts and bought half-hour infomercials to explain his positions. His populist, anti-government lectures were a hit, and he succeeded in getting people to focus on eye-glazing issues like foreign trade and economic policy. Once again, he was the grain of sand, grinding away at the gears of the political status quo.

But his campaign was a mess. He announced his candidacy, then he dropped out of the race. Then he dropped back in. He became more aloof and paranoid. He lost to Bill Clinton but captured 18.9 percent of the vote, the best showing by an independent or third-party candidate since Teddy Roosevelt ran as the Bull Moose nominee in 1912.

Perot ran again four years later. By then he'd started the Reform Party, which vowed to fix the way Washington worked. Reform Party sentiment would resurface in 2009 with the rise of the Tea Party but by then Perot was long gone. He had turned his back on the party he started after it nominated reactionary Pat Buchanan for president in 2000. Just as he had so many times before, when an organization he loved disappointed him, he walked away.

In 2009, he sold Perot Systems to Michael Dell for $3.9 billion and spent his remaining years focusing on his philanthropy, much of it centered on Dallas. Over the years, he gave millions to veterans' organizations, the University of Texas Southwestern Medical Center, and the Morton H. Meyerson Symphony Center (named for his former right-hand man at EDS). Though he once said that "money is the most overrated thing in the world," if Perot ever achieved his goal of becoming a pearl, it was when he was giving away the fortune that never mattered to him anyway.

Whatever irritations he caused, Ross Perot was almost universally admired by the time he passed away in 2019. He didn't look much like the Texan of the popular imagination—no boots, no hat, no Wranglers, no square jaw or chiseled features—but, like many of the men and women who built this state, he was always ready to fight for what he thought was right.

Gloria Anzaldúa

by **Richard Z. Santos** Photograph by Annie F. Valva

The author, scholar, and poet Gloria Anzaldúa was born in the Rio Grande Valley in 1942 and died at the relatively young age of sixty-one, leaving behind an outsized influence in the humanities and social sciences. Anzaldúa was a member of what she said was a once-prosperous and influential landholding family in the Rio Grande Valley that had been reduced to migrant labor and tenant farming, a descent that fueled her sense of injustice and her curiosity about her own identity and place in the world. Her most influential work, 1987's *Borderlands/La Frontera: The New Mestiza*, is a collection of essays and poems based loosely on her own experiences that explores the porous borders between the United States and Mexico, Hispanics and Anglos, men and women, and gay and straight. Writing, teaching, and lecturing widely, she was working toward a PhD in literature from the University of California, Santa Cruz, at the time of her death. She was awarded her doctorate posthumously, and each year multiple academic awards and prizes are bestowed in her memory.

Growing up in San Antonio in the 1980s and 1990s, I called myself Mexican because all the brown kids called themselves Mexican.

Nothing else made sense. I was a Mexican because what else could I be? The brown kids were Mexicans, the white kids were white kids, everyone else was who they were. Nothing more needed to be said.

I was nearly eighteen before I began to real-

ize "Mexican" didn't quite cut it. My mother's family has been living in New Mexico since the 1500s, when her ancestors, a mixture of conquistadores and Sephardic Jews fleeing the Spanish Inquisition, made their way from the ruins of Tenochtitlan to Santa Fe. My father's family has been in San Antonio or Laredo for at least 150 years. There are Indigenous ancestors on both sides—not that any of us knows their tribes or even their names. I knew I wasn't white, but was I actually Mexican if my forebears' presence here predates the existence of both Mexico and the United States?

The realization that the easy categories weren't so easy for me didn't emerge after deep reflection and study. I didn't have long conversations with my elders or write poems that searched for my identity. I wasn't looking for insight because I didn't think I needed any. But the same question kept being forced on me. My white friends in high school asked me, then my college classmates asked me, then my professional colleagues, strangers here and abroad, the families of women I've dated, and all of them usually delivered it with a slightly exasperated tone: "But what are you *actually*?"

"I'm from Texas" wasn't the answer they were looking for, and "Mexican" didn't sit right with me. So at a certain point I switched to saying "Mexican American." This was an answer they understood, or thought they did. Depending on the situation, maybe that would be the end of the conversation, or maybe we'd get to the question they were really asking: "But when did your family come to the United States?"

"About two hundred years before the American Revolution," I'd say.

They'd laugh with a touch of confusion. Only so many stories are possible, and some people have trouble grasping a story about brown people that doesn't involve hiding in the back of a truck or crawling under barbed wire.

I don't entirely blame them, and this isn't always a white thing. When I was teaching high school an occasional student who'd emigrated from Mexico would have trouble wrapping their head around the fact that some of us have been here for centuries. An easier story would have let all of us settle into a comfortable narrative frame so we could get back to not talking about things like race or heritage. The *Mayflower*. Ellis Island. San Francisco. Miami. Laredo. Got it. Just give me a story about the Old World and women with handkerchiefs around their hair.

These aren't racist encounters—not really, or not fully. They're encounters with the limits of our imaginations.

The power of Gloria Anzaldúa's work in books such as *Borderlands/La Frontera: The New Mestiza* was to brush aside simple ideas such as nations, religions, languages, borders, and skin color in order to reach the complex, beating heart of what it means to live in the borderlands of Mexico and the United States. The blending of Spanish and Indig-

enous blood and culture and the United States' annexation of Mexican territory—combined with the relative isolation that came from living in a remote region—led to new languages, religions, cultures, and skin colors.

The end result is Anzaldúa's "new mestiza" who doesn't act, sound, or think like other people and who to this day still can't settle on a word for ourselves: *Spanish, Mexican, Latin, Hispanic, Tejano, Texican, Chicano, Latino, mestizo, Latinx, Latine,* and many others left off or yet to be added. But that's the point. We'll never settle on a single term because a single term can't encompass all the experiences and identities that have emerged in the physical and psychic borderlands.

Anzaldúa recast the new people not as mongrels or mistakes but as hybrids powered by ancient combinations and sometimes violent contradictions. As she said, "I am a wind-swayed bridge, a crossroads inhabited by whirlwinds." Hybridity is not always easy. Occupying an in-between space can be confusing and it's easy to feel unrooted or threatened even at home. In *Borderlands/La Frontera* she wrote that in the Borderlands "enemies are kin to each other" and even those who call the place home might feel like a stranger.

Anzaldúa's philosophy was rooted in her lived experience as a Chicana from the Rio Grande Valley and, more specifically, her lived experience as a lesbian Chicana from the valley. She wasn't just a member of a culture far from the center of power but an outsider among outsiders, dealing with centuries of shame and, worse, the expectation that you should hide your shames.

Anzaldúa refused. "I will no longer be made to feel ashamed of existing. I will have my voice: Indian, Spanish, white. I will have my serpent's tongue—my woman's voice, my sexual voice, my poet's voice. I will overcome the tradition of silence." She faced racism and economic struggles that my middle-class upbringing never exposed me to. I'm an able-bodied, cis-het man, and I know there is an element of her work that I will never fully grasp. But even though Anzaldúa's work is intensely personal, I feel as if she wrote for me and for anyone else who doesn't fit into the easy categories.

Here's where I should have started this essay. Not in high school but in the third grade at an elementary school in the northwest suburbs of San Antonio.

The amount of segregation, official and otherwise, necessary to support a majority-white elementary school in San Antonio is massive, and today Hispanics make up nearly 75 percent of the school's population. But in the late eighties the school was only one-third Hispanic, and at times it felt like there were just a handful of us.

I didn't face outright racism. I wasn't called names as my dad had been or made fun of for eating tacos like my mom. Or, if I was, I buried the memories so deep I don't have access to them. Instead, I was an oddity. My skin was an object of curiosity to be remarked on as if it were a birthmark or a scar, which I suppose it was.

Even then, nine- or ten-year-olds would ask what I *really* was. I insisted to one kid that I was white and I just had a tan.

Today, I can almost smile at those words.

My mom tried to comfort me. She probably told me I was beautiful, that I should be proud, that I should ignore them, that some people were hateful. I'm sure she said all this because what else could she say? Her actual words are lost to me because I knew that she didn't have an answer.

I've come to terms with there not being easy answers, which in itself provides a kind of certainty. In a fragment that appears in her essay collection *This Bridge Called My Back*, Anzaldúa wrote, "The mixture of bloods and affinities, rather than confusing or unbalancing me, has forced me to achieve a kind of equilibrium."

So many of us will never be able to fully explain who we are or where we come from. I'm no closer to answering this question now than when I was a teenager, and I won't be any closer in another forty years. Anzaldúa's gift was to help people like me feel the "exhilaration," as she called it in *Borderlands/La Frontera*, "in being a participant in the further evolution of humankind." There's something to be said for the power of hybridity, of sliding between staid categories, of recognizing that your heritage is something to eternally grapple with, rather than settle into.

69

Bill Hobby

by **R.G. Ratcliffe** Photograph by Pam Francis

The son and grandson of prominent state officials, Bill Hobby was born to be a politician. Growing up in Houston and Washington, D.C., he attended Rice University and after graduating served in intelligence for the Navy. When he returned to Houston, Hobby worked at the family-owned *Houston Post*, becoming president of the publication in 1965. By that point he had already started his political career, having worked as a parliamentarian of the Texas Senate. After serving on President Lyndon Johnson's President's Task Force on Suburban Problems, the Texas Air Control Board, and the Texas Senate's Interim Committee on Welfare Reform, he was elected lieutenant governor in 1972, a job he held on to for eighteen years. Hobby retired from politics in 1991 and went on to serve as the chancellor of the University of Houston System, teach classes at Rice, and even write a book, *How Things Really Work: Lessons from a Life in Politics.*

One day, toward the end of Bill Hobby's tenure as the longest-serving lieutenant governor in Texas history, I was taking a shortcut through the state Senate chamber when I spotted him in the corner and heard the distinctive throat-clearing growl that he used to cover his stutter. He called my name. "Come to my office," he said. "I want to show you some-

cepted for publication," Hobby proudly replied. "Math relaxes me," he said.

It was a classic Hobby moment: the man who had guided Texas through one of its most wrenching transitional eras couldn't help acting like a quant nerd.

In many ways, Hobby was the least natural politician I have ever met. He often dressed in rumpled clothing, and because he was color-blind his bow ties and shoes sometimes didn't match his suit. He frequently appeared in public looking sleepy, and when he made a speech his double-cluck throat-clearing baffled audiences. At receptions, you had to be careful not to get between Bill Hobby and the exit door. He just wasn't a people person.

Nor was he much good at playing the role of a man of the people. He was a patrician figure who had received a significant inheritance and went foxhunting at his country house in Ireland. Yet his love for Texas was as deep as that of any cowhand, and he was a remarkably effective public servant. Between the day Hobby first took office in 1973 and when he stepped down eighteen years later, he had modernized our government in countless ways. He insisted that the state adopt zero-based budgeting, which meant that state agencies would have to defend their current budgets and then justify any increases. He helped reform public education by pushing for smaller class sizes and requiring students to pass all of their courses in order to par-

71

thing." When you're a reporter, if the most powerful elected official in the state invites you to visit, you go.

We arrived at his office, which was strikingly spartan, and Hobby seated himself behind a massive executive desk. As I squirmed in a straight-backed visitor's chair, he handed me a sheet of paper filled with numbers and symbols, the kind of equations that strike fear in the hearts of high school algebra students.

"What's this?" I asked.

"It's a math problem I wrote that has been ac-

ticipate in extracurricular activities, such as band or football. And he fought for tax increases—hardly a popular position in Texas—to pay for improvements in public education and protect higher education from budget cuts. He knew that we needed to create a smarter workforce for the information economy that was fast approaching. *Texas Monthly* political writer Paul Burka, the longtime dean of the Capitol press corps, once wrote that Hobby was "the largest Texan of our time." It's a remarkable claim, and a plausible one.

Bill Hobby's father, Will Hobby Sr., was a newspaper publisher who was elected lieutenant governor in 1914 and then became governor in 1917. Bill's mother, Oveta Culp Hobby, was the first commander of the Women's Auxiliary Army Corps during World War II and then served in President Eisenhower's cabinet as secretary of health, education, and welfare, making her the second woman ever to serve in a presidential cabinet. She returned to Texas in 1955 and eventually took over the family-owned *Houston Post*.

Don Carleton, a Hobby family biographer, believes that Bill decided to run for lieutenant governor in 1972 to get out from under his mother's shadow. Although Bill had important jobs at the *Post*, including managing editor, Oveta was always in charge.

His campaign slogan was typically artless: "Bill Hobby will make you a good Lieutenant Governor. Honestly." And he did, honestly.

The Senate that Hobby took over in 1973 was very different from the one we have today. The business of the Legislature was business: the state budget and taxes, not culture war issues, were its raison d'être. Hobby's genius was to bring warring factions together to hammer out a compromise. As a pro-business conservative Democrat, he tended to fashion agreements that leaned toward the establishment. The senators and lobbyists would gather in a room, and Hobby would reason, cajole, arm-twist, and dangle compromise legislation in front of everyone. Liberals complained Hobby had sold them out. Republicans said he catered to the big-spending liberals and trial lawyers.

But they usually acquiesced, partly because he often had the best arguments. "He just has an incredibly deep intellect," former state senator John Montford of Lubbock said. "There was no way you were going to outdo him on facts." Hobby also had an institutional advantage. Gubernatorial power was severely limited by the state constitution; the Legislature ran the government, and Senate rules empowered the lieutenant governor. Hobby had the upper hand, and he wasn't shy about using it.

Perhaps the greatest test of Hobby's talents as a backroom operator came during the gubernatorial tenure of Bill Clements, who was first elected to office in 1978. Clements wanted to change the political balance of power, tilting it away from the Legislature and back to the governor himself.

Clements and Hobby both had childhoods of privilege: Clements attended the tony Highland Park High School in Dallas and Hobby was enrolled at the private St. Albans School in Washington, D.C. But the commonalities ended there. While the Hobby family's finances flourished during the Great Depression, Clements's father went broke. Hobby went to Rice; Clements went to work as an oilfield roughneck before studying engineering at Southern Methodist University. Hobby inherited the family media empire. Clements built the world's largest oil-drilling contracting company from scratch.

They exasperated each other. Clements once declared that "our institutions of higher education" wasted more state money than any other entity. Hobby responded by saying the Legislature was beset with "a virulent strain of anti-intellectualism" and that Clements was giving it "redneck reinforcement."

Clements lost his reelection bid in 1982, but after he won reelection in 1986 he promised to "scrub the budget" for waste, create jobs, and halt any increase in state taxes. Hobby, by contrast, promised to protect the budgets of state colleges and universities.

Hobby put on a serene public façade while getting into shouting matches with Clements behind closed doors. At a crucial point in the budget battles, John Montford and Republican senator O. H. Harris of Dallas went to Clements to ask him to negotiate with Hobby. "I'm not going to go see that son of a bitch," Montford recalls Clements saying. "If he wants to talk, tell him to come over here." The senators told Hobby what Clements had said. "Well, I'll be a son of a bitch," Hobby replied. "Let's go." In Clements's office, the two adversaries sat at either end of a long sofa. Harris found a bottle of Scotch. By midnight they had a budget deal, and it was more or less on Hobby's terms. To pay for it, Clements signed a $5.7 billion tax increase, the largest in state history.

"He just presided over some amazing things, when the Legislature actually governed instead of just performed," Carleton said. "One of the sad

notes is everything Bill worked for in those eighteen years has been almost destroyed by the later legislatures."

In the decades after Hobby left office, the Legislature went from Democratic to Republican, and compromise became a dirty word. In his 2010 memoir, Hobby lamented how profoundly Texas government had changed; there was no longer any room to reach across the aisle. "The result was a lack of civility, bad legislation, unmet needs, and partisan divisions between the factions that are too deep to bridge," he wrote.

For nearly two decades Hobby did an expert job of bridging those sorts of divides and delivering results to the people of the state. It was tempting to think that he represented the future of Texas politics: a centrist, consensus-driven, results-oriented process that would set an example for the rest of the nation. But if that is the future of Texas politics, from the vantage point of the early twenty-first century it looks like the very distant future indeed.

73

George Strait

by John Spong Photograph by Joe Pugliese

The traditional country music that George Strait played was out of style when he recorded his first single, in 1981; pop-country was topping the charts back then. But the future "King of Country," who was born in Poteet in 1952, knew what he was doing. More than two dozen albums later, Strait is one of the most successful performers of all time. He has won more Country Music Awards and Academy of Country Music Awards than any other artist, chart-toppers such as "Heartland" and "The Chair" have made him a household name across the country, and in Texas his songs can be heard streaming through car speakers, blaring over the PA at football games, and setting the tempo for two-steppers at dance halls. Other than Willie, it's hard to think of a country performer more beloved by Texans and more influential on the state's music scene.

George Strait's eyes are green, somewhere between the color of a Granny Smith apple and pool table felt. He's got the bright white, worry-free smile of a country club golf pro, somebody who makes his living flirting with older women. His face is quietly handsome and friendly, and he usually looks like he's enjoying himself. His expression often suggests he's open to a little mischief, nothing too dramatic, maybe a beer or two too many. He'll always leave room to charm his way out of trouble. In truth, none of that is too terribly extraordinary. He probably reminds you of someone you had a crush on or looked up to in high school.

So move on to his music. Over the course

of his four decades and counting as a major-label recording artist, he's released dozens of studio albums, every one a collection of old-fashioned meat-and-potatoes country music. The songs are barroom weepers and cheating tunes, balanced with others about true love, family, and faith. He delivers them with a warm, expressive voice that is more comfortable than remarkable, keeping to the straightforward style of Merle Haggard rather than the vocal acrobatics of George Jones or the vibrato of Ray Price. The melodies are often poppy and sometimes they swing, but they always come dressed in fiddle and steel guitar.

That sound was distinctly out of favor when Strait started recording in 1981. As that decade wore on, he managed to pull traditional country music back into vogue, and he's stuck with it through every trend that has surfaced in the meanwhile. Improbably, it has made him the most successful singles artist in history, owner of more number one songs than any other artist in any genre—sixty, by one metric. There's no hyperbole in saying that his loyalty to the old sound is the single most important reason it stayed alive and on the radio.

In the spring of 1981, when MCA Records was preparing to release Strait's first single, "Unwound," there was no reason to suppose people would still be listening to him decades later. This was the era that country fans of a certain age deride as the "urban cowboy" period. The term, however, is a misnomer. Though the John Travolta movie that inspired it made unlikely national figures out of middling singers Johnny Lee and Mickey Gilley, *Urban Cowboy* merely capitalized on the sound that already dominated Nashville: watered-down, wide-appeal country. The artists who'd perfected it, singers like Kenny Rogers and Eddie Rabbitt, were selling millions of records by shucking steel guitar and fiddle for a sound so unobjectionable it would have put Jim Reeves to sleep with his head in Chet Atkins's lap. Throughout these years, Nashville was looking past the country chart. The real money was on the pop and adult-contemporary charts. And since country artists had a more realistic shot at the latter, this became Nashville's easy-listening era. If you loved hard-core country, it was a dark age. To paraphrase Voltaire, as any meaty discussion of country music should, had there been no George Strait, it would have been necessary to invent him.

If someone had, however, they almost certainly wouldn't have drawn up a calf roper from Poteet fronting a western swing band. But that's what twenty-eight-year-old George Harvey Strait was: a recent ag grad of Southwest Texas State supporting his pregnant high school sweetheart wife and their ten-year-old daughter by working cattle during the day and playing music at night. He and his band, Ace in the Hole, were a huge draw on the Texas dance hall circuit, which was precisely their limitation in the minds of country A&R reps. Nashville country had originally come down from the mountains. It was hillbilly music, ballads and banjos. Texas country was something else. It was waltzes and shuffles and above all western swing, the upbeat jazz-and-country hybrid that Bob Wills and His Texas Playboys had used to introduce the Grand Ole Opry to the revolutionary notion of drums—to which it came kicking and screaming. Western swing was dance music, and George Strait and Ace in the Hole were a dance band. They would not have had a harder time selling themselves on Music Row playing reggae.

There was also the matter of Strait's appearance. He was sure enough a good-looking guy, but he wore a cowboy hat, an accessory that, for Nashville, had effectively died in the back seat of Hank Williams's Cadillac. He also wore plain brown boots with a low roper's heel and Wrangler jeans, starched and stacked, meaning they were left extra-long so they didn't ride too high up his leg when he rode a horse. Simply put, he was a South Texas cowboy and he looked it, which was not a package that a country record label could hope to cross over to pop with. When Strait made occasional trips to Nashville to shop for a record deal in the late seventies, the labels all passed. He wasn't too country, he was too *Texas*.

And then Erv Woolsey stepped in. In the early 1980s, Woolsey was the head of promotion at MCA's country division. But he was also a Houston native, and he had been working with Strait since he'd booked the Ace in the Hole Band at a San Marcos nightclub he owned during a mid-1970s sabbatical from Nashville. Now that he was at the seat of power, Woolsey pushed Strait on MCA execs, who eventually signed him.

The hits came quickly, though by 1984 there were still wide pockets of the United States where Strait wasn't getting played. In Nashville, a programmer at storied WSM, the station that invented the Grand Ole Opry, flatly refused to play his western swing song "Right or Wrong," explaining to Woolsey, "We don't play that music."

If you were a country fan in Texas at the time, the idea that there might be any resistance to George Strait was unimaginable. I was a junior at Austin's Westlake High School back then, and as far as I could tell, Strait was everywhere. His image hung at the boot store and in record shops, his music played over the PA between innings at baseball games and blared out of pickup trucks in the parking lot after school. There was a cashier at the grocery store who never asked for an ID when I tried to buy beer, chiefly because I always asked to see the backstage snapshot of her and Strait that she seemed to carry at all times. Then my friends and I would drive to vacant lots, drink the beer on open tailgates, and listen to George. He had the exact appeal that Nashville execs always claim to be looking for: girls wanted to be with him, and guys wanted to be like him. One by one my friends and I made the leap from Levi's and Tony Lamas to Wranglers and Justin ropers.

Over the course of the ensuing decades, Strait never did stop sticking to his guns and having that sort of impact. No matter how big he got, he never moved to Nashville; he stayed in Texas, and he kept his music squarely rooted here, too. And while it's hard to imagine that bands playing Texas dance halls would have ever shucked western swing for Nashville's ever-changing flavors of the month—be it Shania Twain's pop confection of the 1990s or the more recent bro-country scourge—it's even harder to imagine the Texas scene being as vital as it is without Strait as its champion. He transformed Texas country music by refusing to let it be transformed, making sure we all knew that our traditions didn't need Nashville's imprimatur.

77

George H. W. Bush

by **Mimi Swartz** Photograph by Platon

"I'd say I have a lot better shot than some in this country of two hundred fifty million people," Vice President George H. W. Bush told *Texas Monthly* in 1983 about his chances at the presidency. That kind of modesty marked Bush's life, from his birth in 1924 to a patrician Massachusetts family to the heights of Washington power. Our forty-first president, who moved to the West Texas oil patch in 1948 to make his fortune, adapted quickly to his new surroundings and was a key player in the state's transformation from a Democratic stronghold to a Republican bulwark. After a couple of failed Senate bids in the 1960s, he landed as ambassador to the UN, then head of the Republican Party, special envoy to China, chief of the CIA, two terms as Ronald Reagan's vice president, and eventually one term as president, during which he oversaw the 1991 Persian Gulf war and the country's response to the Soviet Union's collapse. He paved a path for his sons as well. His namesake, George W., served as the governor of Texas and then followed him to the White House. Another son, Jeb, served two terms as governor of Florida but failed in his attempt to win the presidency; by 2016 modesty was no longer an advantage in American politics. (Jeb's son, George P. Bush, served two terms as Texas land commissioner but in 2022 failed to win the Republican nomination to become the state's attorney general.) By the time Bush died in 2018, his family's dynasty looked shaky; Donald Trump had profoundly scrambled the political calculus for Republicans. Even so, George Herbert Walker Bush helped define American and Texan politics for a generation.

I **always enjoyed** watching George H. W. Bush and the media spar over one of the most contentious issues of the president's life and times: whether he was a real Texan. Even *Texas Monthly*, a respectable (and generally respectful) publication, got in on the act. "He was a lean and lanky six feet two, with crystal-blue eyes, neatly combed brown hair, and the kind of clean-cut, delicately handsome features that seemed to sing out 'I'm a Yankee Doodle Dandy,'" is how we once described a twenty-four-year-old Bush, newly arrived in the West Texas oil patch in the summer of 1948.

The Bum Steer Awards, the magazine's annual razzing of public figures, wasn't above calling into question his Texas bona fides, either. In 1985 we mocked him for claiming that his real residence was his family's compound, in Kennebunkport, Maine, so he could save $123,000 in taxes. "The IRS didn't buy it, but we do," we wrote. "Now we know why you spent the whole year acting like a Yankee. Anybody who'd sell his Texanhood for $123,000 deserves to be Bum Steer of the Year."

Four years later, we gave Bush, who had just been elected president, yet another Bum Steer, this time for calling the presidential suite at the Houstonian Hotel his Texas residence. During their state convention, a group of mischievous Democrats rented out that very suite to needle the Republican candidate.

Even in death, Bush was haunted by the specter of eternal exile: "Forty-first president honored in adoptive home of Texas before being laid to rest," announced a 2018 *Wall Street Journal* story after his Houston funeral. It was as if Bush was never allowed the privilege afforded to just about everyone else who settles in Texas, which is the honor of calling oneself a Texan without a modifier attached. Davy Crockett came from Tennessee, as did Sam

Houston. No one has ever made fun of *their* claims to the Lone Star State.

It's ironic that "poor George"—as small-town Texas native Ann Richards called him—has been singled out for mockery in a place that's famous for opening its doors to everyone. The best thing about Bush's adopted hometown of Houston is that no one has ever cared where you came from or who your people were, especially if you manage to make it big on your own. Houston was transformed into the nation's fourth-largest city by as many outsiders as insiders: the doctors recruited to the Texas Medical Center by Louisiana-born Michael DeBakey; breathtaking ballet dancers like Li Cunxin (from China) and Carlos Acosta (Cuba); philanthropists like Rich Kinder (Missouri) and Laura Arnold (Puerto Rico); any number of athletes, from the fabled Rocket Hakeem Olajuwon (Nigeria) to hard-hitting second baseman José Altuve (Venezuela); and the current Harris County judge, Lina Hidalgo, who hails from Colombia by way of Peru and Mexico. The truth is that the likes of Davy Crockett and Sam Houston set a standard for self-selection. Few come to Texas for the climate (the summers are brutal) or the natural beauty (acquired taste, mostly). They come because they have a sense that this is where they can become who they know they are meant to be. Sometimes that means becoming president of the United States, and sometimes that just means living freely in a small apartment complex with washer-dryers on-site.

Of course, there have been exceptions. People of color haven't always been welcome, and immigrants from Latin America, once welcomed as a constant stream of cheap labor, have now become political pawns. Bush had a different problem. He became a target because he hailed from a world most Texans have historically held in contempt: Yankeeland, specifically the Richie Rich environs of Green- wich, Connecticut, where his dad, Prescott (Prescott!), was an investment banker and, later, a Republican senator. And of course Bush went to that fancy-pants prep school, Phillips Academy, in Andover, and then, af- ter a stint in the Navy during World War II, to hoity-toity Yale. There was also all that patrician stuff: the exceedingly good manners, the prolific writing of kindly notes. (He once apologized in an email to me for declining to participate in a story about his son Neil's bitter divorce.) Real Texans for many years were thought to be guys like oilman Oscar S. Wyatt Jr., who shot hogs from his helicopter. Bush rarely got points for abandoning the staid aristocrats back home for the unforgiving environs of Midland, where he and his wife volunteered in the community, raised two of their six kids, and built an oil business with folks who would become friends for life. Trust me, a person who could pull that off was already a Texan; anyone who has spent much time in Midland knows it makes Asmara look like an oasis.

Maybe the problem was that the struggle over Bush's Texan-ness was internal as well as external. His life in Houston was often an awkward combination of old-money noblesse oblige and, well, the Texas thing. He had Texan interests if not quite authentic Texan tastes. When he and Barbara moved to Houston, in 1958, he chose to live in understated Tanglewood instead of flashy River Oaks, where most other oilmen had made their homes. He loved Mexican food but preferred the West Houston chain Molina's Cantina, which has never been known for using jalapeños in abundance. He loved barbecue too, but his favorite joint was Otto's, a homey dive near Memorial Park that was eventually eclipsed by far tastier spots in more racially diverse parts of town.

On the other hand, he deserves credit for legitimizing the state's virtually nonexistent Republican Party, a brave act for its time. Back in the day, the longtime political operative Dave Walden explained, Houston "basically had three kinds of Republicans: the John Birch Society types, who were really off-the-wall; the hard-core Goldwater people, who were very conservative; and the pro-business, moderate, try-to-get-along-with-everybody, try-to-keep-the-government-out-of-our-lives–type Republican—that's where Bush was." But it wasn't until Bush agreed to become Harris County party chair and started barnstorming the state that the latter group decided it was okay to join up. As Mark P. Jones, a political science fellow at Rice University's Baker Institute, points out, "If you were a politically ambitious person, the strategic thing to do was run in the Democratic Party, not to stick with your Republican brand and run as an outsider."

Of course, even as he launched a political career, Bush had to make some changes to his image. He was stuck with the carpetbagger charge when he ran for Senate against the folksy Democratic liberal Ralph Yarborough in 1964. As the presidential biographer Jon Meacham wrote in *Destiny and Power: The American Odyssey of George Herbert Walker Bush*, the candidate had to give up wearing a necktie and using big words (like *profligate*, as in spending). He had to trade in his Mercedes for a Chrysler. He still lost, but along the way he won a lot of respect from people who weren't members of the Petroleum Club.

Bush was at heart a sentimentalist, but he also came to display a pragmatism that seemed distinctly Texan. His move to the right during the Reagan years and during his own presidential campaign was described, pejoratively, as expedient. In Bush's calculus it was simply the most expedient way to maintain his own power and influence. He may have struggled initially with his electoral losses, but Bush was also one to pick himself up and start over, always looking forward and rarely back.

And, like many Texans, his faith—albeit Episcopalian, not Southern Baptist—was never in doubt. Bush taught Sunday school and had a family pew at St. Martin's, in Houston. His devotion was genuine, as evidenced by the affectionate eulogy given by his minister, the Reverend Dr. Russell Levenson Jr., at the Washington National Cathedral. "They were not political members of that church. They were regular attenders," Jones said.

That Bush wanted a second funeral, in Houston, was itself a testament to his adoration for the place he called home. He and Barbara had been prominent empty nesters here, socializing with longtime friends without big-dealing it, eating Chinese food at the Galleria, and attending Astros and Texans games. I don't expect many people back in Bush's hometown of Greenwich would have ever arranged for a musical tribute to him by the Oak Ridge Boys and Reba McEntire. But Bush wasn't a stuffy guy.

And in the end, there was the choice of his final resting place. Bush didn't pick the family compound in Maine, but Aggieland, a place that many would declare the most quintessentially Texan spot in all of Texas. It was a choice that should put the doubts to rest once and for all. Read my lips: George Herbert Walker Bush was a Texan, full stop.

83

T. Boone Pickens

by Skip Hollandsworth Photograph by Arthur R. Meyerson

When T. Boone Pickens was a twelve-year-old paperboy living in small-town Oklahoma in the early 1940s, he was already thinking like a businessman: spotting an opportunity, he acquired the routes of some other kids and quintupled his customer base. "That was my first introduction to expanding quickly by acquisition," he later said, "a talent I would perfect in my later years." Pickens's family moved to Amarillo not long after that and he briefly attended Texas A&M before returning to his home state to enroll in Oklahoma A&M, where he majored in geology. In 1956, after a few years as a wildcatter, Pickens founded his own company, later named Mesa Petroleum, and grew it into one of the largest independent oil outfits in the world. As he had when he was a child, Pickens engaged in the art of aggressive acquisition, gobbling up smaller oil companies. He also attempted to take over much bigger companies, such as Gulf Oil and Phillips Petroleum. Those efforts failed but left him a lot richer, earning him a reputation as a no-holds-barred corporate raider. Pickens was ousted from Mesa in 1996 after he made a bad call that buried the company in debt, but in the years that followed he founded a wildly successful energy hedge fund and moved into renewables—quite the shift for a born-and-raised oilman. After his health started declining, he retired to his massive ranch in Pampa, and passed away in 2019.

Back in 2008, I ate lunch with Boone Pickens at Al Biernat's, the swanky Dallas steak house. The legendary old wildcatter seemed to be on top of the world. He cheerfully shook hands with other diners who came up to say hello. He talked to one man about how he was itching "to get a hold of a rig" and drill for oil in a field in West Texas, and he told another man that, yes, the rumors were true: he was planning on building a wind energy farm in the Panhandle.

"A wind farm?" said the man. "Really?"

Pickens shot the man his trademark boyish smile. "You know me," he said. "I like to keep things interesting."

Since Spindletop, Texas has been home to countless larger-than-life oilmen. But no one played the role better than Pickens. He lived in a big mansion in Dallas. On weekends, he flew in his $57 million Gulfstream G550 corporate jet to his sixty-eight-thousand-acre Panhandle ranch that was filled with man-made lakes, creeks, and waterfalls, plus more than ten thousand trees trucked in from places as far away as Colorado, Illinois, and Tennessee. He gave away more than a billion dollars to charity. He married five times to five beautiful women.

And Pickens was a master showman. When reporters came around, he spouted off folksy sayings that he called "Boone-isms." "If you are going to run with the big dogs, you have to get out from under the porch," he liked to say in his tangy accent. "Work eight hours and sleep eight hours, and make sure that they are not the same eight hours" was another favorite. And there was this one that he told me at Al Biernat's that summarized his entire business philosophy: "Don't fall victim to what I call the 'ready, aim, aim, aim, aim' syndrome. You must be willing to fire."

Pickens never hesitated to fire away. The son of an oil patch land man, he was born in Oklahoma, moved to Amarillo during high school, graduated from Oklahoma A&M (now Oklahoma State), went to work for a couple of years as a geologist for Phillips Petroleum, and then struck out on his own in 1954, when he was just twenty-six, forming an Amarillo-based exploration company with $2,500 in borrowed money. He hunted for oil in unproven terrains, and by the late 1970s he had turned his company, which was then known as Mesa Petroleum, into perhaps the most successful independent in the country. In one of his most profitable plays, he invested $35,000 in drilling sites in Canada, sank the money he made from those sites into new wells, and in 1979 sold his entire Canadian operation for $600 million.

Then, in the early 1980s, he made a peculiar statement to his board of directors. "Fellas," he said, "it's cheaper to drill on the New York Stock Exchange." At the time, it didn't strike anyone as the kind of line that would one day be studied in business schools: What did a Texas wildcatter know about the intricate machinations of Wall Street? But Pickens persuaded the board to let him use Mesa's money to buy stock in publicly held oil companies that he believed were undervalued and poorly managed. After he accumulated 10 percent or so of stock in one of the companies, he pounced, calling a press conference to announce that he would attempt to get controlling interest in the company so that he could bring in a new team of executives who cared more about their shareholders than about their perks.

He was one of the first barbarians at the gate, going after Gulf Oil, Phillips Petroleum, and Unocal. Corporate executives despised him, but he was a darling of the media, landing on the covers of *Time*, *Fortune*, and *Texas Monthly*.

Although Pickens never acquired any of the companies he targeted, he brought almost all of them to their knees, forcing them to merge with other companies just to keep him away. And as a result, he did, as promised, increase the value of the stock of those companies, reaping millions for their shareholders and millions more for Mesa.

Looking for another opportunity to make a little more money, Pickens used much of Mesa's earnings from the corporate takeover battles to purchase huge reserves of natural gas because he believed that the price was about to go up. It was a spectacular miscalculation. Gas prices declined, Mesa was saddled with $1.2 billion in debt, and the company became a target of its own corporate raider, David Batchelder, who incredibly enough was a former Mesa executive and a Pickens protégé.

Pickens was told by the new team brought in to run Mesa that he hadn't kept up with the times and was booted out of his own company. Pickens attempted a comeback, forming an energy hedge fund that consisted of just him and five employees, who worked out of a modest leased office filled with used furniture. He persuaded many of his wealthy friends to invest with him.

But Pickens quickly made some bad bets, going short on natural gas contracts under the belief that prices would drop, which they did not. By 1999, the fund was down to $2.7 million. "I was scratching a poor man's ass," Boone said, using one of his least favorite Boone-isms.

People who knew Pickens told me they were worried he was suffering from clinical depression; his marriage was falling apart and he briefly saw a psychiatrist and even tried antidepressants for a month. He was off his game: his sense of humor was gone, and he snapped at his underlings. Younger investors would sneer when they saw him at Al Biernat's and say, "Boone who?" When I later talked to him about that time in his life, I told him that I had once seen him walking out of Bob's Steak and Chop House looking glum and carrying a doggie bag. "Yeah, it wasn't my finest hour," he acknowledged. "Most nights, I went with my divorce attorney, and I didn't have much of an appetite. I ended up with about twenty doggie bags of steaks in my freezer."

Did he consider retiring? He was, after all, sixty-eight years old when he lost Mesa—a perfect time, I said, to head off to his ranch, where the quail hunting was superb. Pickens gave me a look, his eyes narrowing. "You think the phrase 'giving up' is in my vocabulary?" he asked.

In early 2000, he made his make-or-break gamble, telling his brokers to take almost all the money they had left and buy long on natural gas. The price, he said, had to be going up. This time he was right: by the end of the year, natural gas had jumped from $2 to $10.10 per thousand cubic feet. The hedge fund was up $252 million, a fantastical gain of 9,905 percent before fees.

Over the next couple of years, he made more smart bets, and by the end of 2005 his hedge fund was up $1.3 billion. At a

Christmas luncheon, Boone passed out $50 million in bonus checks to his employees. Once again, he was being celebrated in the media, getting headlines like "The Resurrection of T. Boone Pickens" and "Comeback Kid."

Pickens still wasn't ready to retire to the ranch. In 2008, when he was eighty, he signed on to spend $58 million on a national advertising campaign to promote his national energy policy, which he called the "Pickens Plan," which envisioned a major shift to natural gas and wind power.

People who knew Pickens were stunned. A devout Republican, he seemed like the last person on earth who would be advocating for environmentally friendly alternative energy. Critics claimed he just wanted to benefit his investments in a Panhandle wind farm and a company that made natural gas–powered automobiles.

Pickens insisted, however, that the world would not, in the long term, be able to produce enough oil to keep up with demand. ("I've been an oilman my whole life, but this is one emergency we can't drill our way out of," he declared in his television commercials.)

Congress never got behind the Pickens Plan. And Pickens's Panhandle wind farm never got off the ground because he couldn't secure the rights to transmit that power to major urban areas. "But the politicians will eventually come around," he told me (correctly, as it turned out: within a decade renewables were a major boom industry). "My plan may not have been perfect, but a fool with a plan is better than a genius without one."

In his eighties, Pickens finally began to slow down. He closed his hedge fund. He gave away a lot of his money to hospitals and to his alma mater, Oklahoma State. But he still remained restless. He decided to drill for oil, of all places, on his own ranch—and it was a huge success.

The last time I saw him was in 2019, a few months before he died. The occasion was the memorial service for his friend Alan Peppard, a *Dallas Morning News* society columnist. The legendary oilman had suffered a series of strokes and was clearly in failing health. Clinging to the arm of one of his friends, he shuffled toward a pew in the front of the church sanctuary. During most of the service, he kept his head down. I thought he was sleeping. When I delivered Peppard's eulogy, I decided to throw in an impromptu line about Pickens being there. "It's good to see you, Mr. Pickens," I said.

For a few seconds, he didn't move. Then he slowly lifted his head and nodded. I smiled. Everyone in the church sanctuary was smiling. There was a scattering of applause, and the great old wildcatter nodded again—a showman to the very end.

89

Dean Fearing, Robert Del Grande, Anne Lindsey Greer, and Stephan Pyles

by **Patricia Sharpe**   Photograph by Zigy Kaluzny

Decades before Texas barbecue bathed the world in post oak smoke, the state jump-started another culinary movement, Southwestern cuisine. Many people had their hands in this, but four Texas chefs were, arguably, the most prominent. Stephan Pyles, a fifth-generation Texan who was born in Big Spring, has headed up nearly two dozen restaurants over the course of his career, most of them in Dallas. California native Robert Del Grande was the chef at Houston's Cafe Annie and its successors from 1982 until his retirement in 2022. Kentucky-born Dean Fearing led several Dallas restaurants over the years and is the author of *The Texas Food Bible*. Chicago-born Anne Lindsay Greer (now McCann) was a longtime Dallas culinary consultant and is the author of numerous cookbooks, including *Foods of the Sun: New Southwest Cuisine*.

By the early twenty-first century it was a given that Texas had a world-class culinary scene. Every time you turned around, one of our chefs was winning a James Beard award or appearing on *Top Chef*. A modern cult was just beginning to coalesce around our most iconic meat, smoked brisket. Once third-tier at best, Texas's major cities had risen into the second rank of American dining destinations, and were on their way to the top level. Tourists who came to visit the Astrodome, the State Capitol, and Neiman Marcus began to add select restaurants to their list of attractions.

How did that change happen? Turns out it had been simmering for over a decade, beginning with a feisty movement known as "Southwestern cuisine" that seized the national spotlight in the 1980s. Drawing on the then-daring idea of marrying Mexican and American ingredients and cooking methods with French culinary techniques, it resulted in dishes that dazzled restaurant goers: Think black bean and corn salsa, goat cheese quesadillas with cilantro pesto, grilled antelope with cactus-pear glaze. Espoused by a cadre of young chefs, Southwestern cuisine was more than a bunch of recipes; it was a revolution. It embraced notions such as eating seasonally and locally decades before the word *locavore* was coined and *farm to table* became a catchphrase. It kicked hoary classic dishes off their pedestal. It promoted an unparalleled creative freedom in restaurant kitchens and turned chefs into rock stars.

How can you pinpoint the beginning of something as sweeping as a culinary movement? You can't. But a key incident occurred in August, 1984, when seven classically trained Texas chefs, joined by a journalist as witness, came together to cook, eat, and talk about dishes inspired by Texas native

traditions. To appreciate the radical nature of that act, it helps to remember how stratified Texas restaurants were then: there was fine dining, defined by French food and "continental" cuisine, and there was everyday dining. Seldom did the two overlap. Yet, at their very first dinner meeting, the Texans recognized one another as kindred spirits who believed that our state's humble foods—enchiladas and salsas, smoked meats and fried chicken, buttermilk biscuits and peach pies—were not just homey favorites. Treated with imagination and refinement, they could equal anything the Old World had to offer.

What followed was an explosion of creativity that grew to be the biggest regional culinary movement in the country's history. Even though it was part of a movement that was called the New American cuisine, Southwestern cuisine was more regionally focused. It had creative centers and active chefs in California and New Mexico, but its roots ran especially deep in Texas, turning critics' eyes to the state for the first time and setting the stage for the kind of dynamic cooking that endures here to this day.

In the early eighties, Texas was riding the tail end of a huge oil and real estate boom, and an unfolding recession, caused by falling petroleum prices and an imploding savings and loan sector, was beginning to shred the state's economy. But in Dallas and Houston, newly minted millionaires still ate out at upscale restaurants, where

A *Dallas Times Herald* photo from the 1984 potluck held by chefs (from left) Anne Lindsay Greer (now McCann), Kevin Hopkins, Amy Ferguson, Avner Samuel, Dean Fearing, Stephan Pyles, and Robert Del Grande.

chefs served refined European dishes such as beef Wellington and trout meunière. "Everybody was buying Dom Pérignon," recalled Dean Fearing, who was the chef at Agnew's and then the Verandah Club, at the Loews Anatole Hotel, in Dallas. The boom had given people the money to travel, to Chicago, New York, Paris, Madrid. "I had customers who would actually fly to London for the opening of a new restaurant," he remembered. Robert Del Grande, who was the chef at Cafe Annie, saw the same thing happen in Houston: "Hard to believe, but back then, Americans thought foreign was better than local."

Yet some Texas chefs were growing bored with the fancy food of the day. Around the country, their peers had begun to challenge the French hegemony and play with a more native approach to cooking: in New

Orleans, Paul Prudhomme was making a splash with Cajun cuisine; in California, Alice Waters and Wolfgang Puck were championing dishes that drew on the local larder; and in New York, Larry Forgione captured the sentiment when he named his new restaurant An American Place. The Texas chefs found the trend enthralling. "We may have learned from the French, but we were here to claim our birthright," recalled Stephan Pyles, who was the chef and an owner of Dallas's Routh Street Cafe.

At first, these were nebulous, independent ideas on the part of a handful of chefs, not a movement. That changed in 1984 when Anne Lindsay Greer, a Dallas culinary consultant, took a pet project to the next level. For months the forty-four-year-old, who had recently published a cookbook, *The Cuisine of the American Southwest*, had been convinced that chefs in Texas should be talking to one another. (She may have been the first person to call the food "Southwestern.") Greer had been on the lookout for others who were interested in indigenous Texas ingredients, and she had already convened a few informal meetings. In August she acted on an idea she had been toying with: get up-and-coming chefs together to cook and trade ideas. She organized a potluck and invited a who's who of talent from Dallas and Houston: Fearing, Pyles, and Del Grande, as well as Kevin Hopkins, Avner Samuel, and Amy Ferguson. The potluck inspired several more get-togethers, and Greer, who was smart about PR, always asked a reporter to join them for dinner.

"We all sort of had the same idea independently: spicy food in fine restaurants!" Del Grande said. "I always felt like we were doing something illegal, that we were outlaws. Anne kept saying, 'You guys don't all go off on your own, you're gonna be better off sticking together.' In other words, it's not just

one lunatic out there, it's a bunch of lunatics."

But what exactly was Southwestern cuisine? The chefs were drawing on certain basic elements of the state's heritage—Southern recipes, cowboy techniques, Germanic traditions—but the dishes their customers loved best were Mexican. It soon became apparent that this would be the heart and soul of their repertoire. There was just one problem: none of them knew much about Mexico's spices or cooking methods. There was a serious learning curve ahead.

To better understand regional Mexican food, they read and took lessons from esteemed cookbook authors Diana Kennedy and Patricia Quintana. For practical techniques back home, they turned to the Mexican line cooks in their own restaurants. "So much of our vision came from the people who worked for us and what they prepared for staff meals or for themselves," Pyles said. "They had come directly from Guanajuato, from Puebla, all over. They would raid the walk-in at Routh Street for cilantro, serranos, chicken thighs, whatever, and they would whip up a great dish or salsa in no time."

"Initially there was this cuisine-transposing—'I'm gonna take a hollandaise and add chiles to it,'" said Del Grande. "The joke became 'Oh, just put some black beans on top.' A lot of things didn't work at first." Little by little, though, the chefs began to figure it out.

By the late eighties, thanks in large part to media coverage, Southwestern cuisine was on the move and Texas in particular got a lot of press. But there were other outposts as well, in places like California, Santa Fe, New York, and Denver. Soon there were Southwestern food festivals across the country, television appearances, and even the Great Southwest Cuisine Catalog, which sold salsas, turkey chorizo, and piñon brittle to its more than forty thousand subscribers. That small group of Texas chefs had sparked a far-reaching movement and found themselves transformed into national celebrities. "There's no question that Southwestern put Texas on the map," Pyles said. "I would go to a festival or on a book tour around the country where people had no idea that there was anything here but barbecue or chicken-fried steak." In a little over half a decade, Texas's place on the national stage was secured. Pyles, Del Grande, and Fearing each won a best regional chef award from the James Beard Foundation—the Oscar of the American culinary world—in 1991, 1992, and 1994, respectively.

But then, almost as quickly as it had arisen, Southwestern cuisine's preeminence began to fade.

The flush economy that had jump-started it had run its course, and the novelty was wearing off. Diners and chefs alike turned to new fads and whims.

Still, the principles that the Southwestern movement had unleashed freed subsequent generations to innovate as never before. "Someone once asked me, 'Whatever happened to Southwestern cooking?'" Del Grande remembered. "And I said, 'What do you mean? It's called American cooking.' When you look at the spice levels today and the ingredients you can find in supermarkets and salsa replacing ketchup as the number one condiment, a huge percentage of American cooking is Southwestern cooking in one way or another."

"To have started a whole movement?" Pyles said. "That's something worth celebrating."

95

The Best of the 1980s

Books

Films and TV Shows

1 *Urban Cowboy*
(1980)

2 *The Best Little Whorehouse in Texas*
(1982)

3 *Tender Mercies*
(1983)

4 *Terms of Endearment*
(1983)

5 *Blood Simple*
(1984)

6 *Paris, Texas*
(1984)

7 *Places in the Heart*
(1984)

8 *Fandango*
(1985)

9 *The Thin Blue Line*
(1988)

10 *Lonesome Dove*
(1989)

Sports

1 Under new coach Eddie Reese, the Longhorns men's swimming team wins the 1980 NCAA championships—its first of fifteen during his tenure.

2 Fort Worth race car driver Johnny Rutherford, aka "Lone Star JR," wins five of twelve races in 1980 and sets a qualifying lap speed record of 215.189 mph in 1984.

3 The University of Houston Cougars win the Cotton Bowl in 1980, followed by the Southern Methodist University Mustangs, who win it in 1983 and then win the Aloha Bowl in 1984.

4 The Houston Cougars basketball team advances to three consecutive NCAA Final Four tournaments between 1982 and 1984 and is given the nickname Phi Slama Jama.

5 After moving to Houston to train, gymnast Mary Lou Retton wins one gold, two silver, and two bronze Olympic medals in the 1984 Olympics.

6 Ben Crenshaw wins his first Masters Tournament in 1984.

7 The Texas A&M football team heads to the Cotton Bowl Classic in 1986, 1987, and 1988, winning the first and last of those games.

8 A young Shaquille O'Neal leads San Antonio's Robert G. Cole High School basketball team to a 3A crown and an undefeated season in 1989.

9 In 1989, twenty-year-old Ty Murray becomes the youngest rider to win the Professional Rodeo Cowboys Association all-around world championship.

10 Refugio native Nolan Ryan strikes out his 5,000th batter on August 22, 1989.

Music

1 **Johnny Copeland,**
Copeland Special
(1981)

2 **George Strait,**
"Amarillo by Morning"
(1983)

3 **Stevie Ray Vaughan,**
Texas Flood
(1983)

4 **Daniel Johnston,**
Hi, How Are You?
(1983)

5 **Laura Canales y Encanto,**
El Mas Querido
(1984)

6 **Steve Earle,**
Guitar Town
(1986)

7 **La Mafia,**
1986
(1986)

8 **Mazz,**
Beyond
(1987)

9 **Butthole Surfers,**
Locust Abortion Technician
(1987)

10 **Lyle Lovett,**
Pontiac
(1987)

1990

TM

the 1990s

Though Ann Richards's victory in the 1990 gubernatorial race seemed to many to augur the beginning of a progressive surge in the state, it was not to be. In 1994, George W. Bush crushed her reelection bid, ushering in a period of Republican dominance that nearly three decades later has only intensified. But not everyone bought into the growing conservative movement. Austin, a once-sleepy college town long regarded as the state's most liberal city, began its march to major metropolis status, thanks in part to the advent of Dell, Inc. in 1984 and South by Southwest in 1987. After the devastation of the 1980s oil bust, business and government leaders grasped the need for economic diversification. More jobs meant more people and a more complicated political scene. By mid-decade, Texas's population surpassed New York's, making it the second biggest state in the country and one whose growing diversity signaled that the longstanding non-Hispanic white majority wouldn't be a majority much longer. The culture reflected that shift: Selena brought Tejano to a global audience before her murder in 1995, and Houston hip-hop began catching up with the scenes in New York and Los Angeles. Eventually, it would join country as one of the state's most famous musical exports.

Michael Dell

by Loren Steffy Photograph by Pam Francis

Like many other University of Texas undergraduates, Michael Dell found himself distracted soon after his academic career began and left school before earning his diploma. But unlike most dropouts, he wasn't led astray by excessive partying or undone by a lack of direction. As it turned out, higher education was the distraction that was getting in the way of his true calling: becoming a groundbreaking tech entrepreneur. Enthralled by computers from an early age, Dell arguably did more than any single person to transform the personal computer from an expensive piece of business equipment into a common commodity, ubiquitous in homes and offices alike. In the decades since he started his eponymous company in 1984, the multibillionaire Houston native has steered it through some rough waters and, so far, stayed afloat. Today he and his wife, Susan Dell, are active in philanthropic efforts, especially in their hometown of Austin, where the Dell Children's Medical Center, the Dell Jewish Community Center, and the Dell Medical School all bear their name.

The global technology company that Michael Dell founded during his freshman year at the University of Texas at Austin started modestly. Back then, Dell, who was on the premed track, was an unusually bright undergraduate who liked tinkering with computers; he cluttered his dorm room with so many PC components that his roommates asked him

to move out. But he wasn't deterred: he turned his hobby into a business, building and selling upgrade kits for computers and turning a handsome profit.

By the time his parents figured out what was going on at UT, their dreams of medical school had been replaced by a fledgling business that in just a few years would change an entire industry. Back then, buying a PC was like buying a car: you went to a dealer and shopped the models that were in stock, which came with a handful of options. You bought the machine that best suited your needs, even if it wasn't a perfect fit, and you paid a high price for it. The parts for a typical IBM PC cost about $700, but retailers sold them for $3,000 or more, which Dell thought was ridiculous.

He had a better idea. He offered customers a chance to pick the components they wanted, then built the machine to their specifications, which reduced overhead because he didn't need to maintain an extensive inventory of pre-built computers. And he sold them for less by cutting out the retailers, which eliminated the middleman's markup. In 1986, for example, Dell sold a 12-megahertz PC with a 286 processor for $1,995. IBM was selling a 6-megahertz machine for $3,995. Dell's machine was twice as fast and cost half as much. That caught the attention of consumers and PC hobbyists, but it was corporate procurement officers who really took notice.

By 2001, Dell's Round Rock–based company was selling more than $43 million worth of computer equipment a day over the internet. It was arguably the fastest-growing company in history, and for most of the 1990s the best-performing stock on the Nasdaq exchange. Investors large and small touted the slogan "Never ever sell Dell" and held backyard cookouts to celebrate the company's earnings statements.

The charcoal cooled by 2013, however. The market Michael Dell created had turned against him. As technology prices dropped, Dell's competitors began selling machines that were faster than most customers needed and offered more capabilities than ever before. Most off-the-shelf PCs could now do anything the average buyer wanted, which made Dell's customization options obsolete. And the company was still heavily wedded to PCs even though customers were shifting to smartphones and tablets.

At the same time, Dell struggled to adapt to the emerging business model of selling servers and data storage systems bundled with the software and consulting expertise that made it all work. The company remained mired in the hardware market, where the margins had become razor-thin and were getting thinner. Since Dell was publicly traded, investors had come to expect growing sales, steady profits, and a rising stock price every quarter, none of which it could deliver.

Michael Dell recognized that he needed to shift the company's focus toward helping businesses set up and run their internal information systems. These business services come with long-term contracts, which create predictable revenue, shielding the company from the ups and downs of the PC market. Other PC makers had tried similar strategies and failed. (In fact, Dell itself had tried to make such a move, buying Ross Perot's Perot Systems for $3.9 billion in 2009. But that attempt didn't add up to much, and Dell remained a marginal player in the field.)

In the face of many analysts' doubts, Michael Dell led an investor group that took the company private in a $25 billion deal and quickly began to reinvent it away from the public eye, where he no longer needed to worry about satisfying the demand for quarterly results. In 2016, he paid $67 billion for the enterprise technology firm EMC, which was almost twice Dell's size. The biggest tech acquisition ever, it created what may be the world's largest company that specializes in selling technology to businesses and then running it for them. To reflect its new direction, Dell Inc. changed its name to Dell Technologies, which made sense. The old Dell wasn't really a technology company; it was a manufacturing wonder that spent far less on research and development than most of its rivals. The new Dell was all about the tech, spending about $2.5 billion a year on R & D between 2020 and 2022. Five years after going private, Dell proved his doubters wrong and took the revamped company to the public markets once again, in a deal worth about $24 billion.

By 2022, the company that started with one guy in a dorm employed 133,000 people worldwide. Nowhere is the impact of Michael Dell's success more obvious than in the Austin metropolitan area, especially Round Rock, where the company set up shop in 1994. Four years before Dell came to town, the city's population was about thirty-one thousand. In 2022, it was four times that. And Austin itself was transformed by the influx of "Dellionaires," who made up much of the city's burgeoning entrepreneurial class, donating money that led to the founding or expansion of such institutions as the Long Center, Ballet Austin, the Austin Lyric Opera, the Blanton Art Museum, Arts Center Stage, and the Austin Children's Museum. Austin soon became a magnet for tech companies, partly because Dell's success acted as advertising for the city and partly because the company's suppliers wanted to set up operations nearby, creating tens of thousands of jobs. The forty-second largest city in the country before Michael Dell arrived to attend UT, Austin had become the eleventh, perhaps tenth largest by 2023, and his company had a lot to do with that.

And yet Michael Dell's journey from college dropout to tech elder statesman was marked by something rare among tech entrepreneurs: a sense of humility and pragmatism to go with his unabashed self-confidence and vision. Dell realized early in his career that as a twentysomething computer geek he didn't know much about running a company. So he hired top talent such as former Motorola executive Mort Topfer, who was instrumental in turning the company into a manufacturing powerhouse.

Pushing back against classic stereotypes of the Texas businessman, Dell never affected the swagger of a T. Boone Pickens or a Mark Cuban. He has never posited himself as a globally transformational figure along the lines of Bill Gates or his fellow Austinite Elon Musk. Nor has he cultivated the sort of mystique that surrounded Steve Jobs. Like the unglamorous computers he made his fortune selling, Michael Dell has always gotten the job done without setting anyone's heart on fire. It wasn't, by many people's lights, the Texas way of doing things. But it changed Texas even so.

103

Ann Richards

by Jan Reid Photograph by Wyatt McSpadden

"If you give us a chance, we can perform," Ann Richards said of women during her legendary Democratic National Convention keynote address in 1988. "After all, Ginger Rogers did everything that Fred Astaire did. She just did it backwards and in high heels." That speech put Richards in the national spotlight, but she was already a known quantity to millions of Texans. Born in Lakeview in 1933, Richards grew up in Waco and received her bachelor's degree from Baylor University and her teaching certificate from the University of Texas at Austin. After teaching at an Austin middle school for a year, she took to the political scene, campaigning for Texas liberals and eventually getting elected to office herself in 1976 as Travis County commissioner. Six years later she became the first woman elected to a statewide office in Texas in fifty years when she became treasurer. In 1990, Richards was elected the forty-fifth governor of Texas, making her Texas's second female governor. As the state's chief executive, Richards revitalized Texas's economy, focused on education, and worked to reform the prison system. After she was defeated for reelection in 1994 by George W. Bush, Richards stayed in the political sphere, championing women's health issues and fundraising for a variety of progressive groups. She passed away in Austin in 2006.

During her lifetime, Ann Richards seemed to have been everywhere, to have seen and done it all, which made her impatient with her friends, such as my wife, Dorothy, and me, who were trying to keep up. In her twenties, she was a card-carrying member of the gang of Austin liberals who gathered at Scholz Garten, a watering hole by the University of Texas campus. At thirty, living in Dallas, she was a homemaker and political activist awaiting a luncheon speech by the president when it was announced that he'd been shot in a motorcade downtown. Back in Austin a few years later, she was a political activist and a member of Mad Dog Inc., a crew of writers and performers that included the likes of Bud Shrake, Gary Cartwright, and Jerry Jeff Walker. (Look at the photos on the cover of Jerry Jeff's storied album *¡Viva Terlingua!*, recorded in Luckenbach in 1973. Ann sits on a picnic table, taking it all in.)

Eventually, after years of helping other people get elected, she decided to run for office herself. Like all successful politicians, she was an opportunist with a run of good luck. Seasoned by working for local candidates such as Sarah Weddington, who was elected to the Legislature after arguing *Roe v. Wade* before the Supreme Court, Ann ousted an incumbent on the Travis County Commissioners Court in 1976. She was good at shaking hands and promising to keep folks' roads fixed. There was a prickly edge to her feminism, but her articulation of those views had an old-fashioned quality that resonated in Texas. "I know there are exceptions," she later wrote, "and that there are men who do the laundry and who go to the grocery store and plan the meals. But most of the men I know go to the grocery store with a list of instructions. And that list is put together by the female of the household. Men drive the car pool or pick up the cleaning because they are

told to. . . . So, if a woman is not there, the whole management of the house suffers."

After she defeated an incumbent Democratic state treasurer who had been indicted for misusing his office, Ann found employees trundling numbers on obsolete calculators and undeposited checks gathering dust on desks. She was no banker or computer programmer, but she hired some, and she set about managing the state's money.

Her first big moment as a public figure, of course, was her keynote speech at the 1988 Democratic National Convention. It's never been clear how Ann was chosen for that gig—she was as surprised as anyone. But when she got the chance, she hit a home run. The lines—about George H. W. Bush's silver foot, Ginger Rogers's dancing backward in high heels, Ann's game of ball with her grandchild Lily—were matched by the beauty of her, all silver and blue, and the sheer joy of her timing and delivery. She went onstage a little-known state politician and walked off a superstar.

In 1990, Ann put that star power to use in a run for governor against Clayton Williams, a rich West Texas Republican. For months, she was so far behind that the race seemed hopeless. Then her luck kicked in. Among other offenses, Williams cracked a joke about rape, predicted in cowpoke terms that he was going to rope her like a heifer, and refused to shake her hand. Appalled women in the suburbs couldn't wait to get to the polls. Ann was the beneficiary of one of the most spectacular self-destructions in Texas political history. On a blustery January morning in 1991, she led an energetic multiethnic throng down Congress Avenue to take back the government. I remember glancing above the sidewalk at windows in the office buildings. White guys in suits were looking down, smiling, charmed by the spectacle, inclined to give her a chance.

Ann made reform of insurance and ethics guidelines early priorities of her administration, but she is best remembered for sending shock waves through the agencies and commissions with her appointments of women, Hispanics, and Blacks. (Among these new appointments was my wife, who Ann named an assistant director of the criminal justice division.)

As governor, Ann tried to veil the fact that she was a liberal, and in chasing the center she sometimes looked awkward, even inept. Though no one questioned her commitment to the ideal of public service, throughout her 1994 race against George W. Bush her own internal polls told her that this time she had just 47 percent of the vote. The national press cast Bush as the underdog, but I had a sinking feeling when I attended her reelection campaign kickoff in Austin. It was her birthday, Jimmie Dale Gilmore performed, and she made a fiery speech. But the event didn't have a pulse.

Ann acknowledged that she ran a poor campaign in a year that saw a nationwide GOP sweep, but she believed her loss came down to one principle she refused to compromise. A clamor had arisen to allow citizens to carry concealed handguns. With strong backing from law enforcement, she vetoed the Legislature's bill in 1993, but the issue wouldn't go away, and the National Rifle Association and the Bush campaign used it deftly. She lost by a seven-point margin and inadvertently helped launch one of the most consequential political careers in our country's history.

At Ann's memorial service in Austin in 2006, Hillary Clinton observed that right after September 11, when so many Americans were inclined to put distance between themselves and New York, Ann chose to join a consulting firm and live in Manhattan. People would call out her name and come up to shake her hand just as they did in Texas. That's the image I dwell on now, not the bouquets of yellow roses in the rotunda of our Capitol. I can see her strapping her purse over her shoulder—having no harried young male aides to lug it around, as she did when she was governor—and barging up those sidewalks grinning, proud of her good heart and thrilled by the journey.

Selena

by **Cat Cardenas** Photograph by John Dyer

By the time she was twenty-two Selena Quintanilla was the biggest Tejano star in the world—a stunning feat in a largely male-dominated genre. The Lake Jackson–born, Corpus Christi–raised soprano was also an innovator who incorporated funk, Latin pop, and R&B elements into her music—sometimes to the consternation of purists skeptical of a native English speaker who had to sing her Spanish-language songs phonetically. But the fans, as always, had the final say, and few Texas artists have ever inspired as much devotion as the "Queen of Tejano" did. More than eighteen million Selena records have been sold worldwide, and songs such as "Bidi Bidi Bom Bom" and "Amor Prohibido" earned Selena numerous honors, including two Grammys and thirty-six Tejano Music Awards. All of this was tragically cut short in 1995 when she was murdered by the founder of her official fan club. Since her death, Selena has been the subject of a major Hollywood biopic and a Netflix dramatic series, and her songs have been streamed hundreds of millions of times.

In the days following my grandpa's death in 2019, I searched his house for old photographs. My family was putting together a slideshow to play at his funeral, and I wanted to find pictures that would remind attendees of the incredible life he had lived: snapshots of him posing with the lions and hippos he cared for at the San Antonio Zoo, training polo ponies in

Tennessee, and relaxing at his parents' home back in Mexico.

In an old dresser at the back of the house, I stumbled upon a worn leather book filled with photos, a handful of which fell to the floor when I opened it up, the adhesive long since dried out. I found myself gazing at images of two family dogs, Chaquira and Spudsie, that were long gone and of my cousins riding horseback.

And then, toward the back of the album, I came across clippings from *People* and the *San Antonio Express-News*, all of them featuring Selena, all dated from the days and weeks after her death. In practically every shot she had a microphone in hand, and her dazzling smile lit up the page. "Thousands of fans mourn Selena," read one headline. "Tejano artist's potential to remain unrealized," read another.

Drowning in waves of despair over my grandpa's death, I was desperate for a distraction. So I sat there at his kitchen table and pored over those stories. I recognized the grief in the faces of young fans sobbing by the chain-link fence that surrounded Selena's Corpus Christi home and clutching the black marble bench at her grave site.

Studying these images of mourning felt strangely comforting. My grandpa's death was a loss so profound that I wasn't sure I would ever recover. But those forgotten articles, by then more than two decades old, made clear to me that there is life after death and power in remembering. And for what felt like the thousandth time, Selena had found me right when I needed her.

I was born in 1996, a year after Selena's death and a year into her sainthood. I don't remember who first told me about her or when I listened to her music for the first time, but it felt like she was always

there, playing in the background while my family members and I browsed the aisles of the Handy Andy supermarket and during drives with my *tías* and *tíos*. For a few years, I had no idea where she was from or what had happened to her. I just knew she felt familiar.

At Las Palmas Elementary on the West Side of San Antonio, my classmates and I swapped stories about Selena, piecing together what had happened to her from whispered conversations we overheard at home. By the fourth grade, we knew the basics: Selena was a girl from the South Texas barrios who sang in English and Spanish and danced around the stage in marvelous, glittering outfits. She was the Mexican Madonna, on the verge of accomplishing things that no other Mexican American singer ever had. And then she was killed, taken from the people who loved her by one of her biggest fans.

In the sixth grade, my family moved to Fair Oaks Ranch, on the outskirts of San Antonio, and I learned that the connection I'd felt to Selena wasn't universal. I went from a majority Hispanic city to a suburb where Hispanic residents made up little more than 10 percent of the population. From the first day of school, I was made keenly aware of my ethnicity. Teachers and students stumbled over my last name. The normalcy of my family suddenly seemed abnormal; while my classmates might have visited a few of their relatives over summer break, my "immediate" family consisted of at least

never heard. On a break, our teacher let us walk around outside and I heard "El Chico Del Apartamento 512" and "Tus Desprecios" for the first time, trying to get my mouth to form the words as quickly as Selena's did.

Selena had a way of making you feel seen, but also of feeling so completely out of your league that you wanted to figure out how to be her. I was particularly captivated by YouTube videos of her performance at Fiesta Broadway in 1992, where she demonstrated how fluent she had become at Janet Jackson– and Paula Abdul–style footwork; I spent months trying to learn her moves.

When I went to college in Austin and was away from my family for the first time, Selena's voice pushed me to seek out attention and not be afraid if someone gave it to me. Texas's capital city had more Latinos than Fair Oaks Ranch, but it still wasn't San Antonio. During my first few years there, I'd get in my car and drive around town, blasting Selena's greatest hits as I scoured East and South Austin for *panaderías* and *fruterías*. With each drive, the city felt a little bit more like home.

When I was a child, twenty-three seemed well on the far side of adulthood. I imagined it as the age when you got married, bought a house, and maybe started a family. Selena's death at twenty-three was heartbreaking, but I felt sure that she had

twenty people: aunts, uncles, and cousins who all lived within a thirty-mile radius of one another and saw one another every week. And I was sure that my grandpa's signature dishes (especially his menudo) would have scared off most of my peers. I felt lost, and Selena was my life raft.

During my junior year of high school, when I enrolled in advanced Spanish, something changed. I finally met friends who knew Selena's entire discography and introduced me to songs of hers I'd

111

gotten a taste of freedom, a brief chance to live before her life was cut short.

But by the time I turned twenty-four, Selena at twenty-three felt impossibly young. Too young to have the pressure of international stardom on her shoulders, too young to think about what she had to give up to achieve it, too young to be turned into a martyr.

Yet she became one, or whatever other label of reverence you might want to put on her: a saint, a queen, a symbol, a role model. Coming along as I did, after her death, I've only ever known her as an icon, as something bigger than herself. That's understandable, given that she died so early in her career and with so much of her story unfinished;

it's no wonder that those of us who were devoted to her filled those gaps with our adoration.

But the problem with sainthood is that it has made the real Selena less tangible. In the early 1990s, Selena was doing something radical. She wasn't sacrificing the imperfect or less commodifiable parts of herself to rise through the ranks; she was putting them on full display for everyone to see. She embraced her Mexican heritage at a time when Latinos were under pressure to assimilate. She didn't hide from her fans on the other side of the border that her Spanish was far from perfect. She designed outfits that showed off her curves and challenged mainstream standards of beauty.

She wasn't just a singer or a fashion icon; she was an enterprising woman making her way in a culture that was—and is still—dominated by men. In that sense, maybe she was a saint—because saints aren't usually passive or peaceable. They're fierce to their cores.

While most of us recognize Selena's tenacity, though, that halo we've placed above her head has turned her into an infallible figure she never pretended to be. To truly understand what was lost when Selena died, new generations of fans will need to see her as a person, not a myth.

Selena left us when she was still inventing herself, when she hadn't made any major missteps. She's forever frozen in amber on the precipice of superstardom, having rarely, if ever, failed at anything.

But if her fans want to honor Selena and find a way to carry her with us as we move through our own lives, then we need to imagine what she might have done if she had lived a full one. That too is a way of ensuring the dead never die. She would have doubtless gone on to greater heights. She might have become an actress or a heavy hitter in the international fashion world; she might have headlined a Super Bowl halftime show. In a bid for relevancy later in her career, she might have recorded a duet with a flash-in-the-pan singer well beneath her talent, or subjected one of her songs to a trendy remix. Because she was human, she would have inevitably made some mistakes. And that would have forced us into a more nuanced and complicated relationship with her.

In this, I'm reminded of my grandpa. Though I see in him many of the same things I see in Selena—a resolute will to succeed against the odds, abiding loyalty to his family, and pride in his roots on both sides of the border—he was also completely unlike her. He lived to be eighty-nine years old, and when I think of him, it's not just of the heroic younger years I've heard so many stories about but of the decades that followed, the years I witnessed. I saw him experience grief and frailty. I watched his temper flare. I saw his pride cloud his judgment. As much as I loved him, I know that he sometimes let his loved ones down.

Selena never got the chance to disappoint us. But if she had lived long enough, she surely would have. And we would have had to struggle to love her. Which is a different kind of love, and maybe a better one.

113

Karl Rove

by S. C. Gwynne Photograph by Henry Leutwyler

Although Karl Rove didn't move to Texas until his mid-twenties, he was the essential strategist of the Republican takeover of Texas in the 1990s. Rove, born in Denver in 1950, first became famous for steering George W. Bush to the governorship in 1994 and 1998, but he also boosted the fortunes of such statewide figures as Bill Clements, Rick Perry, and John Cornyn. After he helped Bush secure the presidency in 2000, Rove joined his client in the White House, serving as senior adviser and, later, as deputy chief of staff for policy. He didn't leave the White House unscathed: a pair of scandals led to his resignation in 2007. In the years since, Rove has continued to work as a political strategist and commentator. He also served as an adviser to President Donald Trump's unsuccessful reelection campaign in 2020, though by then he was clearly playing catch-up with a conservative movement that had passed him by.

In the summer of 1989, a legislator named Terral Smith received a phone call at his Austin office from a young political operative named Karl Rove. The two men knew each other casually. Both were Republicans with rising ambitions. Smith was a state representative. Rove was a political consultant who owned a small company that raised money by mail for candidates. He was calling to ask a favor. He had a friend from Midland he was

trying to persuade to run for governor. He wanted Smith to give his client a little friendly coaching on the subject of criminal justice. Smith, who had been the chairman of the Criminal Jurisprudence Committee in the state House of Representatives, said sure.

He arrived at the small conference room at a downtown Austin hotel, where the meeting was to take place, and Rove introduced his pupil: George W. Bush. For the next hour, Rove listened intently as Bush, who chewed a cigar and propped his feet up on the table, asked questions and Smith held forth. Smith recalls that Bush seemed confident, almost cocky, as though he had already made up his mind on many of the issues. For Bush, it was just one of many such meetings; Rove had lined up a full day of issue briefings in the same hotel room.

None of this might seem noteworthy, except for one thing: there was absolutely no reason to believe, in 1989, that George W. Bush could ever be elected mayor of Midland, let alone governor of Texas. He had little going for him beyond the fact that he shared three-fourths of a name with the president of the United States. He was a forty-three-year-old who had never quite lived up to expectations: a mediocre student, a failed congressional candidate, an entrepreneur in the oil patch who had had access to a large pool of East Coast capital and still had not made it big. He was a hesitant, often ungrammatical public speaker. He had once enjoyed a reputation as a party boy. Though that year he helped organize an investor group to buy baseball's Texas Rangers, it would be several years before he achieved success as the team's managing partner.

Karl Rove had an entirely different notion of George W. Bush. He saw Bush as the future leader who would turn Texas into a Republican state. These briefings had been Rove's idea, part of his campaign to try to get Bush thinking seriously about running for governor. Rove would push hard for Bush to run in 1990, to no avail. Five years would pass before Bush took the plunge, against the highly popular Ann Richards in a race that almost no one but Rove thought he could win.

The making of George W. Bush is merely the most visible of Rove's lengthy list of achievements in Texas. By the time Bush was finally ready to run for governor, Rove had already been the driving force behind one of the great tectonic political shifts in American history: the Republicanization of Texas. When Rove arrived in Texas, in 1977, Republicans held one of thirty statewide offices, John Tower's U.S. Senate seat. A quarter of a century later, they held twenty-nine of twenty-nine. Most of them had been Rove clients. It was a stunning transfer of power, and Rove's fingerprints were all over it.

Yet this story starts not with a triumph but with a catastrophe.

On November 2, 1982, the main client of Rove's new consulting business, Governor Bill Clements, suffered a stunning defeat at the hands of Democrat Mark White, the state's attorney general. No one had seen it coming. Polls had shown the governor up by eight points the night before. For Rove, who was likely the most ambitious person in Texas politics in 1982, it was like being sucker punched by a mailed fist. In 1978, Clements had made history by becoming the first Republican governor of Texas since

Reconstruction. Rove had gone to work for Clements's political operation in 1979 and had become a sort of bargain-basement political Svengali: His expertise was direct mail, which is used for fundraising and campaign ads. In 1981 an optimistic Rove, seeing small gains as harbingers of a Republican future, had been so confident that he went into the direct-mail business for himself. His first client was Governor Clements. He had other clients too, including the Republican candidates for lieutenant governor, agriculture commissioner, and attorney general. In the fall of 1982, things were looking up for Karl Rove.

On November 2, all that came crashing down. All Rove's Republicans lost. It was a bloodbath. Not only were the winners Democrats, they were *liberal* Democrats. As a group, they were the most liberal Texas had ever seen. They were everything Karl Rove was against—people like Jim Mattox (attorney general), Ann Richards (treasurer), and Jim Hightower (agriculture commissioner). Within days the vultures were circling.

"The Mark White operatives started calling my clients," recalled Rove. "They were saying, 'You'd be better off not being associated with the young lad.' I felt completely devastated."

But Rove's personal disaster turned out to be the opposite of what it seemed. His bleak morning after was in fact the beginning of the end of the Democratic Party's hegemony in Texas, the moment when the state's vaunted Democratic forces achieved total domination before beating a slow but steady retreat before the Republican onslaught.

As gruesome as the Republicans' defeat was in 1982, it was not total. One seed of hope was a conservative Democratic congressman from College Station named Phil Gramm, who had won the Democratic primary with Karl Rove's reluctant help. Rove had been ordered by Clements to help Gramm, who had co-sponsored Ronald Reagan's

budget cuts over the objections of the leaders of his own party. Rove ran Gramm's direct-mail and phone bank operations. After his victory in the general election, Gramm switched parties, then resigned and ran again in a special election. Gramm won again, and when John Tower chose not to seek a fifth term in 1984, Rove helped elect Gramm to the U.S. Senate.

Though he could not have known it at the time, Rove's timing had been perfect. Gramm was one of the early bellwethers of the political changes that were about to sweep across Texas. Counties like Collin and Denton, north of the Dallas–Fort Worth area, and Fort Bend and Montgomery, near Houston, were booming with an influx of corporate relocations from the North. Gramm's Senate victory had validated Rove's belief that the rural electorate, long considered a sure thing for Democrats, could be persuaded to vote Republican. His business took off in the mid-1980s, first with direct-mail clients and then with bigger jobs where he was the general consultant, responsible for all aspects of the campaign. Crucially, he was the general consultant in Bill Clements's 1986 revenge victory over Mark White. "The Clements campaign was so focused and had such discipline," recalled consultant Mark McKinnon, who worked for White. "We woke up every morning and got hammered. We were constantly on the defensive. We were constantly responding to something. We would wake up with Karl's fist in our face."

Rove didn't stop there. By the end of the decade, all nine Texas Supreme Court justices were Republican, and Rove had run the winning campaigns of seven of them. Every Republican looking to run a statewide race in Texas went to Karl Rove, who had developed a reputation as someone you did not want to cross.

Karl Rove had waited a long time for George W. Bush. Bush had flirted with the idea of running for governor in 1990 but backed down, believing, among other things, that it was too close to his father's 1988 presidential victory. But by 1994, Clinton was in, and everything had changed. Bush

was ready, and Rove was his man. Rove believed, against all reason, not only that Bush could be made over into a decent candidate but also that the highly popular Ann Richards, whose approval ratings were hovering around 60 percent, was vulnerable as the result of the demographic changes he had been tracking.

The two men have always had an interesting, complementary relationship. The notion that Rove was "Bush's brain," as the title of one book has it—the implication being that Bush does not have one of

his own—is patently false, as anyone who has been around the two men knows. But Bush was certainly an unfinished product when he came under Rove's tutelage. As the race against Richards loomed, Rove began the process of grooming his candidate. Bush had a long way to go. He was a mediocre public speaker whose reedy, tenor voice sometimes seemed to trail away. Rove decided to keep Bush out of the major media centers in the early going so his client could hone his speaking ability in small towns.

Discipline and focus—along with the liberal use of opposition research to discredit opponents—were the hallmarks of Rove-run campaigns. This one would be disciplined but in a new way. Rove and his policy gurus had taken roughly forty issues and reduced them to four: reform of juvenile justice, of public education, of welfare, and of that old GOP favorite, tort litigation. Rove's strategy was to stick to those issues and only those issues. Bush stuck to the message, improved his public speaking, and emerged as a credible candidate, a feat many observers found remarkable.

Bush hewed to Rove's discipline and scored a major upset. Rove, the geologist's son, had always seen the Republican takeover of Texas politics not as an event but as a process, a slow but inevitable erosion of Democratic power. And now it was done. Then, five years later, in an even greater shock, Rove engineered Bush's election to the most powerful office in the world—and then helped him hold on to that job four years later.

The Texas political scene of the first two decades of the twenty-first century is the Texas that Karl Rove imagined—one utterly dominated, at least on a statewide level, by conservatives. Much the same can be said of America during the Trump years. The modern-day Republican Party in numerous respects resembles his dream for the GOP: fearless, aggressive, adamantly conservative.

But in other ways the party looks like the monster that ate its creator. Led by Donald Trump and driven by ideologues like Ted Cruz and Ron DeSantis, the Republican Party has lurched into realms undreamed of by George W. Bush or Phil Gramm. Rove has often been out of step, left behind by the forces that he himself unleashed. He has been castigated by the far right, derided as an obsolete "establishment" Republican, and relegated to playing catch-up. He opposed his party, for example, by refusing to embrace the idea that President Biden stole the 2020 election, which had become a key litmus test for the modern GOP.

There is a rich irony here: Rove is, in many ways, a man who got everything he wanted—but not, perhaps, quite in the way he had intended.

119

DJ Screw

by **Michael Hall** Photograph by Ben DeSoto

Under the nom de turntable DJ Screw, Robert Earl Davis Jr. (b. 1971) created a distinctly druggy version of hip-hop known as chopped and screwed music. Beginning in 1990, when he was still a teenager with a background in classical piano, Screw started producing cassette tapes full of rap tracks that had been slowed down to a crawl, music that sounded especially good under the influence of "lean," a beverage made up of codeine and soda. Screwed music became wildly popular in Houston and eventually beyond. Screw wasn't the first notable Houston hip-hop artist—the Geto Boys, among others, preceded him—and he wasn't the person who brought Houston rap to the rest of the world's attention. That honor fell to artists such as Paul Wall, Chamillionaire, and Mike Jones, who were signed to the Swishahouse label. But Screw was a key figure in the creation of a distinctively Houston rap scene, which has produced such international stars as Bun B, Slim Thug, and Fat Pat. By 2005, five years after Screw's death by a codeine overdose, Houston rap was an international phenomenon.

Although **DJ Screw** came along at a time when gangster rap dominated hip-hop, that's not what he focused on. Yes, there's plenty of rapping about street violence, guns, and drug dealing in his music. But most of the songs he produced concern the vagaries of lei-

sure: ballin' (partying), being a playa (one who excels at partying), making money, and hanging out with your buddies in H-town. The emcees he remixed and collaborated with rapped in detail about driving outrageously colorful, candy-coated slabs (cars), swangin' and bangin' (slowly and artfully swerving while cruising and listening to music), and taking drugs, which include marijuana (sometimes dipped in formaldehyde and PCP and called "wet" or "fry") and especially codeine cough syrup, which is usually mixed with soda pop or lemonade and poured over ice into a large Styrofoam cup. Sometimes called "lean," it's the unofficial drug of the Houston rap scene.

When I first heard a DJ Screw tape, I didn't get

it. Screw's method—slowing down a rap song until it sounded slurred and viscous— seemed like a gimmick. I found it hard to make it through a song, much less a whole tape. I wasn't alone. Houston rapper Mike D told me about driving around with friends who weren't from Houston and playing them Screw tapes. They hated the music. Mike D told them that they had to get high to get the full experience. "They said, 'You people here drink cough syrup, you smoke weed, and you listen to slow music. You are *crazy.*'"

Those friends weren't completely wrong. Listening to DJ Screw's music is like being in a fever dream. It sounds like something's wrong—like the deck is about to spit out the tape, or the batteries are so low the machine is about to grind to a halt. Everything seems to be dying—voice, beat, scratches, melodies. For a lot of Screw's listeners, it was a retreat from the grim realities of life in Houston's Fifth Ward—not into a happier storybook world but one where the hard and the bleak became a texture, not a trap. If you can't really escape where you're from, maybe you can slow it down, make it manageable, make it groove. Screw had found a way to slow down time: he had found another world.

When Robert Earl was growing up in the Central Texas town of Smithville, he wanted to be a truck driver like his father. That was changed forever by two things: seeing the 1984 rap movie *Breakin'*, and discovering his mother's turntable. He would take her B.B. King and Johnnie Taylor records and "scratch" them on the turntable the way deejays did, slowing the spinning disc and then allowing it to speed back up, playing with sound. He began buying records of his own and playing deejay with his distant cousin Trey Adkins, who would rap. If Robert Earl didn't like a record, Adkins said, he would deface it with a screw. One day Adkins asked him, "Who do you think you are, DJ Screw?" Robert Earl liked the sound of that.

At seventeen, after moving to Houston, Screw got his first job as a deejay, at Almeda Skating Rink on the south side. Soon he was working at clubs like Boomerang, where he refined his turntablism, juggling the beats of two different records, scratching, repeating phrases, improvising, watching the dancers' reactions to certain songs, riffs, and rappers. He was always working the turntables at

home, studying the techniques of New York deejays and making mix tapes for friends from albums in his huge record collection. One day in 1989, he was mixing in his apartment with some friends. They were drinking and smoking marijuana and Screw accidentally hit the turntable's pitch button, slowing everything down. Screw liked the way it sounded, though he was incredulous when one of his friends offered him $10 to record a slowed-down mix tape. But he did it, and the next day Screw's friend came back with a couple of friends, who also wanted more of the same.

Soon he was collaborating with local rappers who were sympathetic to his unique sensibility. In a few short years of listening and scratching, Screw had developed the *ear*. He knew which beats would sound good slowed down, when to scratch and when to flow. "Screw would speak to you through the turntable," one longtime fan said. "Say one of his friends died. He'd play certain songs with an RIP feel, keep doing it over and over, chopping words to make a point. It's like he knew what you were going through by the way he was playing." Patrick Lewis, head of record label Jam Down Entertainment, told me he thinks Screw's music had a lot to do with the decrease in Houston gang violence in the mid-1990s. "He was all about slowing down, chilling out, smoking a little weed. No more hating. Screw became a part of *life*."

Music and drugs have always gone together, from jazz and heroin to psychedelic rock and LSD to raves and Ecstasy. If I wanted to understand Screw's music, to grasp even a fraction of what it meant to his most die-hard fans, I needed some syrup. So I got a hookup (never mind how). I measured two ounces of the purple codeine cough syrup into a baby bottle, as I had been shown by a devotee of the craft, and then poured that into a bottle of Big Red, slowly down the sides so the carbonated soda pop wouldn't fizz up. I capped and shook it for thirty seconds, slowly unscrewed the top, and sucked off as much of the escaping carbonation as I could. It was, I was assured, part of the ritual. Then I poured the foamy red potion over ice into a Styrofoam cup. I sipped. It tasted sweet, with a metallic edge. I sipped some more. Then I pulled out *June 27th,* the unofficial anthem of the south side, and popped it into my tape deck.

It began the way all Screw tapes did: his slurring introduction, the dragging beat, the familiar keyboard melody buzzing like a dying gnat. Then, as I sipped, something happened. Like a shift in the afternoon light, the bass got deeper and the keyboards began ringing like bells. I wasn't thinking about the music; I was *feeling* it. To an outsider like me—an old white guy—hip-hop often sounds baffling and repetitious; but here, in this moment, in this altered state, it made sense. *Everything* made sense. I fell deep into the music, swangin' and bangin' in my head, and the tape was over before I knew it. Then I put on *3 'N the Mornin', Part Two,* which also sounded great. Nothing seemed slow anymore; it just seemed mellow, and right.

Since I have a tape player with pitch control, I decided to "screw" some other tapes. Van Morrison's "T.B. Sheets" translated beautifully. Lucinda Williams's "Six Blocks Away" didn't. Willie Nelson's "Night Life" was transcendent, an entirely new song. "Listen to the blues, they're playing," Willie sang as if from the bottom of a pit, and then a guitar solo unwound that sounded like someone

trying to crawl out. "Whoa," I thought. By this point, I was three hours into my trip, and suddenly I got very sleepy.

A few days later, when I put on a Screw tape, sans syrup, I was back on the outside again, an observer, a tourist. Lean was my ticket into the music, and now the magic was gone, the gate to Shangri-la closed once more.

There are, no doubt, many fans who listen to and love screwed and chopped music without the benefit of chemical alteration. But I'll bet many of them, like Mike D's out-of-town friends, thought it sounded ridiculous the first time they heard it—and maybe the second and third times. Some music derives its power from demanding that you screw your ears on differently to hear it properly. Sometimes you get there by having a smoke, or popping a pill, or drinking a little lean. Sometimes you get there by subjecting yourself to something unalterably strange, over and over, until it sounds like a new kind of normal, and you feel like an initiate. Sometimes you have to work a little, or a lot, to enjoy an artist's work. Sometimes it's worth it.

123

Charles Butt

by Dan Solomon

The names of Texas grocery chains that have gone the way of the dodo are legion—Rice Epicurean Markets. Eagle Supermarkets. Weingarten's. Some disappeared due to their own ineptitude or fell prey to consolidation. But in many cases they were simply outperformed by the eight-hundred-pound jar of salsa in the room: H-E-B, the San Antonio–based chain that, as of 2022, had more than 400 stores in Texas and Mexico. H-E-B's roots date back to 1905, when Florence Butt opened the C.C. Butt Grocery Store in her home in the modest Hill Country town of Kerrville. In 1971, the chain was taken over by her Ivy League-educated grandson Charles,. Under more than half a century of his leadership, H-E-B has become one of the most successful privately held companies in the country. And while most corporate behemoths get only bad press when they use their size and muscle to eliminate local competition, H-E-B has seemingly grown only more popular as it has gotten bigger.

In early 2020, while the rest of the country was struggling to determine whether COVID-19 would disrupt the American way of life, H-E-B was already knee-deep in war game exercises. The company's director of emergency preparedness—a full-time, year-round position at H-E-B—gathered with other department heads to run a tabletop simulation, based on information it had received from retailers in China and Italy, to learn how to manage the shortages that would hit American supermarket shelves in the coming weeks.

The company's plans involved navigating supply chain difficulties, diverting resources, and offering hazard pay to workers to keep morale high. The effort didn't go unnoticed. Former California governor Arnold Schwarzenegger called the company's effort "a masterclass in preparation and being ready to support your community."

There are few relationships a consumer can have with a brand that feel like a two-way street, but H-E-B's fans have repeatedly seen the company go the extra mile; in 2017 they watched its trucks drive supplies through flooded highways during Hurricane Harvey. And the community-minded nature of H-E-B's leadership—helmed by longtime CEO Charles Butt—has paid dividends in terms of customer loyalty. Whether or not it's healthy for millions of people to have a parasocial relationship with a $38 billion privately held corporation, there's no way around it: Texans *love* H-E-B.

There is no end to the anecdotes that reflect customers' intense affection. Shoppers line up in the wee hours of the night to purchase limited-edition reusable bags emblazoned with the face of Tejano icon Selena as if they were the latest pair of Air Jordans. They feel so strongly about the store's in-house brands that enthusiasts ship H-E-B-branded Texas-shaped tortilla chips to homesick Texpats.

In part, we can chalk up H-E-B's success to its tight focus on Texas and Mexico, which gives the company the opportunity to tailor each store to its neighborhood, using granular data about demographics to ensure that customers in a zip code with a large number of Latino residents can find the brand of baby formula they want or feel confident the salsa doesn't taste like tomato-flavored water.

The halo that encircles the H-E-B logo can be traced back to one man: Charles Butt, who started working for the company when he was eight years old and ascended to the CEO role in 1971. Under his watch, H-E-B has grown from 6,000 to nearly 145,000 employees and donates 5 percent of its annual pre-tax profits to charity.

That halo shines a bit brighter thanks to Butt's sense of civic-mindedness. In 2017 he founded the Holdsworth Center, which helps Texas public schools elevate their best leaders, while his Charles Butt Foundation strives to bolster the quality of public education across the state. Of course, pushing for children to learn to read, write, and subtract isn't the sort of activism that's likely to cost Butt's company any customers. But in 2020, in the midst of a pandemic and a heated election, he did wade into controversy, writing a letter to the Texas Supreme Court imploring it to protect mail-in voting—to no avail. It likely says something about his stature in the state that H-E-B suffered no significant blowback for his intervention into what has become a very partisan issue.

After fifty years, the mark that Butt has left on the company is hard to overstate: until he stepped down as CEO in 2021 (though he remained as chairman), most Texans had never drawn breath at a time when he wasn't leading the state's most prominent supermarket chain. But the results speak for themselves. Over the years H-E-B has tried out a number of slogans, such as "My H-E-B." There's a reason "Here Everything's Better" and "No Store Does More" are the ones that stuck.

Bob Bullock

by Paul Burka Photograph by Wyatt McSpadden

As lieutenant governor, Bob Bullock was known for getting things done—quickly and with maximum force, whether the issue was tax reform or school finance or something far more arcane. As his aide Bill Collier put it, Bullock was "a one-man fury of reform." The Hillsboro native and Texas Tech grad was one of the most charismatic and powerful politicians twentieth-century Texas produced. Were he not hobbled by alcoholism and a general penchant for excess—he was not a man to be trusted around guns—he might have reached even greater heights before his death at the age of sixty-nine.

Bob Bullock could have wished for nothing more.

When he died in 1999, every living former governor attended his funeral. George W. Bush eulogized the former lieutenant governor as "the largest Texan of our time." The officiating minister praised him as "one of the giant oaks of Texas." Newspaper headlines called him "a leader as mighty as Texas" and "a grand master

of Texas politics." No one who made a living at the State Capitol at that time would dispute his dominance of the period.

And yet, it is important for us, the living, to remember that dominance is not necessarily the same as greatness. Of all the skills that contribute to political success—among them leadership, vision, and compromise—the one that Bullock excelled at is the most difficult and the

most dangerous: the exercise of power. In no other human endeavor is the potential for good and evil so great, nor the dividing line between them so difficult to identify. Was Bob Bullock really "the largest Texan of our time"—or just the most fascinating?

He was someone many people around the Capitol wanted above all to avoid: moody, unpredictable, explosive, unrestrained by normal courtesies. You never knew what might happen when you were around him. Once, Bullock walked into Bush's office while I was winding up an interview with Bush. I was not thrilled to see him. In the banter that followed, something touched him off, and the next thing I knew, he seemed to undergo a chemical change. His eyes sank deep into their sockets and stared out into space. He began talking about the biggest disappointment of his political life: his rejection by the Texas Senate in 1972 for an appointment to the State Board of Insurance. I had worked for one of the senators who voted against him, and Bullock was acting as if he were back in those days again, accusing my former boss and me of corruption (totally without foundation)—right in front of Bush. I found myself being hustled out of the room again. That afternoon, I hand-delivered a letter to Bullock asking him to recant his accusation. The next day Bullock called me at seven in the morning, full of good cheer, to say that some people just can't take joshing.

I tell this story not because it is so uncommon but because it is so common. This is what dealing with Bob Bullock was like for everyone. One of his top lieutenants told me once, "It's part of my job description to take a world-class ass-chewing every day." And yet, we all were mesmerized by the man. How could anyone so good be so awful? How could anyone so awful be so good?

And he was good. Bullock changed state government when he became comptroller in 1975. He turned an agency that was stuck in the green-eyeshade era into the nerve center of the Capitol. He was not the first statewide elected official to upgrade an agency, but he was the first to invent an entirely new power base. As comptroller, he had access to vast amounts of information about the state's economy and tax system. He also had by far the best staff at the Capitol. Pretty soon Bullock was an indispensable player in issues that previously had been the province of the Legislature alone, such as taxes and school finance. In self-defense, the Legislature built up its own staff to compete. No one had a greater role in the professionalization of state government.

His second contribution to Texas was a determination to solve problems. It sounds ordinary enough, but the history of the Texas Legislature is one of avoiding problems until a crisis occurs. Bullock anticipated them. Following his election as lieutenant governor in 1990, he was almost frantic about it: so much to do, so little time. In Texas, the lieutenant governor is unusually powerful, in full control of the Senate agenda and a weighty participant on various boards and committees. Bullock instinctively made the most of these powers. Once he latched on to an issue, he would force opposing sides to negotiate a solution; if they failed, he warned, he would write his own bill. He knew everything there was to know. I was in his office once when a senator came in to talk about the shortcomings of the state's technical education system. The conversation ended with the senator volunteering to close a tech campus in his own district. Politicians are not by nature an unselfish lot; that the offer was made was a reflection of Bullock's insistence that senators do what is right for Texas.

To this list of achievements one more thing may yet be added: Bullock deserves a lot of the credit for George W. Bush's ascendance to the presidency. Many Bullock watchers expected that the two men would not get along after Bush was elected governor—they were from different generations, different parties, and different backgrounds (Bullock couldn't stand people with privileged roots) —but what no one knew was that the two men had already developed a bond. A few weeks before the election, Bush had the inspired idea to call on Bullock at home, alone. He told the older man that he thought he was going to win and wanted to work with him when the time came. Bush remembers that Bullock loaded him down with reports to read and that the driver whom Bush had told to come back in thirty minutes had to wait another hour after returning. "We had good chemistry from the start," he says.

Early in Bush's first term, Bullock began praising the new governor, giving Bush credibility when he needed it most. Later, Democrat Bullock endorsed Republican Bush for reelection in 1998. The relationship with Bullock was the foundation of Bush's national image as a politician who values consensus and goodwill over partisanship—though that image was sorely tested later on.

The good side of Bullock was only part of the story, however. The bad side was always there. The one constant about him was that he was the most feared person in Texas politics. To receive a sum-

mons to his office was enough to make the most powerful senators and the most influential lobbyists shudder.

Those who knew him best say that he was aware of his faults, that he was hardest of all on himself, that he was ashamed of the mess he had made of his family life. (Four of his five marriages ended in divorce.) Even if he had wanted to control his faults, he may have lacked the physical resources to do so. He had been through so many medical problems—the removal of part of a lung, depression, alcoholism (which he overcame), back surgery, hemorrhoid surgery, gallbladder surgery, a heart attack, a heart bypass operation, bouts with pneumonia, lung cancer—that he required constant medication.

In death, he was compared with Lyndon Johnson and Sam Rayburn. Like them, he loved Texas, he wanted to do good, and he knew how to make the political system work. But the comparison will not, alas, stand the test of time. They persuaded; Bullock demanded. He brooked no dissent. He wanted every vote to be unanimous. He had to dominate.

It is going too far to say that Bullock was the largest Texan of our time; that honor belongs to his predecessor, Bill Hobby, who led the Senate for eighteen years and did more for social services and higher education than anyone in Texas history. But Bullock was the most fascinating—and the greatest legend.

129

Louis Black

by Michael Hall Photograph by Annie Ray

No city in Texas has changed as much in recent decades as Austin, which, in a generation, went from college town to world-class city, from hippie Shangri-la to techie boomtown. There are many people responsible for Austin growing up—for better and for worse—but foremost among them is a Jewish guy from Teaneck, New Jersey, who came to Austin in 1975. Louis Black was a hard-eyed twentysomething movie nut trying to find his place in the world after stops in Vermont, South Carolina, and Florida. Then he came to Austin, a city that has always attracted people who wanted to do their own thing. The town was wide-open, and if you had the slightest bit of ambition, you could build something new. And Black did, creating or helping create the *Austin Chronicle* alt-weekly, the South by Southwest (SXSW) festival, and the punches-above-its-weight local film scene. The Louis Black who arrived in town in 1975 wouldn't recognize the place today.

In 2018 Louis Black gave a talk before a showing of the movie *Blaze* at an Austin theater. Louis, who was sixty-seven, stood in front of the screen, speaking rapidly about the biopic of the late Austin country musician Blaze Foley (which he executive produced) and its director, Ethan Hawke (who sat behind him). Louis waved his hands wildly as he spoke, then clasped them together again on his ample belly, then waved them again. Sometimes

he got so excited about what he was saying that he rushed ahead and stumbled over his words.

Louis is the honorary godfather of the Austin film scene, and he had been giving pre-movie talks like this for years. He was funny and self-deprecating ("There's no reason to believe a word I'm saying, except that that's what happened"), rambling, and philosophical. "This film is so much about the really important things in life," he finished. "It's how we make meaning out of life, how we relate to each other." These were the sage words of an elder, someone looking back in wonder.

Austin filmmaker Richard Linklater, who had a bit part in the movie, spoke next and turned Louis's words right back at him. Louis, he said, was a "genius connector" who makes things happen, which Linklater knew full well. He first met Louis in 1985 as a wide-eyed twenty-five-year-old and his life was forever changed when Louis helped him found the Austin Film Society, which was a major factor in turning Austin into a film hub. "It wouldn't be the same town, we wouldn't be living in the same world here without Louis," Linklater said.

For decades, since he arrived in Austin in 1975, Louis has been transforming almost everything and everyone he touched in Austin. I met him in 1981 when he, his friend Nick Barbaro, and several others started the *Austin Chronicle*, the long-running alt-weekly that shaped the city's cultural and political ethos. (A 1990 *Chronicle* cover story on a looming development near Barton Springs pretty much launched Austin's reputation as an environmentalist paradise.) As of this writing, the paper has outlasted more storied alt-weeklies like the *Village Voice* and the *Boston Phoenix*.

A few years into his time at the *Chronicle*, Louis, a film buff since his teens, began mentoring Link-

later, and when the fledgling director put Louis in his debut film *Slacker* a few years later, he was cast as the Paranoid Newspaper Reader who had one line: "Quit following me! You heard me, quit following me!" Everyone who knew him knew that fit him perfectly. Nobody could rant like Louis Black.

By the time *Slacker* came out in 1990, though, Louis had found a new project to incubate. In 1987, he and Barbaro and their friends Roland Swenson and Louis Jay Meyers started the South by Southwest Music Festival. All four men worked hard to turn the by-their-bootstraps festival into a juggernaut, but while the other three toiled quietly behind the scenes, Louis was the public face, the guy journalists called for quotes. "Trust me," he told a reporter in 1994 about the rumors that the four partners were getting rich, "we do not make obscene profits."

He wasn't all talk, though; he kept his eyes on the smallest details. When, in the early aughts, some reprobates were making and selling counterfeit conference badges and wristbands, Louis didn't hesitate to fight back. I remember watching him approach a group waiting in line outside the Paramount Theater one night, spot a counterfeit badge, and yank it over the person's head—oblivious to whether the person realized they had bought a fake.

Louis's beloved adopted hometown was laid-back and mellow, but he was neither. He may have been in *Slacker*, but he wasn't one himself. He had an unkempt black

132

SXSW co-founders Nick Barbaro and Roland Swenson, film director Alan Berg, SXSW executive Janet Pierson, and SXSW co-founder Louis Black at the SXSW Music, Film + Interactive Festival, March 16, 2011, in Austin, Texas.

beard, unruly hair, and a manic energy. His writing followed his thinking: it was free-form, with his own grammar and rules. Though I edited him at the *Chronicle*, I mostly let him be. He typed furiously with one finger, his right pointer, and that passion showed up on the page, whether he was writing about music, movies, or politics. Austin at the time was full of people starting bands, making films, putting out fanzines, organizing protests—and Louis always found himself at the center of the excitement.

Sometimes Louis's enthusiasm got him in trouble. He would go on tirades, chopping his hands through the air, sputtering and railing, then suddenly stop—and his head would vibrate like it was about to explode. He believed whatever it was that he was saying at that moment, and if things didn't go his way, he would throw a tantrum. He would yell, kick trash cans, cause tears.

Everybody who worked for him had a Bad Louis story. Mine—well, one of mine—involved a 1986 party where we were all drinking and snorting cocaine off a framed photo of Lyndon Johnson and the Waco-born Watergate prosecutor Leon Jaworski. Louis, a prodigious substance abuser, was holding court, amiably raving. At one point I asked him if he was having fun. "I'm beyond fun," he said pointedly. "Fun is over here." He gestured with his hands to block off a space next to him. "I am into *good times.*"

It was hilarious—until it wasn't. Later that night, Louis and I and a few friends were standing outside, drinking in a circle, gossiping, telling tales. Then, without warning, something shifted, and Louis started telling a different kind of story. He went around the circle, one person at a time, hurling an insult at each of us, something that mirrored a deep fear he was sure we felt about ourselves. I don't remember what he said to the others but I sure remember what he said to me: I was corrupt, a phony, and then he explained his reasons for thinking so. (I'll spare you the details.) None of us escaped the degradation, and we were all so shocked, we just stood there and took it, laughing nervously. Then, when Louis was done, he wandered off as if nothing out of the ordinary had happened.

Louis definitely had his demons. He hated himself and felt like a failure, which is a hard thing to admit, so he attacked everyone else instead. "I was scared to death," he told me years later. "I thought I was worthless. I had imposter syndrome out the wazoo. I also had a headful of ideas driving me insane."

Many of those ideas look remarkably sane today,

even if they seemed nuts back then. "I'm an entrepreneurial capitalist," Louis liked to say, and though he didn't dress or act or talk much like most entrepreneurial capitalists, he had the gift of seeing opportunities where no one else did. In 1994 he pushed SXSW to expand into film, and soon SXSW Film was one of the biggest gatherings of movie fanatics in the country. SXSW also doubled down on technology—SXSW Tech was where Twitter had its coming-out party, in 2007—and the conference became one of the most important gatherings of influencers on earth. In 2019, SXSW reportedly had 420,000 official attendees—in a city of about one million!—and added $356 million to Austin's coffers. And many of the tech companies weren't just coming here for a week; they fell in love with the town during SXSW and moved their headquarters and their employees here, changing almost everything about the city. They made it more driven, more competitive—more like the intense, fast-talking film buff from the Northeast who had moved here in another era.

Eventually Austin became the number one city in the country for seemingly everything from dating to start-ups to barbecue, thanks in part to Louis and his vision of what a creative city could be. But he almost didn't live to see it. In 2011 he nearly died from congestive heart failure, and people whispered that his years of hard living were finally catching up to him. In fact the experience gave him a new life—or at least some perspective. He finally saw all the things he had accomplished and felt happy to be alive. "I'm learning to kind of like myself," he told me, "although I'm the kind of person, when I start liking myself, I get really suspicious."

Louis seemed subdued at his sixty-fifth birthday bash in 2015, when hundreds of people gathered at the Palm Door bar on Sixth Street and told stories about the old days and listened to musicians like Roky Erickson, Rosie Flores, Malford Milligan, and Joe Ely. Louis sat like a Buddha at a table with his then-girlfriend, Sandy Boone, a beatific smile on his face, the crazed days long gone. My favorite memory of the night was the singer-songwriter Daniel Johnston, whom Louis had championed back in the 1980s, walking around, stuffing candy from each table into his pockets.

A couple of years later, Louis retired from the *Chronicle*. He spent his time writing books on Johnston and the director Jonathan Demme. He launched a couple of production companies and co-directed his first film, a documentary about Linklater. He executive-produced several films, including *Blaze* and documentaries on the great Texas musician Doug Sahm and the 1966 UT tower shootings. He bought a house near Cape Cod and spent most of his time there, but he returned to Austin often for special events and to visit friends. Each time, he would look out the window of the plane as it touched down and think how lucky he was to have landed in Austin so many years before. He would also think about how lucky Austin was that he did.

Molly Ivins

by **Mimi Swartz** Photograph by Kelly Campbell

Molly Ivins had a knack for making trouble. The uninhibited liberal journalist clashed with her bosses at the *New York Times*, ruffled the feathers of city leaders when she wrote for the *Dallas Times Herald*, and referred to a woman who accused her of plagiarism as a "mean bitch." *Molly Ivins Can't Say That, Can She?* was the title of her 1991 bestselling book, and she spent her entire career making sure everyone knew that, yes, she could.

Whenever **Texas politics** shifts rightward, many residents of the liberal persuasion ask themselves a question that is nearly spiritual in nature: What would Molly do? Molly was, to the uninformed, Molly Ivins, the late, great Texas journalist who loved to give our politicians a very bad day. She was especially hard on those who went on to bigger things, like George W. Bush, whom she memorably branded "Shrub." Molly kept at it almost until the day she died at sixty-two in 2007, though her most famous, and funniest, lines still live on.

Sometimes she skewered: President Bill Clinton was "weaker than bus station chili." Sometimes she filleted, as when she said that if a Dallas Republican congressman's "IQ slips any lower we'll have to water him twice a day." Sometimes she char-broiled: the speech ultra-conservative presidential candidate Pat

Buchanan gave at the 1992 Republican Convention, Ivins wrote, "probably sounded better in the original German." As long as fifty years ago, she fought for reproductive rights, labeled unlicensed gun owners a blight, and named global warming a threat we denied at our peril. Threats to democracy, including the overwhelming influence of money in politics, was a topic she returned to again and again: "If what you have is a government of corporate special interests by corporate special interests for corporate special interests—which is indeed what we have—then you've lost the dream on which this country was founded," she said in a 1995 interview.

That she often wrote and spoke in a Texas accent with a Texas patois made Molly a particularly revered figure here at home (and she was always "Molly," just as her fellow icons in political sisterhood, Governor Ann Richards and state representative Sissy Farenthold, were always "Ann" and "Sissy"). Those who, today, get their information from one screen or another cannot possibly understand the power a print journalist could have back in the day. But from the beginning of her time as a writer and co-editor of the *Texas Observer* in the 1970s, Molly was an unapologetic voice in the wilderness who promised like-minded Texans that they were not alone in the belief that a more progressive, inclusive, and just plain saner state was possible. She had the ear of Governor Ann and the powerful lieutenant governor Bob Bullock, and, later, national figures like John McCain and, despite her knocks, President Clinton. And because she was funny, and because she often wrote and talked like someone who was born before most Texans lived in cities and had a modicum of education— Molly simultaneously embraced and exploited our stereotypes—even those who disagreed with her couldn't resist her. As she wrote of her *Observer*

heyday, some "egg suckin'" pol who "ran on all fours and had the brains of an adolescent pissant" would see her and "beam, spread his arms, and say, 'Baby! Yew put mah name in yore paper!'"

Of course, that wasn't who she was in real life. Ivins could play the Pineywoods redneck, but she began life as a true child of privilege. She grew up in tony River Oaks, where her father was a successful oil company executive; she graduated from St. John's, Houston's premier private school, and then from the elite Smith College in Massachusetts. Her father, James, was a domineering, hyper-conservative type, nicknamed by friends and family "the General." Molly, née Mary Tyler, rebelled against him seemingly from birth. Their political arguments—and other arguments, no doubt—inspired her gift for ridicule as well as her debating skills.

Once Molly left home, she found new targets, using her intellect and her imagination to vanquish bullies and dunderheads wherever she found them. The Texas Legislature, and Texas in general, had an abundant supply of both, of course. "All anyone needs to enjoy the state legislature is a strong stomach and a complete insensitivity to the needs of the people," she wrote. "As long as you don't think about what that peculiar body should be doing and what it actually is doing to the quality of life in Texas, then it's all marvelous fun." But the smartest way for a woman to take on the powerful in the 1970s—and maybe even today—was to invent a persona that wouldn't seem like a threat. (At first, anyway.) Ivins was, after all, a female in male-dominated Texas, a place that wasn't partial to women who were smart, who spoke their minds, and who didn't spend an inordinate amount of time prettying themselves up. (Even Farrah Fawcett, a Texas icon who was the antithesis of Molly, had to make her own set of concessions to the place.)

She went at the state's, and then the country's, biggest guns armed with nothing more than her wit, mocking and humiliating them until the populace here and beyond saw them for the fools and opportunists they were. As she explained: "Satire is traditionally the weapon of the powerless against the powerful. I only aim at the powerful. When satire is aimed at the powerless, it is not only cruel—it's vulgar."

Ivins's fearlessness, and the persona she created, got her the fame she craved: the syndicated column in four hundred newspapers, the cable TV appearances, the bestselling books. But there was a price, for all of it—the fans, the honors, the wealth she never embraced. "Fame is like a wave," she once told Bill Minutaglio, who cowrote the definitive Ivins biography in 2009. "You will drown in it if you are not careful," she added, talking about herself as much as the people she daily observed. "It will consume you. It will eat you alive." Molly drank to excess—it was a prerequisite for covering the Legislature—and even though she had her share of lovers (powerful, usually married men) and was surrounded by a coterie of hyper-protective friends, her loneliness was palpable to those who knew her even slightly, like myself. Her brilliance, her wit, her anger, and, eventually, her power were the same gifts that kept people at a distance. She wrote about the needs of ordinary folks and would go to her death defending ordinary folks, but from the beginning to the end of her life she could never have settled among them. In the parlance she understood so well, Molly always had bigger fish to fry.

Which is fine. In a Texas where abortion has been outlawed, where schoolchildren can be mowed down in classrooms by killers permitted to buy semiautomatic weapons, and where political divisions threaten to tear her beloved state to pieces—well, it's no wonder Ivins is missed by her public with a wrenching grief many years after her death. What would Molly do? She'd tell us to stop whining and weeping, put on our big-boy and big-girl pants, and figure this shit out—and that's the word she would use. As she once said, "Keep fighting for freedom and justice, beloveds, but don't forget to have fun doin' it. Be outrageous... rejoice in all the oddities that freedom can produce. And when you get through celebrating the sheer joy of a good fight, be sure to tell those who come after how much fun it was!"

No one made it more fun than she did. And probably never will again.

139

Richard Linklater

by **Jason Heid** Photograph by Dan Winters

Though he has refused to spend much time in Hollywood, much less live there, Richard Linklater has played the show-biz game very well. He has directed mainstream films such as *School of Rock* and *Bad News Bears*; made himself a darling to the art-house crowd with, most notably, his Before trilogy; and acted as a successful talent scout. (His 1993 film *Dazed and Confused* alone helped launch the careers of Matthew McConaughey, Milla Jovovich, and Parker Posey.) And he has done all of this while living full-time in his home state, where he has dedicated much of his energy to building the Texas film scene by founding or co-founding the Austin Film Society, the Austin Studios production facility, and the AFS Cinema, a movie theater he had dreamed of for thirty years before it finally opened in 2017.

Westerns dominate the Texas cinematic canon. Think *Red River, The Wild Bunch,* and *The Searchers*. Picture the Lone Star State on the silver screen, and the mind likely summons up images of hard men driving cattle over wide-open spaces, roughnecks transforming hardscrabble acreage into a fortune in black gold, or a sheriff's posse in pursuit of bank-robbing outlaws.

Yet Richard Linklater, the most quintessentially Texan director, has made only one western, and it was perhaps the worst-received movie of his career. His Texas-set films instead portray the sort of urban and suburban

environs in which he grew up, and where the vast majority of the state's residents live. Linklater was born in Houston, raised in Huntsville, and has spent decades living in Austin.

His breakthrough, 1990's *Slacker*, shone a spotlight on a new generation of Texans. These were the baby boomers' disaffected children, who came to be known as Generation X. Even more than thirty years later, the movie, set in and shot in Austin, continues to shape perceptions of the state capital as a place conducive to the lifestyles of layabout coffee shop philosophers and struggling artists, though that hardly describes the city today.

Hollywood came calling after *Slacker*'s unlikely success, and the production of his follow-up, *Dazed and Confused*, was a troublesome experience for Linklater as he dealt with outside interference for the first time. Other young directors might have caved to the demands of studio executives. But Linklater, demonstrating a certain Texas orneriness, stood his ground to make a comedy about teenagers in a Texas town where there's little to do beyond cruising the streets with their friends, drinking, and getting high. *Dazed* also gets at a deeper idea familiar to so many Texans: the desire to leave your hometown behind while simultaneously recognizing how that place has forever shaped you.

Few filmmakers have been as transparently autobiographical in their work, and *Dazed* drew much from Linklater's teenage years. His primary stand-in on-screen is Pink, the high school quarterback who is resisting pressure from his coaches to sign a pledge not to do drugs. Linklater was a jock who floated among social groups, getting on just fine with the stoners and the smart kids and bristling at the wishes of authority figures. He thought that period of his life "sucked," and he set out to make an "anti-nostalgia" movie in answer to what he felt were the false depictions of teenagers in so many popular films. (Though he ultimately stripped most of the melancholy from *Dazed*.)

Eighteen years later, Linklater returned to East Texas for the true-crime movie *Bernie*, based on a 1998 *Texas Monthly* feature story. In recounting the strange tale of the murderous mortician Bernie Tiede, Linklater deployed faux documentary-style interviews to capture a quirky portrait of tiny Carthage, Texas. Carthage's citizens, in the film's telling, embrace those who play their assigned roles and support its institutions, such as the church, the community theater, and the local western wear shop. Bernie's willingness to meet those expectations—and his victim's truculent refusal to do so—leads most folks in town to side with him, even though his suspected homosexuality would otherwise be grounds for derision.

Linklater has never demonstrated a desire to leave Texas; in fact, his insistence on staying here is perhaps the defining aspect of his career. But in these films his complicated feelings toward his native state are evident. As he shows, Texans often make a big show of professing how highly they value individual freedom—so long as that freedom is exercised within clearly demarcated boundaries.

Linklater's other Texas movies—his less-than-successful western *The Newton Boys*, *Slacker*'s spiritual sequel *Waking Life*, the college baseball comedy *Everybody Wants Some!!*, and the animated nostalgia trip

Apollo 10½: A Space Age Childhood—are suffused with the almost irrationally prideful and optimistic outlook that is a cornerstone of a typically Texan personality, not to mention the driver of so much of Linklater's success.

Whatever good growing up Texan did for him, Linklater has repaid it in more than full by helping turn the state into a major film scene. His success fueled the growth of the Austin Film Society, the nonprofit he founded in the mid-eighties that has dispersed millions of dollars in grants to hundreds of up-and-coming filmmakers, including Jeff Nichols, David Lowery, Andrew Bujalski, and Kat Candler. Linklater also spearheaded an effort to transform hangars at the city's shuttered Mueller Airport into a studio complex that has brought dozens of television and movie productions to Texas.

Not long after Austin Studios opened, Linklater embarked upon the most ambitious project of his career: *Boyhood*. While the film emphasizes the importance of seemingly small moments in our lives, its production was a monumental task: shooting piecemeal over the course of twelve years in order to integrate the natural aging of the actors into a depiction of a boy's childhood and adolescence.

In no film is Texas's influence on Linklater more visible. *Boyhood* shows us the protagonist Mason's childhood in Houston and then San Marcos and brings us to his first steps toward adulthood—heading west like some cowboy riding into the sunset, down a long road to Sul Ross State University in Alpine. One scene in particular gets at something profound about Texas. After Mason's father remarries, he takes Mason for a visit to the home of his stepmother's parents. It also happens to be Mason's birthday, and the step-grandparents celebrate with a cake and presents. They give him a shotgun and a Bible.

It's a stereotype—albeit rooted in plenty of fact— that Texans are a gun-loving, God-fearing bunch.

This older couple fits the profile, presenting the weapon to Mason as an heirloom, and in the next scene sitting with rapt attention during Sunday service at their church. Were they to talk politics, they'd likely have little in common with Mason's father (who earlier in the movie distributed Obama-Biden signs). Nevertheless, they welcome him and his children as part of their family, a form of hospitality that will be familiar to many liberal, urban Texans who find themselves warmly treated when they vacation in the more conservative corners of the state.

Such subtle celebrations of community are present in many of Linklater's films. Perhaps that's because he owes his career to the like-minded cinephiles he gathered around himself when he started the Austin Film Society. It was their help that enabled him to make *Slacker*.

Perhaps because he's one of us, Linklater has, from the start, portrayed us as we are, rather than who our state's mythos tell us we've always been. Not for him the romance or bleakness of the neo-western— let Quentin Tarantino or the Coen Brothers play that game. If we're trying to determine which filmmaker's body of work best represents Texas, let's look to the director who, throughout his career, has demonstrated qualities often considered unmistakably Texan: a recalcitrant commitment to independence, an enterprising spirit, and an ambition to pioneer new frontiers.

143

George W. Bush

by Robert Draper Photograph by Platon

Like many prominent Texans, George W. Bush wasn't a native, but he got here as soon as he could. Born in 1946 in tweedy New Haven, Connecticut, Bush spent the bulk of his childhood in Midland, where his father, the future president, moved the family in 1948 to launch his professional career. Early on, George W. seemed to chafe against the expectations that accompanied birth into a politically connected East Coast family. (His grandfather was U.S. senator Prescott Bush of Connecticut.) He trod the academic path expected of someone of his birthright, from the elite Phillips Academy to Yale, but he graduated with lackluster grades and a reputation as a hell-raiser. Though he earned a master's degree from Harvard Business School, his business career was largely undistinguished. So when he decided to run for the governorship of Texas, it was easy to believe that he was a blue-blood lightweight who rose by "failing upward." Even so, in 1994 he stunned the Texas political establishment by unseating the incumbent, Ann Richards, and went on to serve one and a half terms that were notable for their bipartisan comity. In 2000 he moved to the White House, where, as president, he served two much more contentious terms that will likely be best remembered for his launch of the second, calamitous war in Iraq. After leaving the White House, Bush took up painting and settled in Dallas, not far from the George W. Bush Presidential Library and Museum at Southern Methodist University.

It was on a late morning in 1996, in *Texas Monthly*'s conference room, when I experienced the rather pungent persona of George W. Bush for the first time. Editor in chief Gregory Curtis had arranged for an hour-long discussion between Bush—then a first-term governor—and the magazine's editorial staff. Less than two years into his administration, the son of President George H. W. Bush was already regarded as a rising star and likely presidential candidate.

Bush sprawled in a seat at the head of the table, flanked by his advisers Karen Hughes and Karl Rove. Assured by Curtis that our conversation would be off the record, he waved the privilege off, saying with a smirk, "Nothing's off the record." The topics we raised ranged from the state lottery to environmental zoning restrictions. Bush fielded them with a competitor's Is-that-the-best-you've-got? alacrity.

The meeting's understood purpose was to preview the governor's upcoming second legislative session, following his wildly successful first one, in which Bush managed to pass reforms in education, welfare, torts, and juvenile justice. At the top of his to-do list was a sweeping overhaul of the state taxation system that was ambitious in the extreme. Allies had warned Bush that his proposal, which would reduce onerous property taxes by increasing the business tax, was laudable in principle but sure to fail and could throw his political ascendancy off course. He didn't care. "I've got political capital, and I intend to spend it," he informed us that morning, his eyes as narrow as his voice was defiant. I came away believing that George W. Bush radiated enough self-confidence to melt down a Geiger counter.

A question that day had gone unasked, by me and by everyone else in the *Texas Monthly* conference room. *Why* was Bush hell-bent on such a massive—and, as predicted, such a doomed—legislative initiative? Was it really about Texas and taxes? Or was it ultimately about human psychology—the burdens of birthright felt by the eldest son and namesake of a famous father, forever compelled to swing for home runs even when just getting on base would have sufficed?

What seemed audacious back in 1996 foreshadowed a native compulsion that now appears to be an anchor weighing down the legacy of George W. Bush's presidency (though his governorship remains relatively well regarded, to the extent that anyone thinks about it at all). His abhorrence of what he termed "small ball" repeatedly led him into reckless policy pursuits. In 2003, President Bush pushed successfully for a new prescription drug entitlement, known as Medicare D, that ballooned the federal deficit without demonstrably improving the overall health of its elderly beneficiaries. Freshly reelected in 2004, he pressed to partially privatize Social Security—once again crowing about spending his political capital, and once again failing spectacularly.

Most infamously, in the wake of the attacks on September 11, 2001, Bush saw what he characterized as an "opportunity"—by which he meant a chance "to not only defend freedom but to make the world more peaceful." This willful optimism led him to invade a country that had played no role in 9/11 and posed no threat

to the United States. The decision to go to war in Iraq in order to democratize the Middle East now counts as one of the greatest foreign policy blunders in American history.

Well after that first meeting, I was fortunate to spend a significant amount of time with Bush: first, for a *GQ* profile during his 1998 gubernatorial campaign, as he openly contemplated whether to run for president; and, later, for a book I was writing, in 2006 and 2007, when, as Bush freely admitted to me, "I am *consumed* by this war." Though he loved to promote the one-dimensional portrait of himself as a going-by-the-gut cowboy executive, I found him to be a much more complex figure than he readily let on. Bush could be intellectually aggressive at

times, incurious at others. He devoured books (an affinity he shared with his librarian wife), though he often seemed to read into them what he wished. Bush was a great boss, never one to bully his subordinates, though his frat-boy jocularity took on an edge when dealing with Democrats and the media. (Nearly every interview I had with him in the Oval Office began with him making sport of my necktie or scuffed shoes.) He prided himself on doing what he thought was right, irrespective of what polls dictated—though on campaign matters he routinely deferred to the judgment of Rove, who devoured polling data and occasionally persuaded Bush to put principle aside for the sake of electoral gain. (Bush's support for a constitutional amendment banning same-sex marriage comes to mind.)

Up to a certain point, Bush could be a marvel of self-discipline. Throughout his presidency, he faithfully received daily intelligence briefings. He abided by diplomatic norms. He respected the decorum of the office. He was punctual literally to a fault. (Bush tended to race through his schedule; I always knew to show up to our scheduled interviews a half hour early.) Even his defining error, the decision to invade Iraq, was made over an eighteen-month period and was mindful of pro forma considerations like consulting the UN and allowing weapons inspectors to do a few short months of work in Iraq before his patience finally ran out.

What undid Bush's presidency was his failure to appreciate the seemingly "small-ball" stuff. To the new president, Al Qaeda fit in that category. During the summer of 2001, Bush expressed exasperation with the subject of supposed terrorist plots, telling his national security adviser Condoleezza Rice that he was "tired of swatting flies." He cut short a CIA briefing on the subject with a dismissive "You've covered your ass." A few months later, on the afternoon of 9/11, a bewildered Bush found himself asking the same briefer, "Who did this to us?"

It's a painful irony that Bush, the first Harvard MBA president, rode into Washington with his highly experienced senior staff determined to put on a clinic of efficiency. By the end of 2006, the gross mismanagement of post-Saddam Iraq, combined with the slow-footed response to Hurricane Katrina, conveyed instead an image of incompetence. The culprit was Bush himself: his disin-

terest in details, his belief in vision over execution, and his aversion to dissenting viewpoints. Inside the impermeable White House bubble, the president saw himself as the "decider," firmly on top of everything that mattered. In reality, having an accountable secretary of defense, rather than Donald Rumsfeld, would have mattered. Determining whether Iraq really possessed weapons of mass destruction would have mattered. Seeing to it that hurricane responders actually *were* doing a "heck of a job," rather than simply saying so, would have mattered.

Of course, even a two-term governor of a large state whose father had previously served as president and vice president will face a steep learning curve upon entering the Oval Office. Bush got better at the job over time. By the middle of his second term, he was better staffed, less reliant on Vice President Dick Cheney, and more clear-eyed about what he could and could not accomplish. Though his decision to surge troops into Iraq in 2007 was unsurprising, given his unwillingness to concede defeat, what did surprise was his assiduous follow-through when it came to supporting Iraq's fragile new democracy. Likewise, when the financial markets melted down in 2008, he acted swiftly to ensure passage of the Emergency Economic Stabilization Act and thereby prevent a depression.

How, then, will the dust settle? The answer depends very much on whom you ask. At this moment, the Trumpified wing of the Republican Party denounces Bush with as much vigor as the left once did. Meanwhile, establishment Republicans and many Democrats wistfully cite the forty-third president as a GOP leader who believed in democratic institutions and the rule of law. One thing hasn't changed in recent years, however: the dark cloud of Iraq still looms over Bush's legacy, with a majority of Americans viewing the war as a mistake that has made the U.S. less safe.

When I think of George W. Bush, I find much to admire. He never blamed anyone for decisions that were his own. He never held himself up as superior. In one-on-one conversations, he always seemed uncontrived and present. Though he disdained what he called "navel-gazing," he dared to reveal himself—to talk about the many times he cried while in office and to acknowledge the loneliness of the job. It's not for me to rank his presidency. If pressed to do so, I would feel confident in saying that there have been those who were decent souls

and many others who were not, and Bush fits squarely among the former group.

Recently, I found myself thinking about a story I'd heard years ago about then-governor Bush. It was told to me by Logan Walters, who had served as Bush's personal aide during his final year as governor and the fateful first year of his presidency. One morning in New Hampshire in late 1999, Walters walked into the presidential candidate's hotel room to tell him that the day's campaigning was about to begin. He found Bush there on his bed, quietly studying his Bible.

Walters wasn't exactly surprised when he saw this. Nor was I when he later recounted it to me. It was hardly a secret that Bush was a man of Christian faith. Still, the poignancy of that tableau resonates with me. It serves to remind that there was more to the man than met the eye. Bush never made a show of this morning ritual. He didn't boast of his piety on the campaign trail. Though he wasn't above mocking his political opponents, he never demonized them. He knew the difference between belief and performance art. He was who he said he was. I believe this counts for something.

The Best of the 1990s

Books

Films and TV Shows

1 *Slacker*
(1990)

2 *El Mariachi*
(1992)

3 *The Positively True Adventures of the Alleged Texas Cheerleader-Murdering Mom*
(1993)

4 *Walker, Texas Ranger*
(1993–2001)

5 *Bottle Rocket*
(1996)

6 *Lone Star*
(1996)

7 *Selena*
(1997)

8 *The Apostle*
(1997)

9 *King of the Hill*
(1997–2009)

10 *Office Space*
(1999)

Sports

1 McKinney golfer Thomas Oliver Kite Jr. wins the U.S. Open in 1992.

2 Led by Troy Aikman, Michael Irvin, and Emmitt Smith, the Dallas Cowboys win the Super Bowl in 1993 and then again in 1994 and 1996.

3 Coach Rudy Tomjanovich takes over the Houston Rockets in 1992 and he and star center Hakeem Olajuwon lead the team to its first and second championships in 1994 and 1995.

4 Corpus Christi–born NASCAR driver Terry Labonte wins his second premier series championship in 1996, twelve years after his first championship.

5 Track star and Dallas native Michael Johnson sets an Olympic record in the 400 at the 1996 Olympic Games.

6 The WNBA's Houston Comets, led by Brownsville native Sheryl Swoopes (who had earlier steered Texas Tech's Lady Raiders to a women's basketball national championship in 1993), win the league's first four championships between 1997 and 2000.

7 Texas rodeo star Ty Murray earns a record-breaking seventh All-Around World Championship title in 1998.

8 Legendary track coach Beverly Kearney leads the UT Austin Lady Longhorns to four consecutive NCAA championships between 1998 and 2001.

9 Austin cyclist Lance Armstrong wins his first of seven consecutive Tours de France in 1999.

10 The Dallas Stars win the 1999 Stanley Cup.

Music

1 **Pantera,**
Cowboys from Hell
(1990)

2 **Texas Tornados,**
Texas Tornados
(1990)

3 **Geto Boys,**
"Mind Playin' Tricks on Me"
(1991)

4 **Alejandro Escovedo,**
Gravity
(1992)

5 **Selena,**
"Bidi Bidi Bom Bom"
(1994)

6 **UGK,**
Ridin' Dirty
(1996)

7 **Emilio,**
"Por Siempre Unidos"
(1996)

8 **Erykah Badu,**
Baduizm
(1997)

9 **Dixie Chicks,**
Wide Open Spaces
(1998)

10 **Asleep at the Wheel,**
Ride with Bob: A Tribute to Bob Wills and the Texas Playboys
(1999)

2000

TM

the 2000s

By the time George W. Bush was elected president in 2000—the third Texan to make it to the White House in four decades—it was clear that Texas culture had become a dominant force in America. Beyoncé was on her way to becoming *Beyoncé*; Richard Linklater and Robert Rodriguez were making unprecedented inroads into global cinema; Austin-based Whole Foods was altering the foodscape across the country; the Dixie Chicks would soon become, for a moment, the most talked-about musical act in the nation, and the television series *Friday Night Lights* would, not long after, bring a simulacra of small-town Texas life to millions of viewers. Unfortunately, Texas's influence wasn't all good. The disgraced Houston-based energy company Enron's fanciful accounting and vaporous business model seemed to offer a blueprint for the nation's financial firms, which sparked a global financial crisis in 2008. Yet, despite Enron's collapse, Texas could claim to be the fastest-growing state in the country: fracking reinvigorated the energy sector, and workers from all over the world flocked to the major cities, drawn by cheap rents, good restaurants, and jobs of every sort. Many of these new Texans didn't look much like the people who had dominated the state from the start. Following an unstoppable demographic trajectory, Texas no longer had a non-Hispanic white majority.

Beyoncé

by Brianna Holt Photograph by Wyatt McSpadden

In 2004, relatively early in her career, Beyoncé Knowles appeared on the cover of *Texas Monthly*, done up in a Willie Nelson–style headband and braids and wearing a Willie T-shirt. It was a nifty visual joke—a young Texas musician paying tribute to the state's most beloved musical eminence. But it also ended up being a bit of premonition: not long after, Beyoncé became the biggest star Texas had seen since Willie—arguably, bigger than Willie, since she has spent much of the twenty-first century as the biggest star in the world. A product of Houston's prestigious High School for Performing and Visual Arts, Beyoncé first grabbed the public's attention as the leader of Destiny's Child, then embarked on a solo career that cemented her status as a global icon. All things considered, it's kind of surprising that Willie's never been seen sporting a Beyoncé T-shirt.

For decades, when people in the rest of the country thought of Texas, they often thought of white culture: cowboys and country singers and conservative politicians. (Never mind that plenty of Texas cowboys and country singers and a few conservative politicians weren't white at all.) In the mind of America, Texas was stuck in the past, a place unto itself.

If that attitude has budged in recent years, much of the credit should go to Beyoncé. Over the course of her career, the Houston-born-and-raised star has made her Texan-ness a

major part of her image. Though she now spends most of her time in a $90 million Bel-Air mansion, Beyoncé is, as she sings in her 2014 song "Flawless (Remix)," "Texas forever, like Bun B."

Most of the time, though, Beyoncé has a specific part of Texas in mind: her native Houston. In her 2013 song "Pretty Hurts" she imagines herself as "Ms. Third Ward," after the largely Black Houston neighborhood where she was raised. In "Bow-Down," from the same year, she shouts out "H-Town" institutions like the Geto Boys rapper Willie D and the Frenchy's chain of chicken joints. In the music video for "No Angel" (again, from 2013, a year when Houston was apparently much on her mind), she gives fans a non-tourist's Houston tour that includes the public housing complex Cuney Homes, a shiny red slab car, and a busy strip club, and even wears a cowboy hat as she posts in front of a shotgun-style house, the traditional home found in historic Black Houston. Throw in her occasional donning of a Houston Rockets jersey, her 2004 and 2007 appearances at the Houston Livestock Show and Rodeo, her Houston coronavirus testing initiative, and her disaster relief assistance fund for Texans hit hard by the 2021 blackout, and her hometown loyalty is clear.

In 2003, it would have been difficult to imagine Beyoncé's ascent to Queen Bey status. She was, at the time, the frontwoman of the phenomenally popular vocal group Destiny's Child, and though she had ambitions for a solo career, there was reason to be skeptical. Give or take a Harry Styles or a Diana Ross, it's the rare member of a vocal group who makes a go of it on their own. Beyoncé's bandmates, Kelly Rowland and Michelle Williams, had released their solo debuts in 2002, and though each had done well, neither of them came close to Destiny's Child's

level of success. *Dangerously in Love*, by contrast, touched the stratosphere: eleven million copies sold, five Grammys, two #1 singles, two more top-ten singles, and an attention-getting video for "Crazy in Love." Destiny's Child, it was immediately clear, was destined for orphanhood.

In the two decades since, Beyoncé, the highest-paid Black artist in history, has carved out a career with no precedent in popular culture. Other than a middling acting career that largely petered out, she has succeeded at almost everything she has tried her hand at. She made her mark not only as a musician but as a fashion trendsetter, art patron, social justice advocate, feminist, video auteur, and—along with the rapper Jay-Z—half of popular music's First Couple.

Even more remarkably, she has never wavered from her perch. If we regard Destiny's Child's eponymous 1998 debut album as the beginning of Beyoncé's ascent, then she has, as of this writing, been working for twenty-five years. Few popular music acts make it to the quarter-century mark, and of those who do, almost all are reduced to nostalgia mongering or desperate lunges at trend following. (Think of the Rolling Stones from 1989 onward, or Madonna since 2008.) Yet Beyoncé's 2022 album, *Renaissance*, debuted at the top of the *Billboard* charts (making her the first artist in history whose first seven albums did so) and was treated, aptly, as a tour de force. More than two decades into her professional recording career, every Beyoncé move—every album, every single, every tour, every domestic dustup, every daring wardrobe choice—is regarded as a major event by millions. She is not only still making vital music, she still sets the terms of global pop culture.

And yet, despite it all, she has never wavered in her allegiance to her hometown.

But Beyoncé has done more than act as a prestigious flack for the city of her birth. By emphasizing Houston's Black culture, she has implicitly asserted that the city—which is located an hour or so west of the Louisiana border—is a *southern* city that has as much in common with Black meccas like Atlanta and New Orleans as it does with Dallas or San Antonio. (In fact, one might argue that, thanks in part to Beyoncé, Houston is making a bid to displace Atlanta as the capital of the Black South.) And having made that connection, she's doing more than anyone alive to insert aspects of Black southern culture into the pop mainstream.

When Beyoncé headlined Coachella in 2018, she gave a two-hour performance that drew heavily on the traditions of historically Black colleges and universities (HBCUs), a staple of Black southern life. Her routine featured an all-Black marching band and majorette dancers, a step show, and a stroll. Costumes embroidered with Greek letters brought to mind the Divine Nine, the sororities and fraternities created in the early twentieth century for Black students who were barred from membership in predominantly white national Greek organizations. A poignant performance of "Lift Every Voice and Sing" stirred the largest online audience the festival has ever seen. The song, aka the Black national anthem, is commonly played at HBCU football games, including at the Houston area's two HBCUs, Texas Southern University and Texas A&M Prairie View. This wasn't the first time HBCUs have shown up in mainstream culture: the

sitcom *A Different World* and Spike Lee's *School Daze* brought them to mainstream attention in the 1980s. (Notably, after *A Different World*'s debut season was widely panned, another Houston-born performer, the dancer and actress Debbie Allen, was brought in as producer to salvage it.) But Beyoncé, as happens with everything she touches, took everything to the next level. Her performance was widely viewed as historic, and that year's Coachella was quickly nicknamed "Beychella."

Beyoncé isn't the only member of her family who has been making the case for Houston. Her sister Solange's 2019 album, *When I Get Home*, is chock-full of references to their shared hometown. But there's no doubt that Beyoncé is the prime mover. It's possible that no one since the arts patrons John and Dominique de Menil turned Houston into a major arts capital has done more to boost its reputation as a global metropolis—and, yes, a Black southern city.

157

Rick Perry

by **Paul Burka** Photograph by Jeff Wilson

A fifth-generation Texan, Rick Perry was born in 1950 in the small North Texas town of Haskell to a family of cotton farmers. After graduating from Texas A&M University he served for five years in the U.S. Air Force before returning home to farm cotton. In 1985 he was elected as a Democrat to the Texas House of Representatives; he then switched to the Republican Party just as the GOP's fortunes were rising in Texas. Statewide success followed quickly. He was elected agriculture commissioner in 1991 and then lieutenant governor in 1998, becoming the first Republican lieutenant governor in Texas since Reconstruction. When George W. Bush resigned from the governorship to become president in 2000, Perry assumed the office, which he won in his own right two years later and then again in 2006 and 2010, making him the longest-serving governor in Texas history. During his tenure, Perry advocated for socially conservative legislation and boosted Texas's economy. Hoping to follow in his predecessor's footsteps, he ran for the presidency in 2012 and 2016 but came up short both times. In 2017, he became Donald Trump's secretary of energy and served in that position for two years. After leaving public office, he launched a lucrative career as a lobbyist and a member of corporate boards.

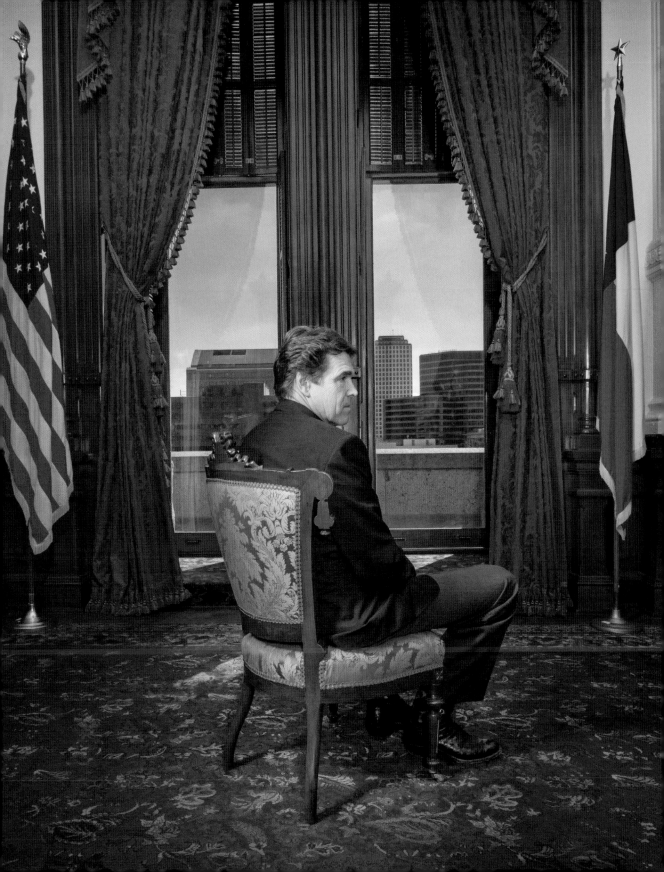

In 2008, I interviewed Rick Perry over lunch at a small Mexican restaurant in East Austin. We dined on typical Tex-Mex fare, and Perry was in high spirits as he recounted his latest triumph: persuading Caterpillar to move one of its main manufacturing facilities to the Central Texas town of Seguin. Perry has always been animated when I've talked with him, and that afternoon was no different. But I'll never forget when he leaned forward, looked me straight in the eye, and gave me a conspiratorial wink. "Do you know how many governors would have liked to have made that announcement?" Perry asked with a grin. He paused for effect. "All of 'em!"

His confidence was understandable. The Texas economy had performed astonishingly well during Perry's tenure. In fact, his success was unequaled among Texas governors.

So was his power. When Perry left office in 2015, he had served nearly twice as long as any other governor in Texas history. I never could have guessed that would happen when I first met him, in the mid-1980s. At that time, he was a backbench Democratic representative who would go on to make his reputation on the Appropriations Committee by asking tough questions about government spending. Given the trajectory of state politics in those years, he had two choices as a conservative Democrat: drop out or switch parties. So he went from a D to an R, and in 1990 he challenged the incumbent agriculture commissioner, Jim Hightower. Rove scraped up enough money to run strong television spots that attacked Hightower—including one that associated him with flag burning—but he also used them to introduce the Texas A&M graduate from Paint Creek to the rest of the state. Perry proved to be a natural on television, and he upset Hightower.

Perry won reelection in 1994, prevailed in a

squeaker against Democrat John Sharp for lieutenant governor in 1998, and became governor in December 2000 when George W. Bush moved into the White House. Politics is about timing and luck, and Perry was blessed with both. Few politicians have had his instinct for being in the right place at the right time. Had he not run a disastrous national campaign in 2012—he will likely never live down his infamous "Oops" moment—there's a good chance he would have made it to the White House.

Texans are used to being represented by heavyweights and stars, but Perry never really qualified as either category; he certainly didn't run in the same company as his predecessors John Connally, Ann Richards, and George W. Bush. Yet Perry accomplished something that none of them did: he completely changed how state government works. Under previous governors, the bureaucracy functioned through boards and commissions made up of citizens who were appointed by the governor—or were holdovers from a predecessor's administration—and operated somewhat independently. For decades, the boards and commissions were the ultimate decision-makers in the executive branch.

Under Rick Perry, however, there was only one decision-maker, and it was Rick Perry. Because of the sheer length of his administration, Perry was able to install political allies in every state agency, effectively establishing a cabinet form of government and making him vastly more powerful than any of his predecessors—and more powerful than the Legislature, which had traditionally held most of the cards. In this regard, the Texas politician he most resembled was LBJ, who, Robert Caro reports, once told an assistant, "I do understand power, whatever else may be said about me. I know where to look for it and how to use it." That's Rick Perry, to a tee. It's ironic, given Perry's professed belief in limited government, that he greatly expanded the power of the governor's office beyond what the authors of the state's constitution intended.

Of the governors I have covered while they were in office, going all the way back to Preston Smith in the early 1970s, I believe that Perry's predecessor, George W. Bush, was the best. He was well liked by members of both parties and presented a clear vision for what state government should do. When I reflect on that era, what stands out is that the government worked—not perfectly by any means, but effectively.

The goodwill and bipartisanship that characterized the Bush governorship evaporated almost instantly after Perry assumed the reins. When I interviewed him during the early days of his administration, it was clear that Texas politics was going to function very differently. "The day George Bush left, the muzzles were taken off," Perry told me. With the Democratic Party reduced to a shell of its former self, Texas in the Perry era quickly became a one-party state, and it has been so ever since.

Despite his long occupation of the governor's office, Perry had few tangible accomplishments to show for his time as chief executive, other than that booming economy. Did public schools improve during his tenure? No—the funding crisis wasn't resolved, and Perry offered no bold vision to solve the challenges and complexities of the modern classroom. Was health care a Perry priority? No—150,000 kids were removed from the Children's Health Insurance Program after the budget crunch of 2003,

and we blithely turned our backs on federal dollars for Medicaid expansion in 2013. Transportation? No—highways remained critically underfunded during his tenure. Did the political conversation grow more civil under Perry? Certainly not—never before had the state been more polarized, never had power been concentrated in the hands of so few, and never had the tone been so hostile. (And it would only get worse in the ensuing years.) By the time Perry left office, the state had turned so far right that Bush wouldn't have been able to survive a primary in his own hometown.

Rick Perry could have been the state's greatest governor. He came to power at the ideal time: he was the unchallenged leader of a newly dominant party, his state was the envy of the business world, and an unprecedented oil boom was piling up huge state surpluses. All those riches could have been put to use improving state services, or raising teachers' salaries, or providing coverage to the uninsured, or recruiting top faculty to the state's universities, but Perry remained unmoved by the possibilities. For years, long-festering needs went ignored. It was the waste of a birthright. Years from now, people will look back on his tenure and ask, "What did Rick Perry do as governor that made Texas a better place for all Texans?" The answer, I regret to say, is "Very little."

161

Robert Rodriguez

Robert Rodriguez, who was born in San Antonio in 1968, had one of the quickest routes to Hollywood success imaginable. For the absurdly low cost of $7,000, he filmed his debut feature, *El Mariachi*, sold it to a major studio, and watched it gross more than $2 million—a nearly 30,000 percent return on investment. From there, Rodriguez basically called the shots on his career, making the movies he wanted to make and keeping his base in Austin, where he has nurtured and inspired a vital Texas filmmaking scene. In all, Rodriguez movies such as *Desperado, From Dusk till Dawn*, the *Spy Kids* franchise, *Sin City, Machete*, and *Alita: Battle Angel* have grossed more than $1.5 billion globally.

When **Robert Rodriguez** was a teenager, he built a film-editing console in his room from two VCRs he'd filched from his dad, a cast-off stereo system, an old TV, and a tape deck and splicer for adding music. He used it to edit short films he made with his nine siblings, as well as school projects and mash-ups of scenes taken from his favorite movies. One day, he took some scenes from a Mickey Rourke movie and cut them together with some scenes from a Rutger Hauer film. The Rourke movie was in black-and-white, so he drained the color out of the Hauer clips by dialing the color down on the TV. Years later, after he had become one of the country's most prolific filmmakers, Rodriguez cast Rourke in *Sin City*, a moody,

mostly black-and-white adaptation of a noir comic book series. At one point Rodriguez needed to shoot a scene in which Rourke's character kills a bad guy, but he hadn't yet cast the bad guy. He decided to go ahead without him, figuring he'd put all the pieces together in post-production. Eight months later, he finally found someone to play the villain: Rutger Hauer.

"It wasn't until I was done that I realized I'd done this before," he said years later, a note of awe in his voice. "There's a lot of weird events like that over the years. I feel like maybe I'm doing the thing I'm supposed to be doing." And what Rodriguez is supposed to be doing, apparently, is making films that have a direct connection to his youthful enthusiasms. It's hard to think of a major film director, other than Tim Burton, whose work seems to spring so clearly from their childhood obsessions. It's one reason why Rodriguez, perhaps, has never garnered the sort of critical praise that his fellow Austinite Richard Linklater draws. Yet it's also one reason he has tapped, over and over again, into a mass audience's desires. Who doesn't want to relive the open-eyed buzz of our wonder years?

It didn't hurt that Rodriguez had an unusually joyful childhood. He was raised in San Antonio, in a stately two-story, five-bedroom stone house in the historic neighborhood of Monte Vista. His father, Cecilio, was a cookware salesman who grew up on the border, in Rio Grande City; Cecilio went to college at St. Mary's University on a jazz drumming scholarship. His mother, Rebecca, was born in El Paso, lived in an orphanage for a short time, and was adopted at a young age. She planned on becoming a nun and entered a religious order, but the nuns sent her off to finish her nursing degree, and in the end she met her husband and had ten kids instead.

Rodriguez is the third child. When he was born, his parents had already produced a jock and a brain, so they encouraged his artistic pursuits, which came naturally. Life at home revolved around the arts: Cecilio kept a drum set in the house, and Rebecca took guitar lessons when the kids were young. "She would have us sing like the Von Trapps," Rodriguez said. "Spanish songs, for anybody that came by the house, even the mailman." State senator Leticia Van de Putte, a family friend, recalled that Rebecca encouraged her kids to draw, write, play music, and dance. "I got the trick of using butcher paper from her," she told me. "She would get butcher paper cheap at a restaurant supply store and put it on the wall so they could paint. Then she'd change it out the next week." Marcel, the sixth kid, remembered that, long before Rodriguez got interested in filmmaking, he was drawing, taking photos, sculpting with clay, and even trying his hand at animation. "By the time I came around," he said, "home was an art school."

Rebecca, a movie buff, liked to take her kids to the Olmos Theatre, a local revival house, where they would sit through multiple viewings of classic double features. She also had a taste for the macabre. "My mom is very Catholic," said Marcel. "And if you want to hear some good horror stories about people being dismembered and ripped apart and nailed to a cross, just read the Bible." Rodriguez maintained a collection of meticulously labeled horror and exploitation bootleg videos, which he kept in a locked cabinet in his room. Between the double features, the Bible stories told with a nurse's tolerance for gore, and the curated home video collection, the kids developed a shared sensibility.

Cecilio's work ethic and self-reliance had a major influence on Rodriguez as well. "He'd come home, and my mother would say, 'We need three more sets of braces for the kids,'" Rodriguez recalled. "And he'd calculate how much extra cookware he'd need to sell, and then he'd go back out and sell it." Much later, after Rodriguez had started his own film studio, he took a tip from his father. He never set out to find other movies to shoot on his stages. Instead, he generated his own work. "It's like my dad selling cookware—'Oh, we're not going to make rent this

month? Well, let me just go write another script, and we'll make another movie to cover us for the rest of the year!'"

One day, when Rodriguez was twelve, Cecilio brought home a JVC video player/recorder. The camera had no viewfinder, so he had to hook it up to the TV with a twelve-foot cable and watch the screen while shooting. Rodriguez's earliest forays into filmmaking involved dragging the whole contraption as far as the back door and then directing his younger siblings in dozens of action and kung fu movies out in the yard. Van de Putte's kids were occasionally recruited as well. "The kids stayed out of trouble, because they were doing what Robert told them to do," she remembered.

In 1981 the film *Escape from New York* was released. Around that time Rodriguez read an article about the film's creator, John Carpenter, who wrote, directed, shot, and edited all his own movies. For *Escape*, a dystopian sci-fi action movie, he had simply declared that New York City was a giant maximum-security prison, which struck Rodriguez as the ultimate creative freedom. So he told his mother that he and his brother wanted to see *The Cannonball Run*, and after she dropped them off, they snuck in to see *Escape from New York*. The deception ate away at him for a few days. ("I was a really good kid," he says.) When he finally came clean, his mother took him and his brother back to the theater to see it again.

165

After that, Rodriguez began to focus on film-making. He attended St. Anthony's Seminary, a Catholic school across the street from his house, where his teachers gave him permission to hand in "term movies" instead of term papers. "All his movies were slasher films or shoot-'em-ups," one high school friend recalled. "For one religion class, he had a terminator-priest-robot–type character, and it made perfect sense."

In 1990, Rodriguez entered film school at UT and shot his first real movie, *Bedhead*, which was based on his experience growing up—with some obvious artistic license. He cast his little sister Rebecca as a kid who develops telekinetic powers after her older brother accidentally knocks her down and she hits her head. The film, which won awards at several small festivals, contains many of the themes that would recur throughout Rodriguez's work: the lawlessness of childhood and the transcendent powers of imagination. (At one point, Rebecca's character fantasizes about becoming "the first Mexican American female president of the United States!")

From there it was a remarkably quick route to success in Hollywood (and at bucking Hollywood). In 1993, Columbia Pictures released his made-on-the-cheap debut feature, *El Mariachi*, a Spanish-language neo-western filmed just on the other side of the Mexican border. Then came the follow-up, *Desperado*, the breakout film for Salma Hayek; the wildly popular *Spy Kids* franchise; a failed attempt at a Hispanic television network, El Rey; a host of other films and TV shows; and a handful of innovations in the fields of digital and 3-D technologies. Along the way, he created his own production studio in Austin so he could keep control of his work and out of the hands of Hollywood suits. Whether or not he meant to, he ended up proving that Texans could make slick, big-budget, technically transformative films without ever leaving the state.

The set of a Robert Rodriguez movie often feels like the warm, antic home he grew up in. One day in 2013, he was at his Austin studio filming an episode of his *From Dusk till Dawn* series that was written by his brother Marcel, who was there to supervise. The atmosphere felt genial and relaxed: Rodriguez played his guitar between takes, and somebody passed around a tray of burgers from a nearby In-N-Out Burger.

Rodriguez does what he can to foster that feeling of hominess. Stacked against a wall of the studio was a cache of paintings—portraits of actors who have appeared in Rodriguez's films: Hayek, Rosario Dawson, Bruce Willis, Joseph Gordon-Levitt. Rodriguez, apparently, paints the portraits, then invites the actors to embellish their own images during downtime when they're shooting. The idea is to make them feel as if they're just kids playing in the backyard; Rodriguez is a firm believer in the snowballing effects of uninterrupted creative flow. "You paint for a while, and you come back to the set, and any problem you had before you can solve immediately, because you've already been solving creative problems on a whole other level," he explained. "Everybody's in that mode, because they're being creative all the time, not just when we go, 'Now, action! Be creative!'"

His own working methods reflect this approach. "I work out of my house a lot,"

Rodriguez said. "That's really the secret to it." When his kids were smaller, he'd have breakfast with them, they'd go to school, and he'd go to sleep. Then he'd pick them up at three and they'd play or go swimming or draw. "I'd cook them dinner, goof off, put them to bed at eight o'clock, and then I'd work from eight until eight. That's twelve hours of uninterrupted work. You can't even find distractions—everything is closed. I'd be editing, and then I'd be done editing and have three hours to go, so I might as well score that scene I just edited. I'd be done so fast. I'd be putting out two or three movies a year, sometimes. And the kids never saw you work. You were like an elf. It was the best schedule. You never came home late because you'd work while they were asleep and sleep while they were at school."

Art, home, and a kind of anarchic freedom are thoroughly intertwined for Rodriguez, and he seems to experience any system that would sort them into separate categories as unnatural. Since the beginning of his career, he has grounded his work in his formative experiences in one way or another. He seems to have emerged from childhood with his artistic vision fully formed—which is probably why his work evinces both a childlike purity and the maturity level of a twelve-year-old boy.

Controlling the means of production has been crucial to this because it has allowed him to replicate the frictionless creative conditions he grew up in. He writes movies with his brothers, his sisters are involved in editing them, his cousins have worked on his sets, his nieces have been cast in his films, and his ex-wife, Elizabeth Avellán, produced many of his films, even after their divorce. How else to interpret it all but as an effort to extend his childhood, only with more freedom and bigger toys?

"Movies take so long," Rodriguez said. "And the process wears you down. A lot of what I've been doing is creating a method where it isn't such an effort to get films or shows out." It's almost a child's idea of how movies are made, with a direct line from the creative urge to the creative act to the finished product, which is profoundly different than the typical process that results in a Hollywood movie. "It's the process that sucks the life out of them," Rodriguez said. "The politics and the methodology of it just sucks. That's why people find it very refreshing to come down here. They go, 'This is what I've always wanted to do! I don't want all the other stuff. I just want to do this!'"

167

George Mitchell

by Loren Steffy

George Mitchell is best known for spearheading the fracking revolution that transformed Texas's—and the world's—energy industry. He's perhaps second-best known for creating Houston's Woodlands, a master-planned community that featured wildlife habitats and protected green space well before such considerations were mainstream. From the perspective of environmentalists, those seem like two diametrically posed accomplishments—on the one hand exploiting the earth and keeping the fossil fuel industry chugging along, and on the other striving to find a balance between the needs of people and the needs of nature. But over the course of his long life Mitchell seemed to be at peace with what his son Todd called the "Mitchell Paradox." A native of Galveston who was born to Greek immigrant parents in 1919, Mitchell graduated as valedictorian from Texas A&M in 1940 with a degree in petroleum engineering and soon founded an independent oil outfit, Mitchell Energy & Development, that became a Fortune 500 company. Mitchell was once estimated to be worth about $1.6 billion, and he spent many of his later years giving hundreds of millions of dollars to charitable causes, with a focus on scientific and environmental endeavors. Mitchell died in 2013, at the age of ninety-three.

In early September 2013, President Barack Obama pushed Congress to authorize air strikes against Syria, roiling the international community and igniting a firestorm on Capitol Hill. In the past, the mere hint that a U.S. president was considering military action in the largest oil-producing region in the world would have been enough to drive traders into a frenzy and send prices soaring. This time, the only measurable effect was a three-day blip in which prices jumped by about $2 a barrel, then quickly settled back.

This ho-hum stability could be chalked up to the fact that domestic energy production had reached fantastically high levels. In 2005 the United States was importing almost 65 percent of its oil. By 2013, that had slipped to about 40 percent. After forty years of reckoning with increasing scarcity, the country was suddenly basking in abundance; in 2018 we surpassed Saudi Arabia as the world's biggest oil producer.

It was a stunning reversal, and virtually all of it could be attributed to George Mitchell, a pioneering Houston oilman who died six weeks before those air strikes demonstrated to the world the importance of his life's work. Under Mitchell's leadership, geologists developed the process for using hydraulic fracturing, or fracking, to unlock previously unreachable reservoirs of oil and natural gas. The oil business is indisputably prone to hyperbole, but there's no denying that fracking has transformed our energy outlook. In Texas, it unleashed a boom unlike anything that had been seen for more than a generation, and it hit Americans in the one place everyone cares about: the pocketbook. According to one study, real disposable income rose by $1,200 in 2012, not because wages increased but because utility bills and the prices of consumer goods decreased, thanks to plentiful and inexpensive energy. Fracking changed global petro-politics as well. Saudi Arabia, the world's oil cop for four decades, began watching U.S. shale production as intently as U.S. analysts once monitored production in the kingdom's oil-rich Eastern Province.

The laboratory for Mitchell's innovation was 350,000 acres in North Texas's Wise County covering a geologic formation known as the Barnett Shale. Natural gas had been found in Wise County in the 1940s; the following decade, a college buddy of Mitchell's introduced him to the shale gas play. Mitchell formed a company with the unimaginative name of Oil Drilling, Inc., and began raising money to lease 3,000 acres in the southwest part of the county. Oil Drilling had success with the first well it drilled, and Mitchell and his partners expanded their holdings. They soon realized they had tapped a sizable reservoir that would require extensive drilling to fully exploit, but various financial pressures convinced Mitchell that he needed to come up with ways to more thoroughly exploit the gas beneath his feet. He knew the Barnett held lots of it, and he was determined to find a drilling technique that could release it.

Mitchell is often dubbed "the father of fracking," but it's not an entirely accurate label. Fracking—in which water, sand, and chemicals are injected under high pressure into shale rock to cause fissures that release natural gas or oil—was first used in 1947 in southwestern Kansas. But it was inefficient and cost-prohibitive, and it relied on dangerous techniques. (At the time, sand was mixed with napalm rather than water.)

Mitchell's company had used hydraulic fracturing in 1979, doubling the production of a conventional gas well in Limestone County, and in 1981 Mitchell decided to try it again, though he felt sure he could improve the technique. At the time, geologists knew that shale was a source for oil and natural gas, but the prevailing theory was that such deposits could be extracted only through natural fractures. Most of those occurred close to the surface. Mitchell decided to try fracturing the rock artificially at greater depths. The early attempts at fracking were all made in vertical wells, and while Mitchell found that production increased significantly, he still thought he could do better. During the next seventeen years, the company's wells would become a fracking test bed, an exercise in trial and error. Mitchell tried fracking at different depths, with different amounts of pressure, in different reservoirs, constantly tweaking the blend of the fracking fluid. By the time Mitchell and his geologists perfected the process, they had unlocked a mammoth play. Even though production began to decline in the 2020s, the Barnett Shale has produced more than thirteen trillion cubic feet of gas, and may hold as much as forty-four trillion.

Mitchell and his band of fiercely loyal employees were obstinate in their pursuit of fracking. And whether this was due to diligence or stubbornness, it reinforced the truism that most advances in the energy industry have come from the independent producers, not the majors, who flooded into shale plays only after the success of Mitchell and others. Today, there are significant fracking operations in West Texas's Permian Basin and South Texas's Eagle Ford Shale, as well as much of the rest of the country.

Other companies took Mitchell's innovation and adapted it to oil, and the boom that followed led to a rash of problems, as Mitchell warned it would. He knew all too well how oil companies reacted to booms. Before he unlocked the Barnett, drilling tended to occur in remote parts of the state; fracking brought it literally into people's backyards. Companies often drilled with little regard for communities, and wastewater disposal—an ugly byproduct—led to an increase in earthquakes.

The fracking boom began to hit the skids in 2019 as investors tired of watching companies blow through cash to boost production without generating much in the way of returns. Banks stopped lending, and private equity firms became enamored with renewables. There was another mini-boom when Vladimir Putin's invasion of Ukraine sent gasoline prices soaring, but the long-term prospects for fracking seem grim.

Mitchell had no illusions that his innovation would save the world. Yet fracking unlocked natural gas reserves that significantly reduced carbon emissions as more electricity was produced with gas than with coal. In the process, the United States, thanks largely to Texas, experienced a level of energy independence unseen in at least five decades. And in helping make that happen, Mitchell offered us a path to a cleaner future.

171

John Mackey

by Tom Foster Photograph by Wesley Mann

To turn Whole Foods Market into the category killer among health food stores, the chain's founder, John Mackey, redefined the sector as one that appealed not to unshowered tofu lovers but to upscale shoppers interested in gourmet foods that did minimal damage to their bodies and their planet. The result was expansive, well-appointed stores where jars of organic wheat germ shared shelf space with grass-fed beef and artisanal baguettes. It proved to be a potent formula, and once Mackey took the company public, Whole Foods became an existential threat to independent health food stores and small chains across the country. Survival seemingly meant becoming more like Whole Foods Market—or being acquired by it. Mackey became a star of the business world and the bestselling coauthor of such high-minded books as *Conscious Capitalism: Liberating the Heroic Spirit of Business* and *Conscious Leadership: Elevating Humanity Through Business*. Eventually, though, the company stumbled, and Amazon—the mother of all category killers—acquired it in 2017. Mackey retired as CEO in 2022, after more than four decades at the helm of one of Texas's most iconic businesses.

The **first time** someone accused John Mackey of selling out his ideals, the founder of Whole Foods was twenty-seven years old, had been in business for two years, and employed a grand total of nineteen people. It was 1980, and the first Whole Foods Mar-

Memorial neighborhood eating the typical mid-century American diet of TV dinners, hamburgers, and mac and cheese. He didn't care a lick for health food until after college, when he moved into a vegetarian commune in Austin called Prana and became the resident food buyer, then took a job with a local health food store called the Good Food Company. He'd attended the University of Texas at Austin, as well as Trinity University in San Antonio, shuttling back and forth between the two over the course of six years, taking classes in religion and philosophy and whatever interested him (certainly not business) without getting a degree.

One night, after he'd worked at Good Food for about six months, he approached his girlfriend about opening their own store. "It'd be so much fun," he told her. They raised $45,000 from friends and family and opened a store called SaferWay in 1978 in an old Victorian. When they got kicked out of their apartment for using it as a stockroom, they moved in above the store and showered in a back room using a hose from the dishwasher.

Mackey's studies and his life in the commune had led him to a predictably progressive worldview. But as he worked to build his store, he developed a new set of beliefs. He'd been reading free-market economists such as Milton Friedman, and after two years of running SaferWay, he realized that building a successful health food store might require some ideological

ket, just a few blocks from today's corporate headquarters in downtown Austin, was only a quarter the size of a typical modern Whole Foods. Nobody had thought yet to call the place Whole Paycheck. And Amazon, the company's eventual owner, didn't exist.

Not even Mackey understood quite how transformational his creation would be—that it would fundamentally reshape the American diet and usher in a shiny new identity for Texas's capital city—but everyone could tell from that first day that he was onto something.

Mackey had grown up in Houston's well-to-do

compromises. "We didn't sell sugar," he later said. "We didn't sell meat. We didn't sell alcohol. And we didn't do any business either."

He persuaded the owners of a competing store, Clarksville Natural Grocery, to merge with him and open a 10,500-square-foot natural-food emporium on Tenth Street called Whole Foods Market. The store was two or three times the size of a typical natural-food store of that era, and it blurred the lines around what such a store could sell. Whole Foods sold meat, alcohol, and sugar; it wasn't just a place to buy bulk grains but an actual full-service grocery. Within six months it was the highest-volume natural-food store in America.

Among the co-op crowd, however, Mackey looked like a craven capitalist, even though he still felt like an idealist. As he saw it, he had just added a dose of pragmatism to his vision. If people were going to buy meat and beer anyway, at least try to sell them the good stuff. More sales meant he could drive more business to producers who were doing sustainable, quality work. It was a philosophy that over the ensuing four decades took him from minding that single store to overseeing a publicly traded company with billions in annual sales.

It was also a philosophy whose contradictions would haunt Mackey over the years as Whole Foods grew its assortment into an ever more dizzying array of healthy and gourmet and not-quite-either products that made it harder to define what the company stood for. Wine bars, pizza ovens, and barbecue stations joined the mountains of sustainably caught salmon and probiotic supplements.

And as Mackey's company started buying up other natural grocers around the country, the gap between his personal mission and that of his company became more and more pronounced. He went through a series of diet awakenings, becoming ever more ascetic in his food choices to the point that he gave up not only animal products but all oils. Whole Foods, on the other hand, was becoming a gourmet specialty food store as much as a healthy one.

And the people, boy, did they come along. While the mainstream grocery world was busy chasing Walmart in a race for the lowest prices, Mackey wowed Americans with bounty and freshness. It worked so well that, before the Whole Foods founder and CEO quite understood what was happening, the rest of the industry—Walmart included—started chasing *him*. By the 2010s, customers who wanted to buy organic produce or heirloom tomatoes could do so at their local supermarket. The regular grocery, in time, became *good enough* on quality—and usually better on price than Whole Foods.

In 2016, Kroger, the nation's largest mainstream supermarket chain, passed Whole Foods in annual sales of natural and organic products. Trader Joe's and Sprouts Farmers Market were attacking on another front with nimbler, cheaper, foodie-focused stores. And Amazon and other online services were nosing into the grocery business. After decades of challenging the American food establishment, Whole Foods had become part of the establishment and faced challenges on all sides. Its stock price, once the envy of retailers everywhere, fell into a prolonged slump, the company's value by market cap dropping to half what it had been just a couple of years earlier.

Which is how, in 2017, Mackey found himself under siege when a New York hedge fund snatched up almost 9 percent of Whole Foods' stock and announced that it would pressure the company to either overhaul its business or sell itself—perhaps to another grocery giant, such as Kroger, or to a less traditional player, such as Amazon. To Mackey, the moment spelled peril for what he saw as his life's most important work: using the free market to herd the masses toward healthier food—positive change at maximum scale, even if it came with a few compromises.

"These people, they just want to sell Whole Foods Market and make hundreds of millions of dollars, and they have to know that I'm going to resist that," Mackey told *Texas Monthly* that spring.

The way Mackey saw it, Whole Foods' fight for survival was a "morality play between conscious capitalism and greedy, short-term financial capitalism." *Conscious capitalism* is his term for a way of thinking about business as having a higher purpose than creating value for its shareholders.

"Entrepreneurs are the true heroes in a free-enterprise economy, driving progress in business, society, and the world," Mackey wrote in 2013. "They solve problems by creatively envisioning different ways the world could and should be." On the other hand, in his view, many business leaders had become greedy, and none more so than the hedge funders who were pursuing him, whom he described, memorably, as "greedy bastards."

He tried to resist. But the fate of Whole Foods was sealed before Mackey could respond. Conscious capitalism works just fine when shareholders are getting their due. When they don't, Mackey found, your company is forced to respond to the same sort of short-term pressures that other, lesser, greedier entities fall prey to. In the end, Amazon swooped in and bought Mackey's creation. On one hand, this was the sort of scenario the hedge funders were pushing on him. On the other, this outcome at least offered him a way to try to save face by touting a future of continued innovation. But the focus inevitably moved to cost cutting and automation; by 2022 the company was rolling out shelf-sensor inventory monitors, motion-tracking shopper cams, and cashierless checkout kiosks that require nothing more than the wave of a hand. Whole Foods had become the proving ground for the future of buying stuff.

The parallels with Whole Foods' hometown are more than a tidy coincidence. Just as Mackey's early version of the company blended economic conservatism with crunchy co-op vibes, Austin had once been the home of the hippie cowboy. And just as the growth imperative eventually turned Whole Foods into something shiny and unrecognizable, a tech and real estate boom turned Austin from a scrappy slacker idyll into a gleaming boomtown.

Change at scale had arrived, and John Mackey had helped set the table for it. It just wasn't exactly the change he'd envisioned.

Sandra Cisneros

by Sierra Juarez Photograph by Nick Simonite

Few people who moved to Texas as adults have had as profound an effect on the state's literature as Sandra Cisneros. The Chicago native, who spent much of her youth moving back and forth to Mexico, relocated to San Antonio in 1984, when she was twenty-nine years old, the same year she published her first novel, the celebrated bestseller *The House on Mango Street*. Cisneros, who may be the country's most prominent Mexican American author, quickly became a force in her adopted home state. As the founder of the Macondo Foundation and the Alfredo Cisneros del Moral Foundation, she fostered the careers of countless Latino writers and encouraged many more by way of example. In 2013 she left Texas and settled in San Miguel de Allende, Mexico, though she returns to San Antonio often.

Pleasantries like *yes, ma'am* and *no, sir* fall as effortlessly from my tongue as my first and last names. My family drilled manners into me at a young age, and no one was more influential than my grandmother Herminia, whom we called Nana. She doted on her seven children and thirty-nine grandchildren and great-grandchildren, cooked and cleaned, and tended to her husband's every need. For most of my childhood, I considered her the gold standard of womanhood—amenable, loving, and kind. The schools I attended, the TV shows I watched, and the books I read did nothing to challenge that notion.

My understanding of womanhood unraveled soon after I left my Houston suburb and arrived in Austin to attend the University of Texas. Suddenly, I was surrounded by all types of women, some of whom weren't interested in family life. Many of my female mentors had dedicated their lives to their careers. In class, women who were my age spoke their minds openly in rooms filled with hundreds of students, which seemed amazingly courageous to me. They were hell-raisers; after Donald Trump was elected president, many of them marched to the Capitol while holding signs featuring puns about their uteri. I was awed by their brashness, but I didn't join them. I was still too reserved to attend a public protest, especially one that was so brazen.

I didn't seem to fit into either of my perceived categories of womanhood. I knew I wasn't going to be a woman in the same way Nana was. I planned to get my degree and pursue a career in journalism, and I wasn't sure that I wanted children. But I also knew that I was different from many of my classmates.

As I wrestled with my ambivalence, I found myself returning again and again to the writings of Sandra Cisneros, especially her 1991 short story collection, *Woman Hollering Creek and Other Stories*. The narrators of many of the stories are Mexican and Mexican American girls and women living on both sides of the border in tradition-minded communities who are struggling to understand their lives. Reading the book for the first time as an undergraduate, I felt as if I were scanning old diaries filled with my most private thoughts. "Do boys think, and girls daydream? Do only girls have to come out and greet the relatives and smile and be nice and *quedar bien*?" Cisneros wrote, mirroring questions I asked myself when I was younger.

Some of the characters abide by conventional notions of womanhood. Cisneros gives them names like Soledad (Loneliness) and Dolores (Sorrow) and suggests their suffering is a result of their absolute devotion to their men. "They were too busy remembering the men who had left through either choice or circumstance and would never come back," Cisneros wrote.

There are other types of women in the stories too, the sort who drive pickups, holler in public spaces, and advocate for other women. "Real women. The ones I've loved all my life," Cisneros wrote. "The ones I've known everywhere except on TV, in books and magazines. *Las* girlfriends. *Las comadres*. Our mamas and *tías*. Passionate *and* powerful, tender and volatile, brave. And, above all, fierce." Some of them shun the idea of married life and motherhood. On the book's author's page Cisneros declared that she was "nobody's mother and nobody's wife."

But for me the most valuable stories and characters made it clear that most women fall somewhere in between these two categories. In one story, "Little Miracles, Kept Promises," Cisneros gathers together a collection of letters written to Catholic saints. In one, a woman confides that for most of her life she detested the Virgin of Guadalupe. Every time she looked at the veiled woman's clasped hands and downcast eyes, she was reminded of "all the pain my mother and her mother and all our mothers' mothers have put up with in the name of God." Yet, after learning about the Virgin's Indigenous roots, she begins to understand the figure's resilience and the strength of the women in her own life. "Because those who suffer have a special power, don't they?" writes Cisneros. "The power of understanding someone else's pain. And understanding is the beginning of healing."

In "*Bien* Pretty"—the book's final story—Cisneros explores how complicated and difficult it can be for independent women to live up to their own convictions. The story's protagonist, Lupe, reeling from a romantic failure, leaves her home in California to start a new life as an art director at a community cultural center in San Antonio. Texas's reputation as a place that's hostile to Latinos scares "the hell out of" her, but, Lupe, who grew up attending grape-boycott demonstrations, is strong. In Texas she throws herself into her work, laboring sixty hours a week. She's exhausted and homesick but she's "kicking *nalga.*"

All that changes, though, when she begins dating a man named Flavio, who hails from Michoacán. At first, Flavio seems enamored: the two of them spend romantic evenings dancing the tango and cozy mornings eating chilaquiles and breakfast tacos. But he gradually begins to topple her self-esteem with a stream of critical comments: he implies that she's not Mexican enough and refers to women as *viejas.* "I wanted to leap across the table, throw the Oaxacan black pottery pieces across the room, swing from the punched tin chandelier, fire a pistol at his Reeboks, and force him to dance," Lupe insists, sounding very much like one of Cisneros's tough-minded heroines. But, undone by a mixture of loneliness and infatuation, she's not tough anymore. "Instead of the volley of insults I intended, all I managed to sling was a single clay pebble that dissolved on impact—*perro.*"

When Lupe discovers that Flavio is married to a woman back in Mexico, has a child with another woman, and intends to return to the country, she's devastated. She drowns herself in telenovelas, skips work meetings, and orders takeout daily. Her sense of who she is has grown twisted. "When I look in the mirror, I'm ugly," she says. "How come I never noticed before?" A proud and brave woman has become a ghost of herself.

Eventually, Lupe hits bottom and starts climbing back up. She grows angry and sets fire to Flavio's letters and poems. She disparages the sobbing women characters she had related to in the telenovelas. The old Lupe has reemerged, though now boasting scar tissue. "We're going to right the world and live. I mean live our lives the way lives were meant to be lived," she says. "With rage and desire, and joy and grief, and love till it hurts, maybe. But goddamn, girl. Live."

At the end of "*Bien* Pretty," though, I wasn't fully convinced that Lupe has completely recovered. There's a hopeful moment where she has "no thought of the future or past," but that's not a frame of mind that anyone can sustain for long. You sense that another tumultuous romance could spell disaster for Lupe, but that solitude isn't really an option for her, either. Being tough, driving a pickup, and hollering in public places aren't guarantees of happiness. Even independent women will falter, fail, and be forced to build themselves back up again. It's an endless struggle, trying to be everything all at once. In many of her stories, Sandra Cisneros reminds us that the fight is worth fighting. But she never makes us the false promise that we'll prevail.

179

The Best of the 2000s

Books

Films and TV Shows

1. *All the Pretty Horses*
   (2000)

2. *Reba*
   (2001–2007)

3. *The Good Girl*
   (2002)

4. *The Three Burials of Melquiades Estrada*
   (2005)

5. *Glory Road*
   (2006)

6. *Friday Night Lights*
   (2006–2011)

7. *Grindhouse*
   (2007)

8. *No Country for Old Men*
   (2007)

9. *Charlie Wilson's War*
   (2007)

10. *Crazy Heart*
    (2009)

Sports

1. Texas A&M football coach R. C. Slocum, the winningest coach in the team's history, leaves in 2002, after fourteen years and a record of 123-47-2.

2. Austin native Andy Roddick wins the U.S. Open in 2003.

3. Following a 1999 championship, Gregg Popovich's San Antonio Spurs dominate throughout the 2000s, winning titles in 2003, 2005, 2007, and 2014.

4. The Duncanville High School girls basketball team wins five state championships in 2003, 2012, 2013, 2016, and 2017.

5. UT Austin softball pitcher Catherine "Cat" Osterman joins the USA Women's Softball Team, which wins an Olympic gold medal in 2004. She and the team also win the silver in 2008 and 2020.

6. Robert Hughes, the nation's all-time winningest high school basketball coach, retires in 2005, after compiling a 1,333-247 record at two different Fort Worth high schools.

7. After Coach Kim Mulkey takes over the Lady Bears basketball program at Baylor University in 2000, the team wins its first of three NCAA championships in 2005, 2012, and 2019.

8. Vince Young scores a last-minute winning touchdown for the UT Austin Longhorns in the 2006 Rose Bowl.

9. The Houston Dynamo soccer team wins the MLS Cup in 2006 and 2007.

10. After twenty-five seasons without a bowl game, the SMU Mustangs win the Hawaii Bowl in 2009.

Music

1. **Destiny's Child,** *Survivor* (2001)

2. **Ramon Ayala y Sus Bravos del Norte, En Vivo…** *El Hombre y su Musica* (2001)

3. **Pat Green,** *Three Days* (2001)

4. **Norah Jones,** *Come Away with Me* (2002)

5. **Scarface,** *The Fix* (2002)

6. **Jason Moran,** *The Bandwagon* (2003)

7. **Mike Jones, Paul Wall, and Slim Thug,** "Still Tippin'" (2004)

8. **Spoon,** *Gimme Fiction* (2005)

9. **Z-Ro,** "Mo City Don" (2005)

10. **Miranda Lambert,** *Kerosene* (2005)

TM

2010

Texas Population, 2010:	Rank of Austin in Population Among American Cities, 2010:	Percent of Texans Who Lived in the Six Major Metropolitan Areas as of 2010:	Texas Gross State Product, 2010:	Energy Created by Wind and Solar Combined, 2010:	Democrat/ Republican Split in Texas House, 2010:	Cumulative Number of Albums Willie Nelson Had Recorded in His Career as of 2010:
25.1 million	14th	71	$1.2 trillion	26,259,618 Megawatt-Hours	49 D, 101 R	122

the 2010s

If there was a limit to how quickly Texas could grow and how much more interesting it could get, it still hadn't been reached by the second decade of the twenty-first century, when the state was widely recognized as a site of culinary excellence, technological innovation, and artistic ferment. In New York and Los Angeles, *Texas chic* no longer only meant cowboy hats and hand-tooled boots; it meant an SXSW T-shirt and a weekend stay in Marfa. But greater cultural sophistication didn't mean our increasingly radical politics got any more responsive to the problems facing the state. The Legislature and governors Rick Perry and Greg Abbott did little to address Texas's economic inequality and desperate need for better health care, instead happily feeding red meat to GOP primary voters. A series of devastating wildfires in the summer of 2011 and the historic flooding caused by Hurricane Harvey in 2017 revealed that the state was ill prepared to deal with a changing climate, despite all those enormous windmills sprouting up across the state. Still, people kept coming. By the end of the decade, Houston was poised to become the third largest city in the country, and once-sleepy Austin the tenth. Texas, once a national punch line, was now the most American place in America—partly because we'd allowed the country to change us, and partly because we insisted on changing the country.

Aaron Franklin

by Daniel Vaughn Photographs by Wyatt McSpadden

Aaron Franklin was born in 1977 in Bryan–College Station, where his parents ran a barbecue stand—and the acorn didn't fall far from the live oak tree. Franklin is, without a doubt, the most influential pitmaster in the history of Texas barbecue, and likely the world. The Austin restaurant he opened with his wife, Stacy, as a food truck in 2009 and then as brick-and-mortar institution in 2011 launched a revolution in Texas barbecue that was still reverberating more than a decade later. Franklin Barbecue was called the best barbecue joint in the country by *Bon Appétit* magazine in 2011 and named the best barbecue spot in Texas in 2013 by *Texas Monthly*. That success was followed by a bestselling cookbook, a television show, a chain of barbecue fusion spinoff restaurants, a food and music festival, a spot in the Barbecue Hall of Fame, and the honor of becoming the first-ever pitmaster to win a James Beard Award.

There have been three dramatic shifts in the history of Texas barbecue. The first came in 1878 when a butcher in Bastrop, possibly a man named Peter Gill, advertised his "stock of ready barbecued meats and cooked sausages." Before then barbecue had been en- joyed largely at community gatherings; this marked the first record of barbecue for sale. The second shift came sometime in the late 1960s when beef processors began separating beef carcasses into individual cuts. Instead of ordering beef by the half or quarter, barbecue

joints and meat markets could procure a box full of briskets. Pitmasters had smoked this cut before, along with the beef ribs, shoulder clod, and chuck, but now they could pick and choose. The brisket was cheap thanks to its toughness, and its high fat content kept it moist during the long hours of smoking that were required to make it tender. It soon became the de facto menu item of Texas barbecue. The third date was much more recent: December 2, 2009. That's when Aaron and Stacy Franklin opened their Franklin Barbecue trailer in Austin.

The location didn't look like a plausible spot for a culinary revolution: a raggedy gravel lot in the shadow of I-35's upper deck, just north and east of downtown. And Aaron didn't look much like your typical pitmaster. Back then, most pitmasters spent decades honing their craft. It's a business that's traditionally been the realm of old-timers, who exhibit the signs of accumulated barbecue mileage: leathery faces, calloused hands, and a smoker's cough. But Aaron Franklin, a sometime punk rock drummer, was in his late twenties, sported grease-stained Vans, cutoff Dickies, horn-rimmed glasses, and a smile that rarely faded. Not your archetypal pitmaster at all—which is maybe why he was the perfect person to upend a cuisine that was badly in need of an energy boost.

As far as the rest of the country was concerned, Texas barbecue back then was a sideshow. "Real" southern barbecue, as food writers and barbecue fans defined it, was cooked in Tennessee, Missouri, Alabama, Georgia, and the Carolinas, and focused squarely on the porcine end of things. They served pork ribs, pork steaks, chopped pork, pulled pork, and whole hog. Much of it was good, even very good, perhaps because making pork tasty doesn't require as much effort as brisket does.

Texas barbecue was the outsider. Our devotion to brisket was playfully mocked by those in the deep South who didn't think smoked beef was barbecue. Yet *within* Texas, we were pretty damn proud of what we had. *Texas Monthly* ran its first barbecue cover story in 1973 and launched its top fifty barbecue list in 1997, which was followed by more lists in 2003 and 2008—all before Franklin opened his trailer. A handful of Central Texas places were already legends in Texas—Cooper's Old Time Pit Bar-B-Que in Llano, Louie Mueller Barbecue in Taylor, and City Market in Luling among them. Sampling the wares of the storied barbecue joints in Lockhart, the "Barbecue Capital of Texas"—Kreuz Market, Black's Barbecue, and Chisholm Trail BBQ (and, later, Smitty's Market)—was a rite of passage for a generation of Texas smoked-meat connoisseurs.

But if you wanted to eat some reliably great brisket anywhere else, you'd have to search for a joint and hope you caught it on a great day. There was an awful lot of sliced brisket being served that today would be relegated to the pile for chopped beef.

One of the places you could go, and feel confident you wouldn't be let down, was John Muellers B-B-Q, which was opened by one of Louie Mueller's grandsons in East Austin in 2001. That's where Aaron Franklin got his first job in barbecue, though he didn't learn much about smoking technique there. He worked the register, sliced onions and, eventually, got to slice brisket. He was, instead, something of an autodidact. Soon after he hired on with

A serving of brisket, ribs, sausage, and pulled pork at Franklin Barbecue.

Mueller, he started smoking meat in his backyard and invited friends to sample his ever-improving efforts. One particularly ambitious evening, he served five briskets to dozens of attendees, free of charge. A friend had the smart idea to collect tips from the crowd and delivered the proceeds to Franklin at the end of the night. It was the first time people had paid for his barbecue, and it felt like a turning point. He opened his truck a few years later.

Franklin Barbecue changed what aficionados thought was possible with a smoked brisket. What's the secret? It starts with all-natural, prime grade beef. Before Franklin came along, most pitmasters tried to find the cheapest briskets they could. Paying a premium for high-quality meat wasn't a consideration, and the idea of spending even more for hormone-free and antibiotic-free beef was pretty much unthinkable. Franklin, by contrast, insisted on finding the best beef he could and then sprinkling it with kosher salt, 16-mesh black pepper, and a seasoning blend that's now bottled under the Franklin Barbecue label. The brisket would then spend hours in a steel smoker built by Franklin and get wrapped in butcher paper until buttery tender. When a brisket hits the counter at Franklin, it ripples like a mini-meatquake. The fatty side of the brisket is, essentially, a beef aspic suspended in cow Jell-O, and the lean side, which will dry out in the hands of amateurs, is surprisingly juicy. Barbecue fans who are accustomed to ordering "moist" know that at Franklin every part of the brisket is worth savoring.

The first time I tried it, in January 2010, I was sitting in an otherwise empty lot in front of Franklin's trailer with a couple of friends. After the first bites, we knew we were tasting something special; we shared knowing nods with full mouths. My second stop was a month later. I got a half pound of brisket to go and drove off. My left hand on the wheel, I opened the butcher paper package on my passenger seat with my right hand as I drove up I-35. The slices were stout enough to keep their integrity when I lifted them but tender enough to disintegrate in my mouth. A rush of melted fat coated my tongue as the rendered fat cap collapsed and was balanced flawlessly with the flavors of vanilla-scented oak smoke, black pepper, salt, and beef. Eddie Money's "Think I'm in Love" was playing on the radio, and the song had never before rung so true for me.

I was hardly alone. Word got around Austin within a week of Franklin's opening and the lines at the truck grew long. (It was located across the highway from *Texas Monthly*'s offices at the time, so staffers were among his earliest customers and converts.) But the lines became insane in 2011, soon after the brick-and-mortar restaurant opened and *Bon Appétit* claimed that Franklin smoked "the best BBQ in the country." Soon after, customers

with folding chairs began lining up outside the front door before sunrise for their own form of tailgating, which can last longer than a UT football game and can be as much fun. The hundreds who gather each day, no matter how far they traveled to be there, bond over their anticipation for barbecue that's still hours away. It's a new Texas tradition.

Unsurprisingly, Franklin's style of barbecue was quickly copied all over the state. No longer did Texans need to drive to Lockhart for top-flight barbecue; you could find Franklin disciples in every major city, and plenty of other locales as well. Suddenly, towns like Pearland and Wolfforth—and even the desert environs of Marfa, far from a steady supply of live oak—were barbecue destinations. Customers who had previously been unbothered if their favorite joint was having an off day were now demanding consistency.

That made life a lot more fun for Texas carnivores, but it also reordered the national barbecue scene. Central Texas–style barbecue joints were opening up across the country. By 2013, it was easier to find great Texas barbecue in Brooklyn than it would have been to find it in Austin or Dallas circa 2008. After Franklin's instructions were laid down in his 2015 bestseller, *Franklin Barbecue: A Meat-Smoking Manifesto*, the rest of the world followed suit. By 2017 you could find credible—sometimes more than credible—Texas-style barbecue joints in places as far-flung as Brussels, Paris, and Melbourne. By the time Franklin won a

James Beard Award in 2015, few people were mocking Texas barbecue anymore.

For Aaron, this has all led to a life he couldn't have possibly imagined for himself when he was first getting his hands and arms and face dirty refurbishing a neglected smoker he had bought for $1,000. He's mentioned in virtually every story about Texas barbecue, sells his own Franklin-brand smokers for more than $5,000 a pop, and these days acts more like a chef than a pitmaster; he doesn't really feed the fireboxes with post oak anymore. It's good to be the king of Texas barbecue.

But there's an irony to his success as well. Franklin has inspired so many people that there are now a host of joints doing traditional Texas-style barbecue as well as he does. And some of them, trying to distinguish themselves from all the competition, have begun innovating, creating fusion barbecue that draws on Asian and Latin American influences (as Aaron has also done, at the fancy sit-down Asian smokehouse Loro that he created with Tyson Cole, the chef behind the renowned sushi restaurants Uchi and Uchiko). The energy had started to shift.

In 2013, *Texas Monthly* named Franklin Barbecue the best barbecue joint in Texas. Four years later, in a close call, it came in second, behind Lexington's beloved Snow's BBQ (which had come in first in 2008). But in 2021, Franklin dropped to seventh place—not because its game had faltered, but because the competition had gotten that much fiercer. Places like Fort Worth, Houston, Dallas, and Seguin were full of young men and, happily, women blissfully free of leathered faces, calloused hands, and smoker's cough who had digested Franklin's lessons and applied his techniques and standards to Laotian-style sausage, hefeweizen-marinated turkey breast, and, yes, whole hog. More than a decade after he made his mark, Aaron Franklin's revolution had already sparked yet another barbecue revolution.

189

Annise Parker

by Mimi Swartz

Is there a more misunderstood city than Houston? If it were located anywhere but in Texas, Houston would almost certainly have a reputation as a first-class metropolis. It has the museums, the parks, the restaurants, the music scene, the booming business sector, and the sort of racial and ethnic diversity that mark a great city. And as of 2009 it had, in Annise Parker, what no other major American city—not New York, not Los Angeles, not San Francisco—had ever had: an openly gay mayor. How did that happen? By way of Parker's canny sense of what Houston voters were ready for, and an almost preternatural ability to seem like a bland, reassuring presence, even as she was making history. By the time she left office in 2016—after serving three terms—her hometown was a little less misunderstood.

Annise Parker has always been an unlikely role model: she is shy and remote, far more comfortable with calculations and spreadsheets than meeting and greeting the public. Before she became mayor of Houston in 2010, she could best be described as a typical Rice grad. She was very book smart, and also kind of a nerd. She might have managed to stay that way, moving up the corporate ladder at Houston's Mosbacher Energy as a wonky oil and gas deal analyst until her retirement benefits kicked in. But then she pivoted to public service, winning three city council races between 1997 and 2001 and then getting elected city controller

in 2003. When, six years later, she became the first openly gay mayor of a major American city, it was, to say the least, a big deal around the world.

As the *Houston Chronicle* reported at the time, "Media ranging from the *New York Times* to the *Tulsa World*, from *The Guardian* in London to *The Age* in Melbourne, Australia, spotlighted Parker's sexual orientation." Nighttime talk show hosts couldn't get over it, either: "You [are] the first openly gay mayor of a major city in America. How is that possible?" Stephen Colbert asked when Parker was a guest on his show. "Texas! Six shooters! Conservatives! George Bush! Rick Perry! How is Houston electing a gay mayor?" He quickly added, "No offense."

If Parker was offended, she didn't show it, though she couldn't hide a glimmer of Rice-like condescension toward Colbert when he drew on the same tired stereotypes that Texans have heard forever from the mouths of Yankees. "As mayor of a Texas city, do you walk around the streets in a ten-gallon hat with, like, your thumbs in your pockets with six-shooters, spitting tobacco?" he asked her, as if Houston were some run-down one-horse town rather than a vibrant global metropolis.

Yet, though there were, at the time, at least twenty other Texas elected officials who were openly gay, Parker's election was the Big One. "The voters of Houston have opened the door to history," the mayor-to-be said on election night. "I know what this win means to many of us who never thought we could achieve high office. But let us at this moment join as one community. We are united in making Houston the city it should be, could be, can be and will be." Though she was a successful mayor by most measures, Parker probably accomplished as much in that moment as she did over the course of her six years in office.

A look at Parker's early life would not have led anyone to predict her political success. Growing up mainly in the middle-class Spring Branch area of Houston, she was so introverted, her family nicknamed her "the turtle." But Parker was also ambitious and understood that if she didn't overcome her near paralyzing reserve—she even drafted scripts for potential encounters—she would never accomplish much. Soon enough, Parker realized she had additional work to do: "I could see that if I could not get more comfortable with who I was in terms of my sexual orientation and if the world was not going to be more comfortable with me, then I could not do what I wanted to do in life," she told the Houston Oral History project in 2010. That journey to self-acceptance wasn't easy. As a teenager Parker even cut herself.

But with the help of an older mentor in Houston's growing gay and lesbian community in the late 1970s (yes, it was there), Parker founded a group for gay students at Rice—and was shunned by many of her dormmates for her trouble. After graduation, she kept at it. Even as she spent almost two decades in the oil and gas business, she ran a lesbian and feminist bookstore and served as president of the Houston GLBT Caucus. (Members got their tires slashed on a regular basis.) By 1991, Parker thought the city was ready for a gay city councilwoman but was perhaps a bit overly optimistic: she lost that year and again when she ran in 1995. (She "curled into a fetal position for a couple of days" after that second loss.) Parker finally prevailed in 1997 and did so without hiding who she was. Her campaign literature included her service to the local gay caucus, but she never made her sexual orientation central to her races, which became the winning strategy. As her longtime campaign manager, Grant Martin, put it, "If you can fix my potholes, I don't care who your girlfriend is."

Still, it should be remembered that as late as 1998—a year after her first victory—the Houston area wasn't necessarily gay-friendly. That was the year that a man named John Geddes Lawrence was arrested in his Harris County apartment for having sex with another man, Tyron Garner. That arrest would lead to the landmark Supreme Court decision *Lawrence v. Texas*, which ended criminal punishment for sex acts between people of the same sex—but not until 2003, just as Parker got elected controller.

And even when she decided to run for mayor, five or so years later, Parker found her support from many of the downtown power brokers—straight, white, and male—suddenly drying up. City council, okay; controller, sure. But a lesbian as the face of the fourth largest city in the United States? The answer was no. She couldn't win, they told her. Parker listened to what they had to say—and then ignored their advice. Houston had sent her to the city council and the controller's office because they knew she could do the job, she figured. In an economic downturn, she was convinced she could build a successful mayoral campaign on fiscal responsibility—and she did just that, proving the big boys wrong. Elected by a coalition of gays, liberals, and women, she showed that she knew her city better than the old establishment did. "A lot of Houstonians were really proud of the fact that we were open enough to elect a lesbian mayor," said Martin. (Not everyone was thrilled, of course: one local anti-gay activist decried the "election of a sodomite who has now proven . . . that her lifestyle IS her public policy agenda.")

In fact, what made Parker an unlikely standard-bearer for gay rights also made her the perfect standard-bearer for gay rights: being gay was the only part of her life that wasn't supremely conventional. She met and fell in love with her future wife, Kathy Hubbard, in 1990 and they've been together ever since. They have four children. She spent most of her years in the oil and gas business at a company run by George H. W. Bush's commerce secretary.

Parker understood that once straight voters saw that she was more like them than not—and that she was wholly dedicated to serving her constituents—the one thing that made her different barely mattered. In doing so, she paved the way for public officials like Transportation secretary Pete Buttigieg, Wisconsin senator Tammy Baldwin, and Colorado governor Jared Polis to live full lives while fulfilling their dreams of serving others. As president and CEO of the national LGBTQ Victory Fund, she went on to help even more gay candidates run for office at a time when the freedoms she fought for were being threatened once again.

But most important for Texans in general and Houstonians in particular, Parker knew that her hometown was more progressive than the downtown power brokers believed, and she trusted the voters to show them. Her victory changed perceptions and open minds in Texas and beyond, maybe even those of late-night comics.

Brené Brown

by **Sarah Hepola** Photograph by Justin Calhoun

One day sometime around the turn of the twenty-first century, when Brené Brown was a PhD candidate at the University of Houston, she was deep in the library stacks and came across this sentence: "The decision to study shame has been the death of many academic careers." It was a warning that Brown didn't heed, with fortuitous results: her research into shame and vulnerability launched a career that spans bestselling books, arenas filled with adoring fans, a podcast, and even a Netflix special. A fifth-generation Texan who was born to a chaotic household in San Antonio in 1965, Brown describes herself as a "control freak," and her willingness to examine her own flaws is one of her major appeals. Early in her career as an academic, she realized that a willingness to be vulnerable was the shared trait of what she called "wholehearted" people—those who had a strong sense of love and belonging. Her message has resonated far beyond the borders of her home state, where she has kept her faculty position at the University of Houston's Graduate School of Social Work.

In 2010, **Brené Brown** was living the busy but contained life of an academic. She worked as a research professor in the University of Houston's social work department. She wrote a blog. She'd self-published a book about women and shame that was later picked up by Penguin, a Cinderella story for any writer, but the ball was short-lived. Brown remembers the wave of shame that passed over her when, six months after its release, the publisher called to

say the book was being remaindered, unsold copies pulped into oblivion.

Then she stepped onto a stage at the University of Houston for a TEDx Talk, and everything changed. She argued that being vulnerable, long perceived as weakness, was actually an act of courage and the true path to connection, which her research identified as our deepest human need. The speech pointed in the opposite direction of a technology age that granted us an unprecedented arsenal of tools to keep our messy sides hidden: the cleverly cropped selfies, the control of block-mute-unfriend, the boom-roasted certitude of a perfect tweet. Our likes and followers accumulated while our souls wandered the dark. "To let ourselves be seen, deeply seen, vulnerably seen," she said, was the only way we could connect.

"The Power of Vulnerability" went viral, becoming one of the top ten most watched TED Talks ever. In the decade that followed, Brown released seven books, five of which hit number one on the *New York Times* bestseller list.

Brown often quotes the famed psychoanalyst Carl Jung, who said paradox is the best way to capture "the fullness of life." It's certainly true of Brown. She's a cross between Oprah and Malcolm Gladwell, harnessing the compassion and brave-warrior language of the former and the social science and data-backed wisdom of the latter. This unique hybrid has granted her a high perch in the culture. Her fans include Silicon Valley CEOs, fellow soccer moms, military leaders, and young progressive activists.

Brown's knack for reaching across the aisle—her political identity as a "radical moderate" who can shoot a gun but supports gun control, the way her emotional vocabulary resonates with women while her sports metaphors reel in men—has made her a

coveted and well-compensated speaker (though she says she does half her appearances pro bono). She started an LLC that employs nearly two dozen staffers who help manage her appearances, facilitate training for educators and leaders, feed her blog and social media, and produce her podcast, *Unlocking Us*. Meanwhile, she has remained on staff at the University of Houston and became a visiting professor at the University of Texas's McCombs School of Business. In a country where nobody can agree on much, we seem to agree on Brené Brown.

The big epiphany in Brown's career came in 2006, a moment she now refers to in books as a spiritual awakening. She'd just given birth to her second child and she was about to turn forty-one. Brown has described midlife not as a crisis but as an "unraveling," in which the defense mechanisms we have long relied on no longer serve us. One day, while searching her data for themes and patterns, she decided to group subjects into categories of dos and don'ts. The former was a group that displayed a more joyful way of living she called "wholehearted."

"The *Do* column was brimming with words like worthiness, rest, play, trust, faith, intuition, hope, authenticity, love, belonging," she writes in *The Gifts of Imperfection*. "The *Don't* column was dripping with words like perfection, numbing, certainty, exhaustion, self-sufficiency, being cool, fitting in, judgment, and scarcity."

She thunked down into a red chair at her breakfast table and stared at the lists for a long time, her hand covering her mouth. Her whole life, she realized, was the *Don't* column. That's when it struck her: she could no longer simply research wholeheartedness. She would have to start learning it.

The Gifts of Imperfection, published a few months before that pivotal TEDx talk in 2010, marks the emergence of the Brené Brown we've come to know. The book traces her transformation from an uptight researcher to a, well, slightly less uptight researcher trying to reprogram her own broken habits born of female socialization, family dynamics, and a consumer and media environment that feeds on feelings of inadequacy. Combining her shame research with personal anecdotes, she shepherds readers through the hobgoblins of perfectionism and people-pleasing and lacerating self-diminishment to reach the terra firma of "I am enough." The book would go on to sell two million copies and become a self-help classic, despite the fact that Brown abhors the term *self-help*. She doesn't think help is something we do on our own.

Brown quit drinking and smoking on the same day, when she was thirty. She had just completed a genealogy project for her master's degree that revealed twisted branches on both sides of her family tree. She'd grown up hearing lore about raucous drinking and outlaw swagger among some of her relatives, but the project rendered those heroes' tales into something more like addiction and mental health problems. She joined Alcoholics Anonymous but left after a year. She found wisdom there but never felt she belonged. She didn't identify as an alcoholic, more as a woman who would drink and eat and smoke and micromanage her family and do whatever she could to outrun uncomfortable feelings.

"Sobriety taught me how to be vulnerable," she said. "It's the reason I'm still married. It's the reason I'm proud of being the parent I am. It's the reason I have success in work."

When the coronavirus pandemic upended everything, Brown took it as a lesson not just in our individual vulnerability but in our collective vulnerability as well. Mother Nature had laid us bare and revealed our lives, our country, and our planet to be more troubled than we'd imagined. The illusion of safety and happiness had been easier once. But that was just a story we were telling ourselves; the virus had taken narrative control.

As it happened, Brown launched her podcast on March 20, 2020, just as the coronavirus arrived. On that first episode, she talked about fear and uncertainty to an audience that was experiencing plenty of both. "Many of us are trying to make our kids feel reassured when we don't feel sure about anything," she said, before delivering the sort of bolt of self-doubt that has made her relatable to millions, even as she has ascended into the stratosphere of celebrity: "I'm a grown-ass person, but I do not know what I'm doing."

197

Liz Lambert

by Robert Draper Photograph by Wynn Myers

Austin and Marfa already had international reputations when Liz Lambert put her mark on them. But the "Hippest Hotelier in Texas" accelerated the trajectories of both locales, and in doing so transformed the state's hospitality industry. Born in 1963 to a famed West Texas ranching family, Lambert didn't start creating hotels until her thirties, after bailing on a successful career as a lawyer. But she made up for her late start quickly enough. Her first project, the Hotel San José, a bungalow-style retro haven with an oasis-like courtyard lounge, opened in 2000 and was probably the signal moment in the shift of Austin's South Congress Avenue from a funky, idiosyncratic commercial strip to a global shopping and dining destination. More projects in the neighborhood followed: Jo's Coffee, the Hotel Saint Cecilia, the Austin Motel, and Hotel Magdalena, all possessed of a sensibility that you could describe as modern hip with a western flare. If Austin is no longer the sleepy college town Lambert knew as an undergraduate at the University of Texas, she can take as much credit as virtually anyone. Along the way, she also created El Cosmico in Marfa, where guests can stay in a decked-out trailer, a yurt, a teepee, or a safari tent, all within shouting distance of the sculptor Donald Judd's famous concrete blocks. Her native West Texas would never be the same.

▼

Growing up in this state, you learn not to ask a West Texas rancher how many acres or head of cattle they own. Still, at some point during my years of visiting the Big Bend, it became apparent that impossible stretches of what I was gazing at in the region—near Fort Davis, Balmorhea, and Marathon—were the property of Liz Lambert's family. Or, as Lambert's cousin Bobby McKnight, the overseer of the cattle business, would one day put it to me of his drives between and across the family ranches, "Yep, we get a lot of windshield time."

It was on that land that Liz Lambert—perhaps the most influential hotelier in Texas today—learned to plow her own path and trust that others would come to appreciate her vision.

Her family doesn't advertise itself as West Texas royalty. And, indeed, the first of them I briefly met was Lou Lambert, Liz's older brother, who at the time was doing the cooking at Reata, Alpine's self-styled "cowboy cuisine" restaurant. That Lou would one day develop a dining mini-empire—including Lamberts Downtown Barbecue, in Austin, and, most recently, the Roy Pope Grocery and the Paris Coffee Shop, both in Fort Worth—was anything but inevitable. I didn't know that their mother, Joann McKnight Lambert, descended from a lineage whose first Texas land grant was issued by Stephen F. Austin in 1824. I didn't know that her ancestors had spent the next century migrating across the state before seizing upon superior grama grassland in Odessa and establishing a headquarters there. Had I known all this, but only this, about the McKnight clan, then I would've figured Lou was just slumming it in the Reata kitchen for a summer, more or less in the same manner that Liz was flushing some of the family money down the toilet of a South Congress hotel.

The missing piece of the puzzle, hidden in plain sight, was that such dynasties don't spring up overnight. Then and now, cattle ranching isn't a short path to prosperity. The McKnight progeny were to heed a work ethic that Bobby McKnight describes as "Get up early, do your fair share, get out and push the wagon, and if you can't remove a stump, plow behind it." With that came privilege, of course. No one in Lambert's family was going to starve. No one was going to struggle to pay the bills. But the West Texas version of noblesse oblige that accompanied their upbringing was, as Lou Lambert puts it, "You *will* be productive. You *will* be a part of your community. Do that, and we'll support you. Whatever path you take is up to you. But you are gonna do *something*."

The "something" that Liz Lambert would do was not prefigured by anything that took place in the first thirty years of her life, other than the preternatural self-assuredness that accompanied her from infancy. The youngest and only girl of four children, she wasted little time staking out contrarian turf in her hometown of Odessa: upon learning that one of her brother Lou's show calves was being served for dinner one night, she declared herself a vegetarian. She wrote her high school senior thesis on Bob Dylan. She followed in her parents' footsteps by attending TCU and becoming Pi Beta Phi pledge class president, but she didn't stick with the debutante life.

She came out as gay soon after transferring to the University of Texas at Austin in

1983. Lambert took one look around the city and its unmanicured early 1980s alt vibe—Barton Springs, Mad Dog & Beans, Les Amis, Liberty Lunch, no one giving much of a crap about money—and pronounced herself an Austinite. She majored in humanities with a concentration in poetry, shared a house with members of the lesbian folk band Two Nice Girls, and took a summer internship at *Texas Monthly*.

Practical advice from family members steered Lambert to UT's law school. After getting her law degree, she moved to New York and spent a few years in the Manhattan District Attorney's Office. Then, on a snowy Manhattan day in March, Lambert flew to visit friends in Austin, borrowed a pickup truck, and took a drive down Congress Avenue, heading south from the Capitol. And there, like her ranching forebears, she discovered greener pastures.

"The sound you hear," sighed Steve Wertheimer, owner of the legendary Austin music joint Continental Club, as he gestured outward toward South Congress Avenue, "is the sound of its soul being sucked out."

We were sitting outside Jo's, a coffee shop that Lambert founded back in 2001, two crusty sixty-somethings performing the time-honored Austin rite of bitching about how much better things used to be before the next asshole showed up right after we did. If we exerted our collective hindsight, we could almost see the *Last Picture Show*–like landscape of South Congress back when Wertheimer purchased the Continental in 1987: a loan insurance company, a carpeting store, the original Schlotzky's—that was about it. Though the strip's many restaurants are homegrown, the street otherwise bears telltale emblems of overgrown Sunbelt cities everywhere: an Equinox gym, a Madewell men's clothing store, even a Soho House.

It wasn't clear to me who Wertheimer was blaming, if anyone. Certainly not his friend Liz Lambert, who years ago would sit at the bar of the Continental with Wertheimer on weeknights, watching the occasional addict or sex worker disappear into the San José Motel, the seedy twenty-four-room motel across the street. Lambert was a notable presence on the Austin social scene back then. She was funny without being jokey, well read, and comfortable letting others have the stage until she had something to say, at which time everyone would fall silent. When the day came in 1995 that she wondered aloud whether she should just go ahead and buy the San José, Wertheimer gave her his blessing.

What ensued is one of Austin's most widely told success stories. Lambert purchased the San José from its owners and, lacking any meaningful experience in the hospitality industry, set out to reinvent the place.

Her dreams of empire were nonexistent at that point. Her only real goal was to find a vessel worthy of pouring herself into. As it turned out, the frustrated poet found her artistic calling in architectural design. Intuiting what Austin's downscale-upscale sensibility was fast becoming, Lambert and her collaborators invented her aesthetic on the fly, all loblolly pine furniture and concrete floors, a kind of Texanized

201

feng shui driven in part by her interest in minimalist artists like Donald Judd but also by her paltry operating budget.

After five years of effort, the made-over Hotel San José officially opened on March 4, 2000. A few other things were happening in the Austin area at the time. Dellionaires, for one. South by Southwest, for another. Overnight, it seemed, the town had developed both an appetite for money and a talent for making and spending it. Timing favored Lambert. Still, the bet she placed—that anyone with a credit card would have the slightest interest in spending a few nights behind concrete walls on South Congress as opposed to, say, the Four Seasons on Town Lake—still seemed dubious at the time. Then one day Patti Smith walked into the lobby of the San José with a guitar over her shoulder. Then Annie Leibovitz decided that she wanted some shots of Lucinda Williams in an unmade bed in the San José. Then David Byrne came to play in the courtyard. All of a sudden, the only place where Austinites wanted to be was poolside at Lambert's hotel, basking in the reflected grooviness of whichever reigning hipster was in town.

She formed the management group Bunkhouse, so named after the guest cabin on her family's ranch just north of Marfa. Then came the Hotel Saint Cecilia, a twenty-room urban enclave canopied by immense oak trees that cemented her place as America's newest superstar of what she calls "aspirational" lodging. The Saint Cecilia positioned itself as one of the most expensive hotels in Texas from the time of its opening—at the height of the financial bust in 2008. Asking big bucks for a night on a cul-de-sac just off li'l South Congress during the Great Recession? Why not? Pearl Jam, Beck, and Radiohead each swooped down and claimed every room. Well-heeled visitors to the city took notice. So did commercial real estate agents.

At some point, sleepy Austin transformed itself into the most expensive city in Texas.

Two more South Congress projects followed. First came the Austin Motel, a small masterpiece of motor court cheesiness that was acquired by Bunkhouse in 2017 and promptly transformed into a more stylish celebration of slumming. Citing the brazenly garish wallpaper in the guest rooms as well as the vibrators for sale in the gift shop, Lambert proclaimed it "the most gay hotel we've ever done." Then, in 2020, came the Hotel Magdalena, the largest Bunkhouse property, with eighty-nine rooms as well as a full-service restaurant—signaling that Lambert and South Congress were taking in all comers.

Today SoCo, as the developers term it, bears little resemblance to the white-punks-on-dope underbelly it was when I first started hanging out at the Continental Club as a college student in 1979. There's a profusion of casual high-dollar restaurants and boutique clothing stores that announce themselves as Texan in the most ironic ways. South Congress is increasingly replete with offices and posh apartments, and monied millennials cram the sidewalks.

Much of this can be credited to—or, depending on your point of view, blamed on—Lambert. The San José jump-started the area's transition, as well as an enviable career for Lambert. Bunkhouse has since opened hotels in San Antonio, San Francisco, Salado, and Baja California Sur, transforming how we regard places like Austin and Marfa and, for that matter, the whole circle-squaring of liberal consciousness with growth-crazed capitalism.

But as of 2019, Lambert was no longer in charge of most of this. After she sold an interest in Bunkhouse to the international hospitality conglomerate Standard International, a series of corporate struggles led to her firing. The day before Lambert's fifty-fifth birthday, the company's CEO called her to tell her that she had become an "unmanageable employee."

Not that this has slowed her down much. Soon after, she was exploring opportunities to start new projects in New Orleans, the Bahamas, and Aspen. West Texas women don't fold that easily. Even after a massive setback she remained, forthrightly, a mythic hard-charging West Texas lesbian pro-growth lib-backing motorcycle-riding unbounded dreamer. Which is to say, someone distinctly from these parts. Even if, thanks to her, you don't recognize some of these parts anymore.

Tim Dunn

by R.G. Ratcliffe

Though Tim Dunn isn't a household name—not even in Texas—he is as responsible as nearly anyone for pushing Texas politics to the right at the precise moment when many experts thought that demographic changes would be shifting the state purple if not bright blue. Dunn, a wealthy West Texas oilman, has helped displace a relatively centrist, business-friendly version of Texas Republicanism with a distinctly Christian conservatism. Through a series of groups, only some of which he is openly associated with, he has bankrolled dozens of insurgent candidates and attacked numerous well-established politicians. His influence is likely as great as that of far-better-known figures such as lieutenant governor Dan Patrick and governor Greg Abbott.

In November 2010, as he was readying for his second term as Speaker of the Texas House of Representatives, Joe Straus invited Midland oilman Tim Dunn to breakfast. It was an attempt, after a bruising election season, to extend an olive branch. Dunn had helped bankroll the Tea Party surge in Texas, and an organization he started, Empower Texans, had participated in rallies across the state protesting property taxes and excessive government spending. Straus, a San Antonio businessman from a well-off Republican family, had been chosen as Speaker in 2009 by a coalition that comprised GOP fiscal conservatives like himself and all the chamber's Democrats.

But in the 2010 election, the Democrats lost

twenty-four seats, thanks largely to the Tea Party's energy. Dunn, in other words, had done much to shrink the Speaker's base of support. Nevertheless, Straus thought he and Dunn might find common ground on the subject of fiscal responsibility.

With plates of eggs before them, Dunn and Straus sat at a table in the Speaker's Conference Room, surrounded by Audubon prints and photographs of Straus family members posing with George H. W. Bush and the late Republican U.S. senator John Tower. Dunn never lifted his fork. He didn't seem interested in hearing what the Speaker had to say. But he did have an agenda. He demanded that Straus remove a significant number of committee chairs and replace them with Tea Party activists supported by Empower Texans. Straus refused. Then the conversation moved on to social policy, and, according to Straus insiders, Dunn astonished Straus, who is Jewish, by saying that only Christians should be in leadership positions.

After the meeting, a stunned Straus told aides that he had never been spoken to in that way. Though Straus's aides considered the statement anti-Semitic, others might argue that it was more likely an expression of Dunn's pro-evangelicalism. In sermons and other public statements, Dunn has asserted a belief that born-again evangelicals who follow biblical laws are graced by God and given a duty of political leadership. "If you are an evangelical and you don't vote, that means you are not doing your duty because you are the ones that God gave the authority to," Dunn once said.

"The real biblical approach to government is—the ideal is—a kingdom with a perfect king," Dunn told a Christian radio audience in 2016. "But pending that, yes, the ideal is a self-governing society." Dunn's notion of self-government, though, is different from that of most Americans. He has stated repeatedly that our democracy must be brought into line with biblical laws. When secular governments stray from the Ten Commandments and try to make their own rules, he says, "you have a false perfect government with a false messiah."

Dunn is probably the most influential donor in twenty-first-century Texas. Between 2002 and 2022, he gave at least $16.1 million in publicly reported campaign donations to Texas politicians and PACs. Federal candidates and super PACs received $5.7 million of Dunn's money between 2010 and 2022. Quite likely, a similar amount of his money has flowed in obscurity through a maze of nonprofit foundations, some of which he controls and many of which hide their true identity and never report their donors.

The driving ideological forces behind Dunn's organizations are small-government libertarianism and a socially conservative agenda. It wasn't long after Dunn and Straus met for breakfast that conservatives around the state started sending out emails and press releases pushing for a House leader who was both right-wing and a Christian; as one member of the State Republican Executive Committee put it in a private note to another member of the committee, "We elected a House with Christian, conservative values. We now want a true Christian conservative running it."

"**Nothing comes easy** to West Texas," former First Lady Barbara Bush once said of living in the Permian Basin. "Every tree must be cultivated, and every flower is a joy." It's a harsh environment where sand creeps under the barbed-wire fences and across the roadways, ever threatening to erase civilization. Here, the fleeting nature of life is evident and religion blooms. But beneath the brown desert lies an ancient seabed containing some of the richest oil and gas deposits on earth. Oil is the reason people live there. With each boom, the roughnecks and petroleum engineers come; with each bust, most of them leave. The oilmen remain, having converted some of those fossil fuels into gold.

Amid this austere landscape, Dunn embraced evangelical faith and made a fortune financing wells to extract oil that he once told a British journalist was deposited beneath the earth's surface by God four thousand years ago, not the two hundred million years as determined by earth science.

The youngest of four boys whose father was a Howard County Farm Bureau insurance agent, Dunn grew up in Big Spring, about forty miles from Midland. In high school he was an Eagle Scout and a guitarist in a rock band. He left home to study chemical engineering at Texas Tech University, where he met his future wife, Terri. They married in 1977, and eight months later she was pregnant with the first of their six children. Dunn went to work for Exxon, then spent several years working in commercial banking. The family moved to Midland, where he worked at a bank before joining Parker & Parsley Petroleum as director and, eventually, chief financial officer.

Already on a path to wealth, Dunn formed his own oil and gas company, now known as CrownQuest Operating LLC, in 1996. Over the years it has done quite well; in 2017, for instance, it produced 6.6 million barrels of oil. At the average price of West Texas Intermediate crude at the time, that would translate into about $335 million in gross revenue.

Dunn and his wife attend the nondenominational Midland Bible Church, where the Bible is viewed as inspired by God and without error. Along with several other families, they homeschooled their children; the older ones followed a course of instruction that Dunn created, in which they would read great works of literature and philosophy and then be challenged to square their readings with the Bible. In a promotional video for a private school he founded, Dunn says, "It's our job to give the kids a faith crisis every day and then lead them to what the true answer is and let them decide."

To Dunn, Texas and the entire country are in a crisis, and he eventually figured out an answer to it: Focus on Republican primaries. After the 1998 elections, it was apparent that Democrats were unlikely to win statewide office in Texas anytime soon and that their grip on the Legislature was slipping away. The real action for someone wanting to change the political landscape wasn't in the general elections, which were a lock for the GOP. It was in the Republican primaries, where many establishment politicians were getting their party's support.

One seemingly unlikely target of Dunn's groups was Natalie Lacy Lange, of Brenham. Lange would seem to be the epitome of a modern, small-town Republican woman; she attends church regularly and serves as the president of the local school board. A former teacher, Lange believes that public schools are the future of a thriving Texas workforce.

On the Saturday before early voting began in the 2018 Republican primaries, a fellow school board member texted Lange a photograph of a letter that had been sent to voters in Brenham, headed, "Subject: Is school board president Natalie Lange breaking the law?" The letter, sent by Empower Texans, questioned whether Lange and the Brenham school board had violated state law by approving a "Culture of Voting" resolution urging students and teachers to vote. Empower Texans claimed the resolution was promoted by "liberal activists" who might be illegally using school district tax dollars to get students and teachers to vote against conservative candidates.

Lange had never heard of Empower Texans or Dunn, but being called a liberal in Brenham could be a political kiss of death. How many of her neighbors now thought she was liberal or perhaps a criminal? She was mortified, and a little bit frightened.

She was not alone. Similar letters had been sent out assailing school board presidents in Sealy, Nederland, Marshall, and Coppell. Empower Texans' likely motivation was clear: though the organizations that promoted the voter drive were nonpartisan, the drive was fueled by teachers' groups that were angry about the Legislature's failure to pass school finance reform and its attempt to create private school vouchers.

The day after the letter arrived, Lange met with her minister to pray for strength and then posted angry responses on Facebook, where they were widely shared. Attacking volunteer school board members with "slick propaganda meant to stir false discord sinks to a new low," she wrote, "even for an organization known for ruthlessness and bullying."

"[Dunn] may be a Christian, but his tactics are not very Christlike," she later said. And in this instance, not successful: Lange was reelected to her position that year, and then again in 2022.

In a talk he gave to his church three days before the Fourth of July in 2018, Dunn spoke of his belief that the laws of man have strayed from the laws of God. The federal government has amassed immense power, he said, and used it to bad ends. Christians were under attack, he said, and the resistance begins in church.

The Bible, Dunn explained, instructs Christians to submit to authority, but in the United States the people are the authority. "So participate in government," he said, urging members of the congregation to seek elective office. His voice filled with emotion—some anger, some frustration—Dunn reminded them that challenging the establishment can have a cost. "If you go to the right places, you'll find that I am the bogeyman that hides under the bed of every lobbyist every night and comes out and jumps up and scares them," Dunn said. It was an odd note of aggrievement, coming from a man who uses secret money and innuendo to defeat his enemies.

"The most important thing to do is don't surrender," he said as he closed his sermon. "God is our king. It doesn't matter what they tell us. It doesn't matter what kind of trashing they do to our reputation. If we stand and we are vigilant, we will win."

207

Hugo Ortega

by José Ralat Photographs by Jody Horton

If Houston is a city of immigrants, Hugo Ortega may be its first citizen. The celebrated chef, who arrived in Houston from Mexico in the trunk of a midcentury Chevrolet Impala, started with virtually nothing but some cooking skills he learned from his grandmother and a burning desire to make something of himself. And he did. His five Houston restaurants, Backstreet Café, Hugo's, Caracol, Xochi, and Urbe, are beloved institutions that have profoundly changed the way Texans look at Mexican food. Yet Ortega, the author of *Hugo Ortega's Street Food of Mexico* and *Backstreet Kitchen: Seasonal Recipes from Our Neighborhood Cafe*, remains an approachable, modest figure who continues to push himself and his customers well after he could have happily rested on his laurels.

The puffed tortilla, darkened a shimmering black with squid ink, formed a thin, delicate bowl. The opening at the top, carefully cut out in the kitchen so as to not crack the vessel, bore the weight of thin ropes of chile-seasoned rabbit. Called an infladita de conejo (inflated tortilla with rabbit), this combination of masa and a wild-game waterfall is a common dish in the Mexican state of Veracruz. But it's not the sort of thing one would have found in Houston—or Texas, or, perhaps anywhere in the United States, really—until Hugo

Ortega came along. The infladita is a signature dish at Ortega's modern Mexican restaurant Xochi, which opened in 2017, part of a small culinary empire that he and his wife, the restaurateur Tracy Vaught, launched in 2002.

With each restaurant, Ortega has exposed Texans to the ever-widening, ever-changing gastronomy of Mexico, from the sidewalk stands of Mexico City to the mercados of Guadalajara to the neighborhood cafés and high-end establishments of Monterrey. Along the way, he has inspired disciples who are building reputations of their own, such as his former employee Fabian Saldaña, co-owner of Houston's late, lamented Maize, and Edgar Rico, of Austin's Nixta Taqueria. He has gotten Houstonians to eat roasted grasshoppers, helped Texans realize that wood-fired oysters are a thoroughly Mexican dish, and received a James Beard Award for Best Chef: Southwest.

What is so attractive about his food? He has brought techniques and ingredients previously scarce or uncommon on this side of the border and not only deployed them but done so with an expert hand. Take nixtamalization, the process that dates back millennia in Mesoamerica. This method of preparing corn entails cooking and steeping it in an alkaline solution to loosen the outer hull of kernels and release trapped nutrients such as niacin. The corn is then easier to grind into a dough (masa) that's the basis for tortillas and other preparations. From kernel to masa, the process can take up to twenty-four hours to complete. Ortega, who introduced many Texans to nixtamalization at his first restaurant, Hugo's, didn't advertise his use of the ancient technique. He didn't think he needed to; he just wanted to cook good food—and ended up cooking great food.

Hugo's was where Ortega first figured out how to thrive in one of the most competitive dining cities in the world. His use of mole is perhaps the prime example. The most commonly known mole is mole poblano, a luxuriously silky brown-hued preparation that is a slowly cooked amalgamation of chiles, spices, and herbs with chocolate and myriad other ingredients. Many Texans had eaten mole poblano and perhaps a few other mole varieties before Ortega arrived here. But in Ortega's hands, mole has moved beyond something found draped over enchiladas.

Mole is a crystallization of Mexican food's regionality and creativity, and Ortega has thought much about its essence. "It's about seeing what is local and the abundance of the ingredients," he once told me. Though many mole recipes have been passed down for generations, they leave room for improvising, depending on what's available. Several years ago, a friend gave Ortega a fig sapling; he was moving and didn't want to see the tree wither. Ortega planted the clipping in a mulchy median in Hugo's parking lot. He waited. The tree grew. "I picked whatever the birds didn't help themselves to," he says. Then he began to consider what would go well with figs in a mole. He settled on ancho and mulatto chiles to balance the fruits' sweetness and ended up with a limited-edition mole, one of dozens he has made over the years.

Ortega credits much of his success to his beloved maternal grandmother, Delia, who was a profound influence on him when he was growing up poor in Mexico City and a small town on the border of Oaxaca and Puebla. "For my grandmother to break a smile, it was very difficult," Ortega recalls. He thinks she was so serious because she was devoted to turning young Hugo into a good man with a good heart. "We would get up at 5:00 and she would start the fire" for the nixtamal and the tortillas, he says. Ortega would then saddle his donkey and ride to the well to fill jugs with water. Then he would tend to the farm animals. When he returned, he would do as Delia commanded, whether it be shucking corn or roasting cacao for chocolate. "I carry her with me everywhere I go," he says of his late grandmother. "She is my inspiration."

Ortega carried the memories of Delia's food and Mexican culture to Texas in 1984, when he arrived in Houston at the age of nineteen. The only person he knew in Houston was his cousin David. He spoke no English, and his only ambition at the time was to work. Ortega's first job was as a janitor. When he wasn't unclogging pipes, he was playing soccer. It was during a match that a friend told him of a job opening at Backstreet Cafe in Houston's tony River Oaks neighborhood. His friend didn't make any promises but did introduce Ortega to the restaurant's co-owner, Tracy Vaught. Ortega began working there that very same day, as a dishwasher. Eventually, he was asked if he wanted to cook. He moved up the ranks, enrolled in a local culinary school, married Vaught, became a citizen, and dreamed of opening a restaurant that would serve traditional dishes from across Mexico.

At the time, Mexican cuisine in Texas was limited. Houston's Mexican food options were dominated by Tex-Mex joints like the Original Ninfa's, which offered little that a Mexican might find familiar. A restaurant called Doneraki, which had opened in 1973 in the shadow of the intersection of 610 and I-45, was a relative oasis, a place that served rice and beans, carne asada, tortillas, pico de gallo, and salsas that gave Ortega a taste of the food he missed. He didn't have a car or a bike, so he had to walk about an hour from his home to get there. The effort was worth it.

In Austin, Fonda San Miguel opened in 1975, making it one of the first Texas restaurants to serve region-specific Mexican dishes in a fine-dining format. Founding chef Miguel Ravago served many Texans their first bite of cochinita pibil or mole poblano. It was a major step for Mexican cuisine in Texas, and spawned many imitators, but some diners came away with the misimpression that interior Mexican was the only legitimate Mexican food. There was still a lot for Texans to learn.

In 2001, before founding his dream restaurant, Ortega, his brother Ruben, and his cousin David hit the road in Mexico, not only to reconnect with their homeland, but to seek inspiration in regions they had never visited. When they arrived in Puerto Vallarta, on Mexico's Pacific coast, they had just missed a January festival. The group got the leftovers, Ortega remembers. It was enough. They feasted on pescado zarandeado (fish held in a metal folding basket and grilled over open flames). It was a wondrous alternative to the typical fried seafood served across Texas.

Hugo's opened in the summer of 2002 and quickly secured a reputation as one of Texas's most exciting restaurants. Mexican food, Ortega made clear, isn't just interior Mexican, delectable as that cuisine is.

211

Mexican food is found in the desert border states, the coasts, the verdant mountains and their hidden valleys, in nearly inaccessible Indigenous villages where Spanish isn't spoken, as well as the curbsides of towns and cities. It's the street foods that make Mexican food, according to Ortega, "the most vibrant and the most refined food."

That includes tacos, which are on the menu at all his restaurants. Not that long ago, Latinos in the Southwest were mocked for eating tacos. Though those days are gone, many still think of tacos as little more than a tasty cousin of fast food. Ortega knows that tacos can function as a convenient, casual commodity, but he also knows they can be much more. Take the tacos dorados de papa at Hugo's. Tacos dorados are, traditionally, a folded or rolled fried taco, often filled with mashed potatoes. At Hugo's, however, the tortilla is done away with and the potato is used as the vessel. The cloud-like interior is filled with many of the traditional taco dorado fillings: crunchy ropes of shredded cabbage; diced, slightly spicy jalapeños; and tart pickled onions, with a side of soothing tomatillo and serrano salsa de albañil. It's at once a familiar, comforting finger food but also a show of innovation.

Perhaps none of Ortega's restaurants expresses his desire to bring Mexico to Texas as powerfully as Xochi, which opened in 2017. The restaurant, which specializes in Oaxacan dishes, offers pressed rectangles of cabrito (kid goat); glazed pork ribs stacked above a pool of mole de chicatanas, a nutty mole made with flying ants; and triangular corn masa tetelas. There's also a customizable mole flight, which includes such options as earthy, almond-studded mole almendrado; huaxmole, which uses edamame-shaped guaje seeds; and sunset-colored amarillo.

One evening, as Ortega and I were chatting in one of Xochi's dining rooms, he decided to show me a collection of raw masa preparations before they were finished for service. He left for a moment and then returned bearing a glazed platter of dried blue and yellow corn kernels separated by dried corn husks. Another platter bore balls of masa bigger than a fist. One was black, one was bluish gray with dark speckles, another was green from blending with cactus. Another was unadulterated white. A small bowl with a deep center and scalloped edges contained swooshes of the Mexican corn fungus huitlacoche, gray and blue fading into white. It's unheard-of for a Mexican restaurant in Texas to have such a range of corn products available at any one time. Ortega's sourcing in Oaxaca is unparalleled, a reflection of his devotion to the region of the country where he spent much of his childhood.

Hours later, this raw masa was transformed into a dizzying variety of dishes arranged on a silver platter: thumbprint cookie-like chochoyotes; sopes, which are cake-like thick white corn discs with high, finger-pinched edges; torpedo-shaped molotes filled with plantains; blue, green, and white tetelas fanned next to smaller squid ink sopes; a small huarache, an oblong tortilla shaped and named after the Indigenous Mexican Purépecha word for sandal, resting atop rolled tortillas; and a couple of tamales in corn husks stacked in an X shape next to tumbles of infladitas.

It's almost too much to take in, but Ortega, gazing at this platter, began talking about other tortillas and masas he has eaten in Mexico. He spoke of the tricolor tortillas and the tortilla ceremoniales stamped with intricate designs that he snacked on in Michoácan and the two-masa tamales and single-masa tamales mixed with squash blossoms that he devoured in Oaxaca. "It's very artisanal, the way they define who they are and what they like, and they are very proud," he said of the cooks who created those dishes. "It's unbelievable how wonderful these people are." Ortega went on to admit how little we still know about Oaxaca. In the far, hidden corners of the Mexican state, he says, people have their own recipes and their own communities. "We don't know anything about these very traditional ways of cooking," he explained. For a moment Ortega seemed lost in a culinary reverie before announcing his next ambition. "I need to reach those places," he said.

As he put it to me once on another occasion, "I would like to be homeless in Mexico for a month."

Dan Patrick

by Christopher Hooks Photographs by Jason Madara

Once, not that long ago, there were two kinds of Texas politicians: conservative Democrats and liberal Democrats. Republicans barely existed. Then, as the GOP started to grow in popularity in the state, you could find a wide variety of Republicans, including pro-choice Republicans, pro-business Republicans, and socially conservative Republicans. Today, though, there's basically one kind of Republican sitting in the Legislature and holding statewide office: hard-core right-wing Republicans. Though this is in step with trends in many other states, in Texas it was accelerated, most prominently, by the efforts of one man: Lieutenant Governor Dan Patrick, who has held that office since 2015. In Texas, the lieutenant governor, who presides over the Texas Senate, is effectively the most powerful officeholder in the state, and Patrick hasn't been shy about wielding that power. More than anyone, he is responsible for making Texas inhospitable to Republican politicians who don't closely hew to the party's orthodoxy—which, also thanks largely to him, is an increasingly conservative, religiously driven orthodoxy. And the Democrats? In Dan Patrick's Senate circa 2022, there was only one kind: powerless Democrats.

In the early summer of 2014, as Texas slouched its way toward the Republican primary runoff elections, a sixty-seven-page spiral-bound booklet arrived in the mailboxes of reporters around the state. The four-way primary for lieutenant governor had come down to the twelve-year incumbent, the inveterate establishment figure David Dewhurst, and former state senator Dan Patrick. According to the polls, Patrick, who made his name as an incendiary Houston talk radio host, was on the verge of becoming one of those most powerful elected officials in Texas.

The fourth-place finisher in the first round of the primary, the straight-talking land commissioner Jerry Patterson, considered Patrick a fraud and a danger. So the former Marine fanned the hammer on his six-shooter. The booklet, titled *A Research Document*, was Patterson's oppo file, and the cover promised information on Patrick's "bankruptcy," "tax liens," and "assumed names." It chronicled Patrick's tumultuous 1980s, before he found Christ, when he owned a sports bar in Houston, drank, fought, and lived large during his boom years and the subsequent oil crash. In a follow-up, Patterson released medical records showing that Patrick had been hospitalized for depression and once tried to slash his wrists.

There was no shortage of material, but Patterson saw fit to highlight, in the first line of the first page, the fact, already known by many Texans, that Patrick was "Born in Baltimore, Maryland as DANNIE SCOTT GOEB." That Patrick hails from Charm City, and that he used to go by a different name, is his detractors' favorite fact. Sometimes it's raised as a counterpoint to Patrick's public image, which trades in schmaltzy Texas imagery. Sometimes disdainful Texas liberals mention it to deride Patrick as an undocumented migrant, a foreign infec-

tion bringing alien ways of thinking to our shores.

What they forget, and what Patterson and Dewhurst did too, is that Texans—contrary to their self-perception as a people who value straight talk and authenticity—have always celebrated scoundrels, chameleons, and impresarios. Davy Crockett was a showman; James Bowie a con artist. Sam Houston was run out of Washington after beating a sitting congressman with a cane. Texas is for reinvention, and for leaving old debts behind, and the fact that Patrick had done quite a bit of both was far from disqualifying. The oppo dump accomplished nothing, and Patrick did 24 points better in the runoff than in the first round.

Baltimore is as good a place as any to start this fable. Dannie Goeb was born on April 4, 1950, to Charles, who worked on the circulation side of the *Baltimore Sun* for three decades, and Vilma Jean, a bookkeeper. When he turned twelve, Patrick began working as a newsie. Many politicians would kill for a working-class background like this; it's the stuff that makes a good story. And Baltimore, in that period, must have left a tremendous impact on him: on his eighteenth birthday, Martin Luther King Jr. was assassinated, and Baltimore rioted for more than a week. But it's rare to hear Patrick speak of that time in his life.

In college, he was a disk jockey. After college, a salesman. In Scranton, Pennsylvania, he took a job doing sports and the weather for a local TV station. In 1979, he became the head sportscaster at Houston's KHOU. In one segment, later publicized in Dewhurst's 2014 campaign, his body was painted blue on live TV by Houston Oilers cheerleaders. When he and the station parted ways, he ran a restaurant, a jazz bar, a nightclub, a sports bar. For a while the sports bar thrived, largely on the strength of Patrick's personality, but he soon fell prey to the same financial lunacy that infected so many Houstonians in the early eighties. He bought another bar and restaurant, and then another, expanding, finally, to five. But then it all went south. In 1986, Patrick declared personal bankruptcy, reporting debt totaling $816,000.

But a year later, Patrick was well into yet another reinvention. He put together the money to purchase a discounted talk radio station and gave himself a prime spot on the schedule. His show blended stunts—he aired his own vasectomy live on the air—with his then-distinct brand of commentary, which could be overtly racist, as when he took to calling Chinese American journalist Connie Chung's CBS show *Eye to Eye* "Slanted Eye to Eye," or implicitly racist, as when he railed against the goings-on in Houston's urban core to his suburban audience. More importantly, his station became the first in the Houston area to air an up-and-coming New York broadcaster named Rush Limbaugh. Patrick, thanks to a little luck and more than a little foresight, was riding a revolution in media that would make him politically prominent and personally wealthy.

Those who knew Patrick at the time speak about his personalities diverging. There was Dannie Goeb, "very self-conscious" and "very insecure," his former business partner Mark Miller told the *Austin American-Statesman*, and Dan Patrick, the "flamboyant on-air personality." In 1991, Patrick told the *Houston Chronicle* that he too thought "the way I act on the air is strange, because off the air I'm not like that. I'm kind of quiet. But I change when I get on the air."

In 1994, the broadcasting company Clear Channel offered to buy Patrick's once-humble radio station—and a second one he had acquired later on—for $27 million. Patrick knew instinctively who was responsible for his windfall. "I knew my limitations—I wasn't smart enough to have orchestrated the last seven years," he wrote in his 2002 tract *The Second Most Important Book You Will Ever Read: A Personal Challenge to Read the Bible.* "I wasn't that talented, I wasn't a visionary. I instinctively knew this was all a 'God thing.'" He was ready to be redeemed. At the time the offer came in, he was in Las Vegas at a radio industry convention. So he went to the Shrine of the Most Holy Redeemer, a Catholic church squeezed between the Tropicana Casino and McCarran International Airport, and "prayed as I have never prayed before or since." It stuck.

Not since the renegade East Texas congressman Charlie Wilson reportedly did cocaine in the Fantasy Suite of Caesars Palace has such a momentous event in Texas politics occurred in Vegas. Patrick's newfound faith gave him the emotional stability he had long lacked—and a certain crusading impulse. The Clear Channel money didn't hurt, either. He continued broadcasting, and then, in 2006, he ran for the state Senate. The number one issue facing the state, he

217

said then just as he says now, is illegal immigration—the cause, he insists, of so many of the other ills: the crime rate, a failing education system, a bloated state budget. They brought "third world diseases" like "tuberculosis, malaria, polio, and leprosy."

That year promised a bad election for Republicans, and some responded by tacking left. Not Patrick, who spotted something growing in the suburbs of Houston. He won his primary, and then the election. He received no warm welcome from his fellow Republican senators. One, John Carona of Dallas, left the head of a hobby horse on his desk, in the manner of *The Godfather*. Patrick argued that the Senate should eliminate the "two-thirds rule,"

which requires the buy-in of a supermajority and the consent of both parties to do much of anything. The freshman senator, in a body marked by a worshipful respect for seniority, argued that the chamber's foundational tradition was useless and archaic. He was nearly laughed off the floor.

But eventually they stopped laughing. Carona lost reelection, and then most of his "moderate" colleagues joined him in retirement. Texas politics started to look more and more like Patrick's radio show, and Patrick began to look less fringe and more prescient: despite the fervent wishes of Texas Democrats, the state wasn't going to be painted blue anytime soon. In 2014 he took on Dewhurst directly and whipped him. He railed even harder against illegal immigrants. At the GOP convention that year, his campaign distributed signs in the shape of a white picket fence—with a padlock on the front for good measure. During the campaign, Patterson alleged that Patrick had knowingly hired undocumented workers at his bars. One undocumented employee reported that Patrick had been a kind and generous boss. Patrick denied not only that he hired the man but that he had been kind.

According to the polls, Patrick has never been especially popular. And as lieutenant governor, he hasn't always succeeded in accomplishing his goals. But he is perhaps the only truly great politician to emerge in Texas this century. Rick Perry and his contemporaries were minted last century, and Ted Cruz had a few good years but no more than that. Patrick saw where Texas was going, arrived there a few years before to wait for circumstances to catch up, and transformed his insight into tremendous power.

When Patrick became "lite gov," he neutered the two-thirds rule. He went to war with the House,

using his office to bully and cajole moderate House Speaker Joe Straus. Even when he didn't ultimately get what he wanted, his priorities shaped the conversation at the Legislature, and his demands were the ones that made lawmakers dance. For nearly a year, the state was held hostage to Patrick's demand to pass the "bathroom bill," targeting transgender Texans, and his procedural maneuvering ultimately forced a special session. For a while, there were Republican senators in the upper chamber who would occasionally rebuff him—no more. Patrick treated Democrats with undisguised contempt, and they treated him with deference. He understood power, and had figured out how to wield it.

In Texas, God bless this land, you can become anyone you want to be.

219

The Best of the 2010s

Books

Films and TV Shows

1. *Machete*
   (2010)
2. *Bernie*
   (2011)
3. *Tree of Life*
   (2011)
4. *Dallas Buyer's Club*
   (2013)
5. *Prince Avalanche*
   (2013)
6. *Fixer Upper*
   (2013–2018)
7. *Boyhood*
   (2014)
8. *Halt and Catch Fire*
   (2014–2018)
9. *Hell or High Water*
   (2016)
10. *Dumplin'*
    (2018)

Sports

1. The Dallas Mavericks earn their first NBA championship in 2011.
2. The Texas Christian University Horned Frogs beat the Wisconsin Badgers in the 2011 Rose Bowl, 21–19.
3. Baylor University quarterback Robert Griffin III wins the 2011 Heisman Trophy.
4. Simone Biles, who was raised outside of Houston, begins her elite career at the 2011 American Classic and eventually goes on to become the most decorated gymnast in American history.
5. In 2012 the Baylor Lady Bears become the first college basketball team to finish 40–0, winning their second national NCAA Women's Division I Basketball Championship.
6. In 2012, after years of fighting accusations of blood doping, Lance Armstrong admits he cheated and is stripped of his seven Tour de France titles.
7. Texas A&M beats the Oklahoma Sooners in the 2013 Cotton Bowl.
8. Golfer Jordan Spieth wins the Masters Tournament, the FedEx Cup, and the U.S. Open in 2015.
9. The Houston Astros become the first Texas team to win the World Series, though their 2017 championship is tarnished by a cheating scandal.
10. With twenty-four world champion titles from the National Finals Rodeo and fourteen all-around titles under his belt, Amarillo native Trevor Brazile takes his final win in 2018 and announces his retirement.

Music

1. **Grupo Fantasmo,**
   El Existential
   (2010)
2. **Leon Bridges,**
   Coming Home
   (2015)
3. **Beyoncé,**
   Lemonade
   (2016)
4. **Solange,**
   A Seat at the Table
   (2016)
5. **Post Malone,**
   Stoney
   (2016)
6. **St. Vincent,**
   Masseduction
   (2017)
7. **Kacey Musgraves,**
   Slow Burn
   (2018)
8. **Travis Scott,**
   Astroworld
   (2018)
9. **Megan Thee Stallion,**
   "Hot Girl Summer"
   (2019)
10. **Lizzo,**
    Cuz I Love You
    (2019)

TM

ABORTION IS HEALTHCARE

GIRLS JUST WANNA HAVE FUNDAMENTAL HUMAN RIGHTS

2020

Texas Population, 2020: 28.6 million	Rank of Austin in Population Among American Cities, 2020: 11th	Percent of Texans Who Lived in the Six Major Metropolitan Areas as of 2020: 73	Texas Gross State Product, 2020: $1.8 trillion	Energy Created by Wind and Solar Combined, 2020: 100,977,920 Megawatt-Hours	Democrat/ Republican Split in Texas House, 2020: 67 D, 82 R	Cumulative Number of Albums Willie Nelson Had Recorded in His Career as of 2020: 143

the 2020s and Beyond

Going Forward

An Afterword by Mimi Swartz

When I think hard on it, I've always lived in two Texases. In the San Antonio of my late 1950s and early 1960s childhood, I knew everyone on my dead-end street, and everyone knew and looked after me. Respect for others was nonnegotiable—"Yes, ma'am" and "No, sir" accompanied any response to my elders. I went to excellent public schools, learned to ride horses, learned to speak Spanish, watched the neighbor boys play Little League—no Title IX back then—and tolerated visits to West Texas ranches that East Coast kids could only dream of. The stereotypical Texan—superrich, flashy, kind of a boor—was rarely in evidence; mine was a childhood where conformity was the rule, one shaped by the wealthy, conservative Protestants, aka Anglos, who ran the town.

But there was another reality that was just starting to awaken in other parts of San Antonio, a growing awareness of everyone excluded from that closed circle of power. That included the desperately poor. The average income for 28 percent of San Antonio families in 1967 was less than $3,000 a year—about $27,000 in today's dollars. The listing shacks and rutted caliche roads on the west side were indisputable evidence that our mayor, Walter McAllister, didn't believe our Latino population was worth the investment. He told NBC News in 1969 that they "make good maids, garbage collectors, restaurant workers, and gardeners. They aren't going into politics. They lack ambition."

I suspect many San Antonians of that time agreed and felt similarly about the ambitions of the city's Black population and its women. (The Joske's Department Store charge card that my mother carried in her wallet was stamped solely with my father's name.) The gay population was hiding in plain sight: a gay friend recently suggested to me that the uniforms of King Antonio and the Texas Cavaliers, with their shiny medals, elaborate epaulets, and plumed hats, satisfied, for a certain segment of those in the closet, a deep-seated need to be themselves. The federal government? It was still seen as the enemy, sticking its nose where it didn't belong, even though few objected when Lyndon Johnson gave us Medicare and NASA.

I would love to tell you that, fifty or so years later, San Antonio and Texas have changed dramatically. I sort of can: The population shift from farms and small towns to the biggest cities, already well underway when I was a child, has only intensified. Today 90 percent of our population lives in metropolitan areas—two of which, Houston and Dallas, are among the ten biggest in the country. We are a majority-minority state, with brown people, Black people, gay people, and women running everything from police departments to major cities, where you can have Ethiopian *injera* with *doro wat* for lunch and ramen for dinner. In the old days, we revered the rich because there were so few of them, and their extravagance and eccentricity were really entertaining. Now plenty of Texans routinely make the *Forbes* list, and many favor the understated behavior of old money Boston Brahmins.

What hasn't changed is this. After a semi-progressive interlude led by Governor Ann Richards in the early 1990s, Texas's leadership started moving in the opposite direction. "I wish I could say in parting that the twenty-first century has been good for Texas politics, but I can't," *Texas Monthly*'s late, great political writer Paul Burka wrote in a valedictory column in 2015. "If Texas politics once produced giants, our time seems more like the dark ages. There are no John Connallys or Ann Richardses or Bob Bullocks. These were people who loved Texas and, because of that love, knew how to reach across the aisle, set their egos aside, and put the best interests of the state first."

Since then, the divisions have only gotten deeper: our once porous southern border has become a site of bitter enmity, our Legislature has refused time and again to support public education or public transportation, voting rights are being scaled back, women have been stripped of their reproductive freedom, and as I write, school boards across the state are banning books with a zeal that would have impressed the seventeenth-century residents of Salem, Massachusetts.

The results have been predictable. According to a report released by the Annie E. Casey Foundation in 2022, Texas ranked forty-fifth in the nation for overall child well-being, forty-eighth in child health, and thirty-third in education. In 2019, 70 percent of Texas eighth graders weren't proficient in math, while 70 percent of fourth graders weren't proficient in reading. Don't even ask about the number of uninsured. (Okay, we're first in the nation.)

I don't remember a Texas that was as divided as we are now, though that's partly because back in the day our differences couldn't be proclaimed on social media, and so many who were subjugated reluctantly accepted their fate. Today, for better and worse, we all get to have our say in public. Yet few of us are listening to one another.

What's happening now is nothing less than what Paul Burka would have called a battle for the soul of Texas. As we move into the future, and we decide what to keep and what to discard from our storied past, we will also learn whether the Texas we've built will rise or fall, or just settle into a dreaded mediocrity. In this moment we're being pulled in two directions, and few dare to look for, much less step into, the middle ground.

I thought about that metaphorical DMZ when I was binge watching **Taylor Sheridan**'s *1883*, a series that chronicles the journey west for a disparate group of travelers who set out for Oregon from Fort Worth. In case you don't know, Sheridan, fifty-three, grew up roping and riding in Cranfills Gap, Texas—north of Killeen and south of Fort Worth—before spending twenty years as an actor in television shows and movies. He has lately achieved mega–Hollywood status as the creator of nine different shows, most of which have western themes. ("I'm drawn to the sparseness of the West because that's where I've spent most of my life," he told the *New York Times*.) Like his major influences, Larry McMurtry and Cormac McCarthy, Sheridan updates western mythology—infused with his own Texas-shaped worldview—for a generation new to it, balancing reconsidered histories with the old, well-loved stories. *Bonanza* this is not, but neither is it *Deadwood*.

In *1883*, for instance, Sheridan has supplemented the archetypes of the crusty lawman with a heart of gold and the sweet-natured cowboy who blushes at the sight of a woman with the story of European immigrants who hadn't read up on the dangers of the plains. There's also a young white heroine who is prettier than Annie Oakley, rides better than any Comanche, and initiates a lot of sex. Sheridan's big hit, *Yellowstone*, which picks up the story of

Taylor Sheridan and his wife, Nicole Sheridan, at the seventieth annual Cannes Film Festival on May 20, 2017.

those Texans' descendants decades later, in Montana, has been hailed as a conservative fantasy: one stalwart man—Kevin Costner, his face sufficiently weathered—trying to hang on to his land against everyone who wants to take it from him (his scheming, spoiled kids, Native Americans, developers, etc.).

Sheridan's work is more nuanced than that of many of his predecessors—heroes sometimes act like villains and vice versa—but more important is his larger theme: that the world as we know it, and our place in it, is changing before our eyes. What do we do to hold on, and when do we let go? And in making those decisions, what do we gain and what do we lose? Who will we be, in the end? Those questions may provide entertainment for millions of viewers, but in real-life Texas they are genuinely complicated, fraught, and consequential. Whether we like it or not, we are still sorting through the past every day as we move toward the future.

Today, our suburbs and strip malls are more or less indistinguishable from those outside Washington, D.C., or Miami, and when we speak, most of us sound like we could be from Anywhere, USA—or, for that matter, from El Salvador or West Africa. A great many residents don't know Fort Hood from Fort Davis, and don't care. Fusion and dilution coexist here in equal measure, but recognizing either or both requires a degree of institutional memory that fewer and fewer Texans can lay claim to.

I wonder how many young Texans, Latinos and South Texans in particular, can discern the accordion-laced rhythms of decades-old conjunto tunes that undergird the "nu-cumbia" of Corpus-born Grammy nominee **Horatio "El Dusty" Oliveira**. And I wonder how many older types can hear past Dusty's hip-hop stylings and recognize that he's brought a new audience to the melodies they grew up with. (His web bio poses a challenge for anyone over, say, forty: "El Dusty's self-taught approach is as collaborative as it is singular," it reads, "drawing from a crate-digging and turntablist tradition that links Latin classics with the new generation of bass-heavy soundsystem and hip-hop cultures.") At the same time, he's used his power to help make downtown Corpus an artistic center for young artists, just one of many statewide reclamation projects for an ethnic group long subject to erasure. That will be impossible going forward, of course, with the Latino population of Texas having recently overtaken the state's non-Hispanic white population. As their numbers grow, there will be cultural and artistic fusions and collaborations we can hardly imagine today.

According to the 2020 census, 95 percent of the state's population growth during the decade prior came from people of color. Which is why it's difficult to imagine that the people who are running the

DJ and producer El Dusty in Corpus Christi.

227

state now—those who kowtow to superrich donors while limiting the rights and opportunities for just about everyone else—will continue to do so indefinitely. Failing to improve health care and education and ignoring a rapidly approaching climate crisis doesn't seem like a great strategy for sustainability, much less stability. Our current leaders talk incessantly about the so-called glory days of Texas but always seem to leave out the parts of our history in which Texas politicians worked together—often with the support of the dreaded federal government—to make life better for everyone. Instead, they talk of freedom, freedom, freedom—a term that gets used maybe ten zillion times in *1883* to describe the human desire to be untethered from civilization. In our current reality it's employed by each side to accuse the other of fencing them in.

When I look to the past for help in understanding where we are as Texans and where we're going, it's the lives of women that inspire me most, lives that today seem both unchanged and totally transformed from those of the women I grew up knowing and hearing about. Of all the characters in *1883*, for instance, it's Margaret Dutton, played by Faith Hill, who rang truest to me, despite the distraction of Hill's perfect, glacier-white teeth. (I don't think there were that many cosmetic dentists in 1883.)

Margaret loves her husband and her children, knows the risks and hardships of dragging them (and herself) into the wilderness to support her husband's dream of—yep—freedom, and is, for reasons that are never quite explained given her genteel life back home, fearless and deadly with a shotgun. She's warm without being effusive, a shrewd judge of character, and has the patience of a Zen master. She's accepting of her perilous situation without being resentful, committed to making the best of whatever comes her way. She knows how to bring opposing forces together, whether its warring factions on the wagon train or the timeless struggle (for freedom!) between mother and daughter. In short, Margaret has two qualities I associate with my female forebears: an unshakable optimism and what used to be called common sense, a quality I hadn't really thought about in years, maybe because it has been so little in evidence lately.

It's heartening to see that, in fact, neither quality has disappeared if you know where to look. I think, for instance, of Fort Worth's current mayor, **Mattie Parker**, who grew up in Hico—population 1,335 and twenty-five minutes northwest of Cranfills Gap—where the motto is "Where everybody is somebody"

and the majority of kids are on free or reduced lunch, as they were when she was in high school. Parker is a Republican who has shown remarkable tenacity in suggesting that political partisanship isn't the best way to run a city where 84 percent of kids are economically disadvantaged and 75 percent of public school third graders aren't reading at grade level. "I know one thing we're not talking about—how kids are doing," she said in a speech soon after her election. "You could blame Republicans. You could blame Democrats. But I don't really think that does you any good."

Some of Parker's ideas border on GOP heresy: she favors expanding Medicaid and, after the murder of schoolchildren in Uvalde, went public with a call for greater gun safety and noted the hypocrisy of allowing an eighteen-year-old to buy an assault rifle but not alcohol or tobacco. "Let's not overcomplicate things," she wrote in a blog post, words Taylor Sheridan could have used as inspiration for Margaret.

Renu Khator at the University of Houston in October 2018.

Sister Norma Pimentel at the Shaughnessy Family Center in Boston on February 26, 2020.

Texas, much to the disappointment of Democrats, isn't likely to turn blue anytime soon, but maybe that's for the best. A purple equilibrium would keep both sides from the kind of extreme positions we've seen of late, particularly from those currently in charge, whose scorched-earth policies have destroyed the potential for goodwill for years to come. "Power is worth nothing if you don't use it," an Austin politico told me once, but I suspect those who aren't given to extremes—that would be most Texans—are losing their taste for bitter battles over issues drummed up by pollsters when our real problems are nearing the crisis stage.

Notably, the mantle of leadership has in many places now been passed to determined, clearheaded women of color who for centuries never had a seat at the table, much less access to the room. Indian immigrant **Renu Khator**, for instance, is representative of an Asian population that has increased in Texas from just under 1 million to more than 1.5 million in ten years. According to the 2020 census, nearly one in five new Texans are Asian American, making them, by one measure, the fastest-growing racial and ethnic group in the state. Since taking office as president in 2008, Khator has taken the University of Houston from a backwater commuter school to a Tier 1 public research institution, poured $2 billion into a campus construction program, added a medical school, and arranged to join the Big 12 with a grace that obscures a certain hands-on-hips, take-no-prisoners approach to making change.

The same is true of **Sister Norma Pimentel** of McAllen. Texans of a certain age recall *la frontera* as a harmonious place where families and workers crossed and recrossed the border almost as if the boundary between Mexico and Texas weren't there. But in the last few decades it has become a political battleground, often exploited by people who don't know the difference between Laredo and Nuevo Laredo. Through it all, Sister Norma stood stalwart against the captains of cruelty who turned their backs on, or exploited for political gain, the desperate people fleeing violence in their home countries for the safety of Texas. Pimentel isn't a person who waits on help from the God she has devoted her life to, or from anyone in the government, federal, state, or local. As executive director of Catholic Charities of the Rio Grande Valley since 2004, she has been combatting what she and Pope Francis call "the globalization of indifference" in the most basic ways, feeding, clothing, and providing shelter to the dispossessed arriving in McAllen, without ever giving in to anger or cynicism. "Helping another human being is never wrong," she has said. "That's never a wrong thing to do."

229

Elon Musk at a SpaceX event in Boca Chica Beach, Texas, on August 25, 2022.

And finally, I think of **Simone Biles**, born in 1997, who survived an early childhood in foster care to become an Olympic medalist in gymnastics seven times—and to win just about every other award given in the sport. In performance, the four-foot, eight-inch Biles is a study in both weightlessness and superhuman strength, both mentally and physically, and appears as unstoppable as any great Texas athlete, including the likes of Roger Staubach and Nolan Ryan. But beyond her spectacular gifts, Biles possesses a degree of self-knowledge that belies her twenty-six years, a powerful inner core—no pun intended—that allowed her to speak out against the sexual assaults she and other teammates suffered at the hands of Olympic team physician Larry Nassar, and against USA Gymnastics and the U.S. Olympic and Paralympic Committee that covered up for him. Equally important was Biles's partial withdrawal from competition in 2020 when she knew that trying to compete with a case of the "twisties"—losing her place while in the air—could maim her. Biles changed the conversation around mental and physical health in a state whose sports heroes have heretofore been *muy macho*, power-through-the-pain guys, many of whom wound up broke, hurt, and forgotten. Whether catapulting through the air or striding purposefully on the ground, Biles embodies the victories of so many Texas women who stared down trauma to get where they needed to be.

So what about *the guys*, you may be thinking right about now. I have two words for you: **Elon Musk**. Aside from Native Americans, every Texan since 1845 has been an immigrant or the descendant of immigrants, and most have embraced our mythology in one way or another. Musk is a case in point, living proof that our mythology changes to fit the times but never disappears. Yes, he's trying to wean us off gas with his battery-powered Teslas, which might be threatening to the CEOs of Big Oil, but what real Texas entrepreneur would dare to whine about innovation? And Musk has launched his own mini space program in Boca Chica, because who can wait on those government slugs at NASA any longer? Also, Musk's swaggering, incautious takeover of Twitter is right out of the Texas wildcatter playbook. He's flamboyant, insanely wealthy—currently the second-richest guy on the planet—and, as his crass tweets about women and early mockery of the coronavirus demonstrate, boorish. (Congratulations, Elon. You're home.)

Most important, Musk is an optimist in the classic Texas vein. Electric cars and personal rockets are just another way of betting on the come, of believing, as most Texans always have, that tomorrow can be better than today. So what if he gets even richer in the process? He could just be following in the tradition of previous Texas rich guys who have rolled up their sleeves and bought their way to redemption. Think how those billions could be applied if he could tear himself away from Twitter, where, as I write, he's been indulging in some pretty grotesque political commentary. The Elon Musk

Institute for Clean Energy. The Elon Musk Center for Cancer Cures. The Elon Musk Award for Hurricane and Mosquito Reduction. The Elon Musk Humanitarian Grant for Eradicating Poverty and Rebuilding Education. Or the Elon Musk University for Better, Smarter, Fairer Governance.

Who knows: maybe even the Elon Musk Institute for Uniting Texans, One and All. Right now, given his recent ideological positioning, that seems pretty unlikely. But it makes me smile just thinking about it.

231

Acknowledgments

A s it turns out, it takes a lot more than fifty Texans to celebrate the lives of fifty Texans. If you've already leafed through this book, then you've seen the names of the dozens of writers and photographers who contributed to *Lone Stars Rising*. But behind the by-lines and photo credits stood a few dozen more people who deserve a great deal of credit, too. A few of them aren't even Texans.

Many of my colleagues at *Texas Monthly* were extraordinarily helpful on the front end of this project, when we were generating lists of prominent figures we wanted to include in the lineup (which was fun and easy) and then deciding who would and wouldn't make the cut (not fun, not easy). Virtually everyone on staff participated in that process, though Skip Hollandsworth, Dan Solomon, Mimi Swartz, and Katy Vine should be singled out for exceptional enthusiasm and discernment.

About a third of the pieces included here are from our archives, but in every case they required significant updating and abridgement. (Our founding editor William Broyles was extremely gracious about his lengthy 1976 profile of Barbara Jordan being cut down to 1,300 words: "I have no idea what I said in the other 11,000 words or so, but these read fine to me.") Yet, despite all those changes, there's no doubt that the lion's share of the editing on each of those pieces was done by the original editor. There's no easy way to go back and figure out who that was for many of these stories, but our colleagues and former colleagues William Broyles, Paul Burka, Gregory Curtis, Anne Dingus, Katy Flato, Chris Keyes, Nick Lemann, Dave Mann, Paula Mejia, J.K. Nickell, Joseph Nocera, Kate Rodemann, Jake

Silverstein, Evan Smith, Griffin Smith, Jr., Mimi Swartz, and Brian D. Sweany may well have been among their number.

The bold-faced intros at the beginning of each portrait were written by a host of contributors, including the writers of the portraits themselves, various staffers, longtime *TM* freelancer Rich Malley, and super interns Lauren Girgis and Jacqueline Knox.

Though I edited most of this book, I would like to tip my hat to *Texas Monthly*'s editor for new story platforms, Megan Creydt, who shepherded through a few key pieces when she wasn't busy nailing down exciting Hollywood deals for us. Thanks are also due to Stephen Harrigan, who was a source of immense wisdom when difficult decisions had to be made about updating stories by colleagues who are no longer with us. Ultimately, I made the calls I thought were best, so any errors of judgment are mine alone.

Speaking of errors, there are, I hope, none in this fact-filled book. If that is indeed the case, we can chalk that up to the efforts of our crackerjack writers and an ace team of fact-checkers: Ena Avarado, Akiko Ichikawa, Sara Ivry, Paul Knight, Jack Mc-Cordick, Chris Rickert, Jess Rohan, and Ben Weiss.

TM's dauntingly capable director of editorial operations Anna Walsh did a terrific job lining up those fact-checkers, and also made sure I could take some time off from many of my monthly duties to work on this book. (I was, of course, mortified to learn that my colleagues can put out a first-rate magazine just fine without me.)

If you think *Lone Stars Rising* is beautiful (and how could you not?) much of the credit goes to *TM* creative director Emily Kimbro and her team of designers and photo researchers—Victoria Millner, Jenn Hair Tompkins, Kim Thwaits, Claire Hogan, Kayla Miracle, and Darice DeLane Chavira, who

collaborated with Harper Wave to come up with a lovely, understated design and did mountains of photo research. Every month *TM*'s writers and editors get to experience the joy of seeing our lowly sentences and paragraphs transformed into an object that delights the eye; it's nice to see that sensibility translated into something that won't eventually find its way to the recycling bin.

Making sure that we had the rights to all of this collection's archival pieces—some written as long as a half century ago, some by freelancers operating under a variety of contracts over the years—was no easy task, and I'm grateful to senior operations manager Erin Kubatzky and our legal counsel, Patricia Totten and Charlie San Miguel, for relieving me of the need to think about that stuff at all. Patricia and Charlie were also of invaluable assistance with a host of other legal questions.

Our agent, Amy Hughes, of Dunow, Carlson & Lerner Literary Agency, was instrumental in securing the deal with HarperWave that has led to three excellent books—*Being Texan* and *The Big Texas Cookbook* preceded this one, and there are more to come—and has been a loyal advocate for us.

Speaking of HarperWave—editorial director Julie Will has been an enthusiastic collaborator throughout a long editorial process, asking tough questions, offering smart suggestions, and reining in some of our worst excesses. (Believe it or not, there was once a version of this book that included a profile of Alex Jones.) *Lone Stars Rising* is immeasurably better because of her oversight and editorial vision. The members of her team have also been terrific collaborators: designers Leah Carlson-Stanisic and Joanne O'Neill worked intensively with *TM*'s art team to make the inside and outside of this book stunning, assistant editor Emma Kupor smoothed our path in a hundred different ways, and publicist Yelena Nesbit and marketing director Amanda Pritzker have done their utmost to make sure all this great work gets in front of as many eyes as possible. David Chesanow's copy editing skills made our work read much better than it would have otherwise.

I don't really know where to begin when it comes to our editor in chief, Dan Goodgame. Without Dan's leadership, it's unclear that *Texas Monthly* would have survived the recent travails of the magazine industry, when many fine, storied publications have gone out of business. (R.I.P., *Bookforum, California Sunday Magazine,* and the print editions of *Entertainment Weekly* and *Popular Science.*) And it's almost impossible to imagine us creating books as ambitious as this one (not to mention a host of podcasts, video endeavors, and Hollywood projects) without him at our helm. He was also, of course, a full partner in the task of envisioning this book and deciding who exactly we would include here.

And then there are Dan's full partners in *TM*'s multimedia success—our owner, Randa Duncan Williams; our president, Scott Brown; and *TM*'s entire business team, who make everything we do possible, and profoundly respect the separation of "church and state" that has been the rule at *Texas Monthly* since its founding in 1973.

As I said at the top—a lot more than fifty people. All of whom are committed to telling the stories of Texas and Texans and making this most fascinating and perplexing of states a little more comprehensible. We certainly hope the book you're holding in your hands accomplishes both of those goals—and offers a good deal of fun along the way.

—JEFF SALAMON,
deputy editor, *Texas Monthly*

234

Contributors

Baytown native **WILLIAM BROYLES** is the founding editor of *Texas Monthly*, where he worked from 1972 to 1982. He also served as the editor in chief of *Newsweek* from 1982 to 1984, wrote the screenplays for *The Polar Express*, *Jarhead*, and *Cast Away*, cowrote the screenplay for *Apollo 13* (for which he was an Academy Award nominee), and created the television series *China Beach*.

Galveston native **PAUL BURKA**, the widely recognized dean of the Texas Capitol press corps, wrote for *Texas Monthly* and mentored dozens of writers and editors from 1974 to 2015. He died in 2022.

San Antonio native **CAT CARDENAS** was a staff writer at *Texas Monthly* from 2019 to 2022.

Dallas native **GARY CARTWRIGHT** began writing for *Texas Monthly* with its very first issue, in 1973. He was a finalist for a National Magazine Award in 1986 and the author and coauthor of ten books. He died in 2017.

San Antonio native **JULIÁN CASTRO** is the former mayor of San Antonio, the former United States Secretary of Housing and Urban Development during the Obama administration, and a former candidate for the Democratic presidential nomination.

CARINA CHOCANO is a contributing writer for the *New York Times Magazine*. Her essay collection, *You Play the Girl: On Playboy Bunnies, Stepford*

Wives, Train Wrecks & Other Mixed Messages, won the National Book Critics Circle Award for Criticism in 2018.

Houston native **ROBERT DRAPER** worked at *Texas Monthly* from 1991 to 1997. He is currently a staff writer for the *New York Times* and is the author of eight books, including *Dead Certain: The Presidency of George W. Bush*. He has been a finalist for two National Magazine Awards and won once.

TOM FOSTER is an editor at large at *Inc.* magazine and has been an editor at large at *Texas Monthly* since 2017.

LAURA FURMAN is the former series editor of the *O. Henry Prize Stories*, founding editor of *American Short Fiction*, professor emerita at the University of Texas at Austin, and author of two novels, four short-story collections, and a memoir.

DAN GOODGAME is the editor in chief of *Texas Monthly* and a former White House correspondent for *Time* magazine.

S. C. GWYNNE has been a staffer and then a writer at large at *Texas Monthly* since 2000. He is the author of six books, including *Empire of the Summer Moon: Quanah Parker and the Rise and Fall of the Comanches, the Most Powerful Tribe in American History*, which was a finalist for the National Book Critics Circle Award and the Pulitzer Prize.

MICHAEL HALL has been a staffer at *Texas Monthly* since 1997.

STEPHEN HARRIGAN, who was on staff at *Texas Monthly* from 1980 to 1991 and is now a writer at large, has written for the magazine since 1973. He is a screenwriter, essayist, and the author of eleven books, including *The Gates of the Alamo* and *Big Wonderful Thing: A History of Texas*.

Denton-raised **JASON HEID** has been an editor and writer at *Texas Monthly* since 2019.

SARAH HEPOLA is a writer at large for *Texas Monthly*, the author of *Blackout: Remembering the Things I Drank to Forget*, and the host of the *Texas Monthly* podcast on the Dallas Cowboys Cheerleaders, *America's Girls*.

SKIP HOLLANDSWORTH has been a staff writer at *Texas Monthly* since 1989. He has been a finalist for the National Magazine Award four times and won in 2010. He cowrote the 2012 Richard Linklater film *Bernie* and is the author of *The Midnight Assassin: The Hunt for America's First Serial Killer*. He is currently working on a collection of his true-crime journalism for Harper Wave.

Dallas native **BRIANNA HOLT** is a staffer at Insider and the author of *In Our Shoes: On Being a Young Black Woman in Not So "Post-Racial" America*.

Austin native **CHRISTOPHER HOOKS** is a former *Texas Monthly* staffer who writes frequently about politics.

San Antonio native **SIERRA JUAREZ** was an assistant editor at *Texas Monthly* from 2020 to 2022.

MARK LAMSTER is the architecture critic for the *Dallas Morning News* and a faculty member of the Harvard Graduate School of Design. His biography of the architect Philip Johnson, *The Man in the Glass House*, was a finalist for a National Book Critics Circle Award.

JOSÉ R. RALAT has been the taco editor at *Texas Monthly* since 2020.

Dallas native **R.G. RATCLIFFE** is a former Texas political reporter for the *Houston Chronicle* and *Texas Monthly*, where he began freelancing in 2012 and was on staff from 2017 to 2018.

Abilene native **JAN REID** began writing for *Texas Monthly* with its fourth issue, in 1973, and contributed to the magazine as a staffer and freelancer until his death in 2020. He was the author of sixteen books, including *The Improbable Rise of Redneck Rock*, which is widely regarded as the authoritative text on the early days of the Austin music scene.

AL REINERT began writing for *Texas Monthly* with its second issue, in 1973, and contributed to the magazine as a staffer and freelancer for the next four decades. He cowrote the screenplay for the feature film *Apollo 13* and directed and produced the NASA documentary *For All Mankind*. He was a finalist for an Academy Award twice. He died in 2018.

Beaumont native **JAN JARBOE RUSSELL**, a former *Texas Monthly* staff writer, is the author of *Lady Bird: A Biography of Mrs. Johnson*.

JEFF SALAMON has worked as an editor at *Texas Monthly* since 2009.

San Antonio native **JOHN PHILIP SANTOS** is a writer at large for *Texas Monthly* and the author of three books, including *Places Left Unfinished at the Time of Creation*, which was a finalist for the National Book Award.

San Antonio native **RICHARD Z. SANTOS** is the author of the novel *Trust Me* and a former board member of the National Book Critics Circle. He has written for *Texas Monthly* since 2020.

PATRICIA SHARPE is the main food writer at *Texas Monthly*, where she has been on staff since 1974. She won a James Beard journalism award in 2006.

DAN SOLOMON is a staff writer at *Texas Monthly* and is the author of the YA novel *The Fight for Midnight*.

JOHN SPONG has been a staffer at *Texas Monthly* from 1997 to 2016 and again since 2020. He has been a National Magazine Award finalist three times.

LOREN STEFFY has written about business for *Texas Monthly* since 2013. He is a former columnist for the *Houston Chronicle* and the author or coauthor of six books, including *The Last Trial of T. Boone Pickens*.

San Antonio native **MIMI SWARTZ** has been a staff writer at *Texas Monthly* since 1984, except for the years 1997 to 2001, when she was on staff at the *New Yorker* and *Talk Magazine*. She is the coauthor of *Power Failure: The Inside Story of the Collapse of Enron* and the author of *Ticker: The Quest to Create an Artificial Heart*. She has been a finalist for four National Magazine Awards and won twice.

DANIEL VAUGHN, the world's first full-time "barbecue editor," has written for *Texas Monthly* since 2008 and is the author of *The Prophets of Smoked Meat: A Journey Through Texas Barbecue*. He has eaten at more than two thousand barbecue joints.

KATY VINE has been a staffer at *Texas Monthly* since 1997.

237

Credits

COVER SOURCE PHOTOGRAPHY
Jordan: AP; Richards: Rusty Kennedy/AP; Musk: Hannibal Hanschke/Sipa USA/AP; Biles: Ashley Landis/AP; Selena: ©John Dyer; Perry: Peter Yang/August Image; Longhorn: codyphotography/Getty; Caracara: Jeff R Clow/Getty; Roadrunner: Jeff R Clow/Getty; Flora/Fauna: GettyNelson: M. Tweed/AP

TITLE PAGE
Photograph by James H. Evans

CREDITS PAGE
WBAP-TV/NBC5/KXAS-TV/University of North Texas Libraries/The Portal to Texas History

CONTENTS
Ash: AP; Strait: David Redfern/Redferns/Getty; Cisneros: Leonardo Cendamo/Getty

FOREWORD
PhotoQuest/Getty

INTRODUCTION
LBJ: Hulton Archive/Getty; Bluebonnets: AustinArtist/Getty; Astrodome: McFaddin-Ward House Museum/UNT Special CollectionsLibraries/Portal to Texas History; Landscape: Duncan1890/Getty
Introduction secondary: LBJ: Bettman/Getty; NASA: NASA/AP

1970S
Illustration: Flora: Getty; Southwest: Museum of Flight/CORBIS/Getty; Nelson: Tom Hill/WireImage
Willie Nelson: Photograph by Michael O'Brien
Lady Bird Johnson: Photograph by Michael O'Brien
Americo Paredes: Photograph by Jesse Herrera/Courtesy of The Dolph Briscoe Center for American History/The University of Texas at Austin
Barbara Jordan: Keystone/Hulton Archive/Getty
Tom Landry: Photograph by Ron Scott; secondary: AP
Mary Kay Ash: Photograph by Danny Turner
Dominique de Menil: Hickey-Robertson/Courtesy of Menil Archives/The Menil Collection
Herb Kelleher: Photograph by Pam Francis
O'Neil Ford: The Alexander Architectural Archive/University of Texas Libraries/University of Texas at Austin
Willie Velasquez: Southwest Voter Registration Education Project Records/UTSA Libraries Special Collections

BEST OF 1970S
Dallas: CBS Photo Archive/Getty; Cowboys: Focus on Sport via Getty; Fender: Michael Putland/Getty

239

About the Author

Since 1973, *Texas Monthly* has chronicled life in contemporary Texas, publishing long-form literary storytelling on the state's most interesting characters and trends, along with reporting and analysis on vital issues such as politics, the environment, business, and education. Recognized for its editorial excellence and outstanding design, *Texas Monthly* is one of the most respected publications in the nation and has won fourteen National Magazine Awards.